LEGISLATIVE XML FOR THE SEMANTIC WEB

AF788046

Law, Governance and Technology Series

VOLUME 4

Series Editors:

POMPEU CASANOVAS, *UAB Institute of Law and Technology, Bellaterra, Barcelona, Spain*

GIOVANNI SARTOR, *University of Bologna (Faculty of Law CIRSFID) and European University Institute of Florence, Italy*

Scientific Advisory Board:

GIANMARIA AJANI, *University of Turin, Italy*; KEVIN ASHLEY, *University of Pittsburgh, USA*; KATIE ATKINSON, *University of Liverpool, UK*; TREVOR J.M. BENCH-CAPON, *University of Liverpool, UK*; V. RICHARDS BENJAMINS, *Telefonica, Spain*; GUIDO BOELLA, *Universita' degli Studi di Torino, Italy*; JOOST BREUKER, *Universiteit van Amsterdam, The Netherlands*; DANIÈLE BOURCIER, *CERSA, France*; TOM BRUCE, *University of Cornell, USA*; NURIA CASELLAS, *Institute of Law and Technology, UAB, Spain*; CRISTIANO CASTELFRANCHI, *ISTC-CNR, Italy*; G. CONRAD JACK, *Thomson Reuters, USA*; ROSARIA CONTE, *ISTC-CNR, Italy*; FRANCESCO CONTINI, *IRSIG-CNR, Italy*; JESÚS CONTRERAS, *iSOCO, Spain*; JOHN DAVIES, *British Telecommunications plc, UK*; JOHN DOMINGUE, *The Open University, UK*; JAIME DELGADO, *Arquitectura de Computadors, Spain*; MARCO FABRI, *IRSIG-CNR, Italy*; DIETER FENSEL, *University of Innsbruck, Austria*; ENRICO FRANCESCONI, *ITTIG, Italy*; FERNANDO GALINDO, *Universidad de Zaragoza, Spain*; ALDO GANGEMI, *ISTC-CNR, Italy*; MICHAEL GENESERETH, *Stanford University, USA*; ASUNCIÓN GÓMEZ-PÉREZ, *Universidad Politécnica de Madrid, Spain*; THOMAS F. GORDON, *Fraunhofer FOKUS, Germany*; GUIDO GOVERNATORI, *NICTA, Australia*; GRAHAM GREENLEAF, *The University of New South Wales, Australia*; MARKO GROBELNIK, *Josef Stefan Institute, Slovenia*; JAMES HENDLER, *Rensselaer Polytechnic Institute, USA*; RINKE HOEKSTRA, *Universiteit van Amsterdam, The Netherlands*; ETHAN KATSH, *University of Massachusetts Amherst, USA*; MARC LAURITSEN, *Capstone Practice Systems, Inc., USA*; RONALD LEENES, *TILT Institute, The Netherlands*; ARNO LODDER, *University of Amsterdam, The Netherlands*; JOSÉ MANUEL LÓPEZ COBO, *Playence, Austria*; PIERRE MAZZEGA, *LMTG - UMR5563 CNRS/IRD/UPS, France*; MARIE-FRANCINEMOENS, *Katholieke Universiteit Leuven, Belgium*; PABLO NORIEGA, *Edifici IIIA-CSIC, Spain*; ANJA OSKAMP, VU *University Amsterdam, The Netherlands*; SASCHA OSSOWSKI, *Universidad Rey Juan Carlos, Spain*; UGO PAGALLO, *Università degli Studi di Torino, Italy*; MONICA PALMIRANI, *Università di Bologna, Italy*; ABDUL PALIWALA, *University of Warwick, UK*; ENRIC PLAZA, *Edifici IIIA-CSIC, Spain*; MARTA POBLET, *Institute of Law and Technology, UAB, Spain*; DANIEL POULIN, *University of Montreal, Canada*; HENRY PRAKKEN, *Universiteit Utrecht, The Netherlands*; HAI-BIN QI, *Huazhong University of Science and Technology, P.R. China*; DORY REILING, *Amsterdam District Court, The Netherlands*; PIER CARLO ROSSI, *Italy*; EDWINA L. RISSLAND, *University of Massachusetts, Amherst, USA*; COLIN RULE, *University of Massachusetts, USA*; MARCO SCHORLEMMER, *IIIA-CSIC, Spain*; CARLES SIERRA, *IIIA-CSIC, Spain*; MIGEL ANGEL SICILIA, *Universidad de Alcalá, Spain*; RUDI STUDER, *Karlsruhe Institute of Technology, Germany*; DANIELA TISCORNIA, *ITTIG, Italy*; JOAN-JOSEP VALLBÉ, *Institute of Law and Technology, UAB, Spain*; TOM VAN ENGERS, *Universiteit van Amsterdam, The Netherlands*; FABIO VITALI, *Università di Bologna, Italy*; MARY-ANN WILLIAMS, *The University of Technology, Sydney, Australia*; RADBOUD WINKELS, *University of Amsterdam, The Netherlands*; ADAM WYNER, *University of Liverpool, UK*; HAJIME YOSHINO, *Meiji Gakuin University, Japan*; JOHN ZELEZNIKOW, *University of Victoria, Australia*

For further volumes:
http://www.springer.com/series/8808

LEGISLATIVE XML FOR THE SEMANTIC WEB

Principles, Models, Standards for Document Management

Edited by

Giovanni Sartor
University of Bologna and
European University Institute of Florence, Italy

Monica Palmirani
University of Bologna, Italy

Enrico Francesconi
ITTIG-CNR, Florence, Italy

and

Maria Angela Biasiotti
ITTIG-CNR, Florence, Italy

Springer

Editors
Giovanni Sartor
Faculty of Law CIRSFID
University of Bologna
40126 Bologna, Italy

and

European University Institute
Department of Law
Via Boccaccio, Villa Schifanoia 121
50016 Fiesole, Florence
Italy
giovanni.sartor@gmail.com

Enrico Francesconi
ITTIG-CNR, Institute for Legal
Information Theory and Techniques
Via De' Barucci 20, Florence
Italy
francesconi@ittig.cnr.it

Monica Palmirani
Faculty of Law CIRSFID
University of Bologna
40126 Bologna
Italy
monica.palmirani@unibo.it

Maria Angela Biasiotti
ITTIG-CNR, Institute for Legal
Information Theory and Techniques
Via De' Barucci 20, Florence
Italy
biasiotti@ittig.cnr.it

ISBN 978-94-007-3703-7 ISBN 978-94-007-1887-6 (eBook)
DOI 10.1007/978-94-007-1887-6
Springer Dordrecht Heidelberg London New York

© Springer Science+Business Media B.V. 2011
Softcover reprint of the hardcover 1st edition 2011
No part of this work may be reproduced, stored in a retrieval system, or transmitted in any form or by any means, electronic, mechanical, photocopying, microfilming, recording or otherwise, without written permission from the Publisher, with the exception of any material supplied specifically for the purpose of being entered and executed on a computer system, for exclusive use by the purchaser of the work.

Printed on acid-free paper

Springer is part of Springer Science+Business Media (www.springer.com)

Preface

The Internet already is the broadest and most used source of legal information: in the web one can find most statutory texts (all in some jurisdictions), a vast amount of case law, huge repertoires of doctrinal contributions, many blogs and fora discussing different legal issues. Moreover, as legal activities (legislative, administrative, judicial procedures) are increasingly supported by computerised tools, computer networks (Internet or intranets) become the place where many legal events are primarily taking place (voting, presenting petitions or interrogations, promulgating legislation, acting in judicial and administrative proceedings, etc.). Consequently, the documentation constituted by, and constitutive of, such activities consists of electronic documents that are from the beginning, or can become subsequently, components of the web. For instance, not only the final statutory instruments, but also all preliminary documents, such as proposals, amendments, comments, transcripts of debates, can be produced over, or at least distributed though, the web.

In the emerging framework of the semantic web (where information can be directly processed by computer, according to its meaning), legal documents and in particular legislative documents, are undergoing a fundamental change. Being directed to the Internet, rather than to a print house, such documents need to be identifiable in the web, structured according to document models and enriched with machine processable meta-data. This is achieved using standards based on XML (the eXtended Markup Language) to express document structures and insert in the documents meta-textual information. XML standards can be supplemented with ontology languages (for specifying conceptual structures), and rule languages (for capturing the logical content of legal rules).

Shared standard may indeed address different aspects of legislative documents:

- ways of identifying legislative documents, so that they can be named and retrieved, in their different versions;
- ways of structuring legislative documents, so that they can be made available over the Internet and their elements can be automatically identified and processed;
- ways of adding metadata to legislative documents, to univocally identify the authorities producing them, procedural events, and references to other documents;

- ways of dealing with changes in the law, so that textual modifications can be clearly identified, the current content of legal texts can be automatically constructed, the applicable law can be more easily determined;
- ways of defining and applying conceptual classifications to law texts so that legal conceptualisations can be used in understanding and retrieving laws;
- ways of building rich executable representations of legal knowledge, which can capture the essential components of legal norms, can be transferred from one computer platform to the other, and can provide the basis of knowledge-based systems supporting the application of the law.

The present volume is meant to capture only the lower levels of the standard-based creation and usage of legislative documents, namely, the levels pertaining to the identification of legal documents, their structure, the basic metadata and legislative change. For these layers we already have mature technologies and established practices, so that their appropriate treatment represents a necessary aspect of the up-to-date management of legislative resources (the higher layers, namely ontologies, rules, and knowledge models will be addressed in a subsequent volume of this series).

The first three chapters of the volume are meant to provide an overview of the context for the use of XML standards in legislation, addressing the way in which information and communication technologies can contribute to the functioning of Parliaments (Chapter 1), the digitalisation of legislative information and its distribution on the semantic web (Chapter 2), and the managements of legislative documents (Chapter 3).

Chapter 4 provides a presentation of the rationale of standard-based management of legislative documents, introducing the objectives and scope of standards for legislative documents, and discussing the relevance they assume for different stake holders and computer applications.

Chapter 5 addresses the issue of naming, i.e., it examines how legal documents can be assigned unique identifiers that enable retrieval and referencing.

Chapter 6 presents Akoma-Ntoso, the most comprehensive document-model today available for legal document (and in particular for legislative ones). While having been developed by UNDESA (the UN division for social affairs) with particular regard to African Parliaments, Akoma-Ntoso has been created on the basis of various national and international experiences, and provides a reference for all standardisation efforts in the legal domain. Its rigorous and abstract foundation makes it particularly useful for teaching the principles of legislative XML.

Chapter 7 focuses on how standard-based document management can contribute to handling legislative dynamic, introducing the ways in which the Akoma-Ntoso standard deals with amendments and modifications.

Chapter 8 addresses meta-standards or interchange standards, which enable documents produced on the basis of specific or idiosyncratic standards (compliant with a meta-standards) to be exchanged and compared. In particular, it describes MetaLex, the standard proposed by the CEN Workshop on an Open XML Interchange Format for Legal and Legislative Resources.

Chapter 9 considers the terminological and ontological resources that may be used in order to enrich legislative documents with keywords and conceptual information.

Finally, Chapter 10 provides an international review of systems and project in the management of legislative projects, covering all major standardisation efforts so far realised in the domain of legislative information.

The adoption of XML standards for legislative information constitutes an important precondition for the fruitful deployment of web technologies in legislation, for improving legislative workflows as well as communication between legislative bodies and society, for increasing the usability of legislative documents and transparency of the legislative process. We hope that this volume can contribute to these goals, and represent a useful reference for all those involved in the management of legislative documents.

We would like to thank the Global Centre for Information and Communication Technologies in Parliament (and in particular its director Gherardo Casini) for their support in preparing the report *Legal Informatics and Management of Legislative Documents* [1] which has provided the background for the preparation of this volume.

Reference

1. Sartor Giovanni, Monica Palmirani, Fabio Vitali, Maria Angela Biasiotti, and Enrico Francesconi. 2008. Legal informatics and management of legislative documents. Working Paper no. 2, *Global Centre for ICT in Parliament*. http://www.ictparliament.org/node/683

Contents

Contributors

Maria Angela Biasiotti ITTIG-CNR, Institute for Legal Information Theory and Techniques, National Research Council of Italy, 50127 Florence, Italy, biasiotti@ittig.cnr.it

Alexander Boer Leibniz Center for Law, University of Amsterdam, 1000 BA Amsterdam, The Netherlands, A.W.F.Boer@uva.nl

Enrico Francesconi ITTIG-CNR, Institute for Legal Information Theory and Techniques, National Research Council of Italy, 50127 Florence, Italy, francesconi@ittig.cnr.it

Monica Palmirani Faculty of Law CIRSFID, University of Bologna, 40126 Bologna, Italy, monica.palmirani@unibo.it

Giovanni Sartor Faculty of Law CIRSFID, University of Bologna, 40126 Bologna, Italy; European University Institute, Department of Law, 50016 Fiesole, Florence, Italy, giovanni.sartor@eui.eu; giovanni.sartor@gmail.com

Tom van Engers Leibniz Center for Law, University of Amsterdam, 1000 BA Amsterdam, The Netherlands, vanengers@uva.nl

Fabio Vitali Department of Computer Science, University of Bologna, 40127 Bologna, Italy, fabio@cs.unibo.it

Chapter 1
Introduction: ICT and Legislation in the Knowledge Society

Giovanni Sartor

1.1 ICT and the Predicaments of Legislation

In recent years parliamentary legislation has been under criticism for being unable to provide adequate regulatory solutions, for not coping with the needs of our time. I shall argue that ICT can support the mission of legislatures, helping them to address effectively the present challenges.

1.2 Predicaments of Legislation

It has been often affirmed that the primacy of legislation—namely, the production of the law through authoritative statement by democratically elected collegiate bodies, typically parliaments—is coming to an end. We are moving into a new age, where the normative regulation of social behaviour would be primarily entrusted to other sources: administration (specialised authorities), jurisdiction (judicial decision-making, possibly supported by the analyses and suggestions of jurists), private regulations and customs (as emerging from commercial practice, contracts, self-binding regulations by companies and groups of them, decisions by private arbiters, etc.), technical standardisation (though ISO, Internet bodies, etc.), or even computer code (though software enabling or constraining human action in virtual environments). The end of legislation's primacy would be required by a variety of factors:

- legislative authorities are national, while economic and social networks are global;
- legislation is slow, while current problems require quick solutions;
- elective assemblies are political bodies, while complex problem require technical, economical and legal competence;

G. Sartor (✉)
Faculty of Law CIRSFID, University of Bologna, 40126 Bologna, Italy;
European University Institute, Department of Law, 50016 Fiesole, Florence, Italy
e-mail: giovanni.sartor@eui.eu; giovanni.sartor@gmail.com

G. Sartor et al. (eds.), *Legislative XML for the Semantic Web*, Law, Governance and Technology Series 4, DOI 10.1007/978-94-007-1887-6_1,
© Springer Science+Business Media B.V. 2011

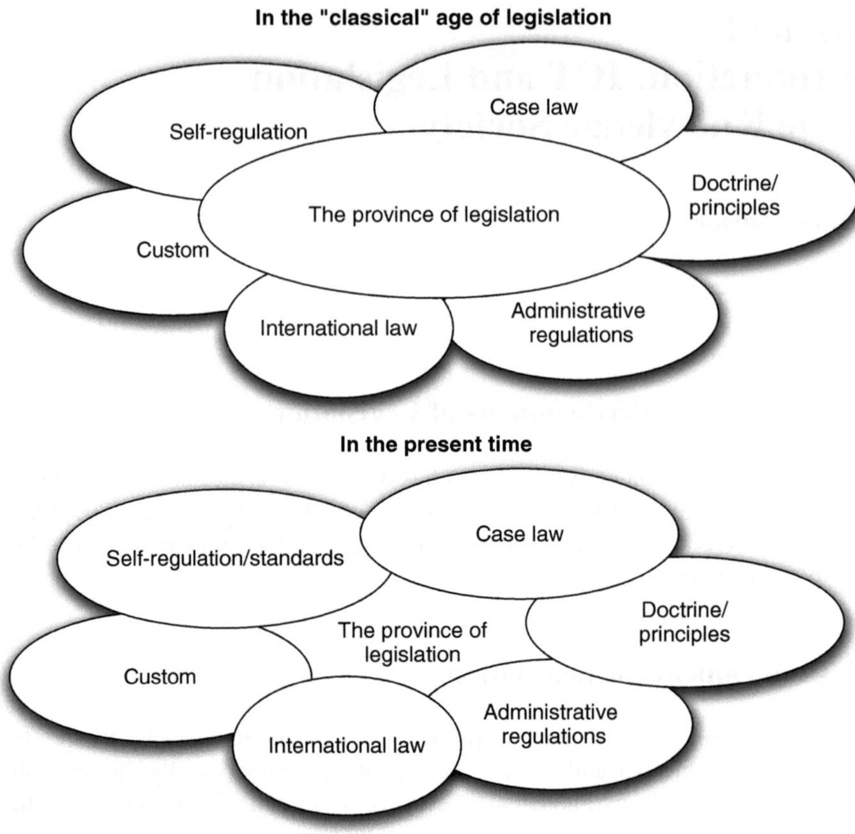

Fig. 1.1 Legislation and other legal sources

- legislation is static, while accelerated economical and technical progress requires continuous adjustments.

This picture has undoubtedly some elements of truth, and indeed nowadays parliamentary legislation is just one among the sources of legal regulation, as it appears from Fig. 1.1, showing how the province of legislation is being encroached by other sources of the law.

It is true that legislation has lost his absolute primacy in our age, but the implications of this fact should not be pushed too far: though legislation needs to coexist with other sources of the law, it still plays a pivotal role in the legal system, having the ability to provide a unique contribution to societal governance. Let us shortly consider what values are inherent in parliamentary legislation, as goals a good legislation should implement:

- Means-end rationality and proportionality. Legislation should provide regulations that are likely to solve effectively the problems they address, according to the best available knowledge. According the ideal of proportionality, while pursuing their

policies, legislators should duly take into accounts impacts on further valuable social or individual interests which may be affected, giving them an appropriate weight.
- Discoursive rationality. Legislation should emerge out of a debate as open as possible, where all interests at stake are considered, the relevant pros and cons are balanced, and the possible alternative are taken into account.
- Responsiveness to citizens' need and preferences. Legislation should reflect the reasoned views of citizens on the common good, while filtering out emotional and unreasoned reactions.
- Progress (ability to change). Legislation should be able to adjust to social change, adapting the legal framework to new needs, and in particular to introduce comprehensive reforms which other sources of law (such as custom or case-law) are structurally unable to deliver.
- Legal certainty. Legislation should contribute to the certainty of the law, providing normative information that gives effective guidance to citizens and legal decision makers. By providing all citizens with a common focus it should coordinate their expectations and prevent the exercise of arbitrary power.
- Citizen's rights. Legislation should enable citizens to have a clear idea of what their rights are, so that they may be able to make justified complaints when these rights are violated.

Preserving the role of legislation in the information age requires that the values above indicated are approximated, at least to a certain degree, by legislative action: it is not sufficient to imagine an ideal legislator, it is necessary to show how ideal legislation can become, to a reasonable extent, a concrete reality. The need to improve the quality of legislation is indeed the focus of a number of national and international initiatives (among the latter, see for example [1–4]).

1.3 The Role of ICT

ICT can contribute to all the purposes we have indicated at the end of the previous section:

- Means-ends rationality and proportionality. ICT can contribute to align legislation to its intended purposes, paying due regard also to foreseeable side-effects, by providing legislators with tools for assessing the impacts of new (or existing) laws on the legal system, on administration, and on society.
- Discoursive rationality. ICT can promote critical debate around legislation, by providing communication tools for promoting the informed debate within parliaments and outside of them, by facilitating the preparation of legislative proposals, and by offering citizens and their associations new ways to participate in the legislative process.
- Responsiveness to citizens needs and preferences. ICT can facilitate the contact between citizens and their representatives, offering the citizen new ways to

express their views and providing them with feedback about the choices of their representatives.
- Legal certainty. ICT can enable citizens to anticipate the effects of legislative rules on their projects and activities, by enabling the drafting of better (more structured, coherent and easily readable) legislation, by providing access to laws, cases, and information materials, and by helping citizens in applying the laws to their particular cases.
- Citizen's rights. ICT can contribute to ensure that laws may effectively protect citizens's rights by making knowledge about rules and remedies more accessible and by ensuring publicity of information about the officers' behaviour.

On the one hand ICTs make it more difficult to govern our societies:

- they provide the infrastructure of globalisation, enabling economic and social networks transcending borders;
- they are the engine of economical and social development, increasing their speed of change;

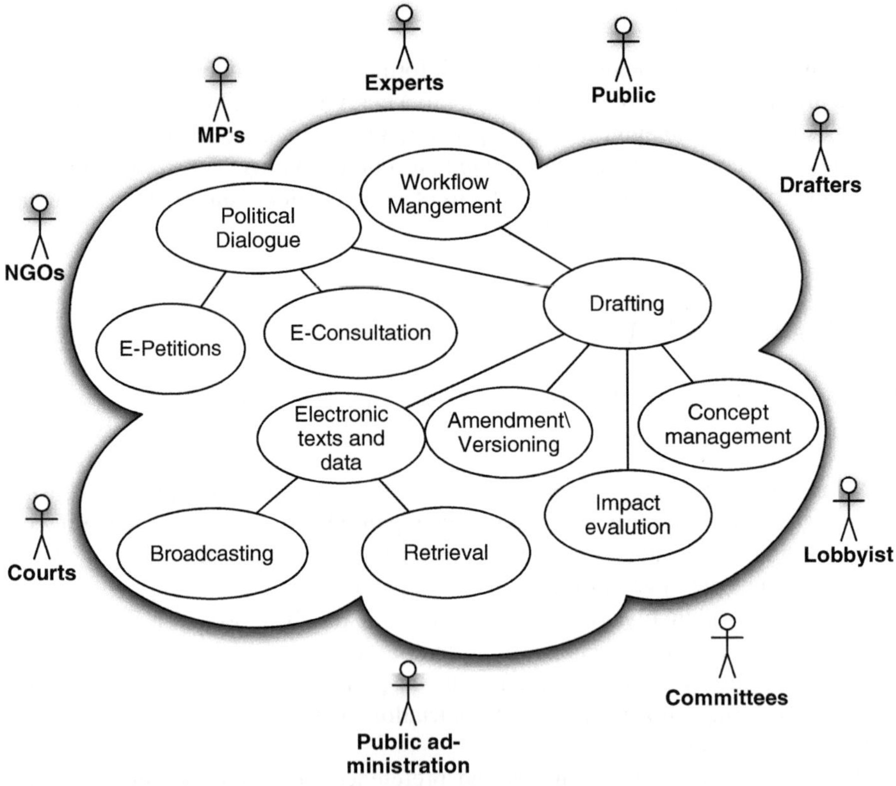

Fig. 1.2 Legislative information system: supported activities

- they are the enzyme of complexity in social interaction, by increasing knowledge and possibilities available to individual actors.

On the other hand, however, ICTs may contribute to an effective governance:

- they provide network infrastructures for legislative bodies, favouring shared (or coordinated) replies to global issues;
- they support dynamic regulation, enabling us to manage and intervene upon the increasing mass of regulatory materials;
- they provide information systems for legislators, helping the latter in modelling social complexity and responding to it.

ICTs are going to play a fundamental role in the working of parliaments. As many other societal institutions, parliaments are increasingly relying upon a ICT-based information systems (as opposed to the use of paper as the exclusive medium for storing and communicating data, only processable by humans). The various agents—internal and external to parliaments—involved in legislation increasingly access information and communicate through computer systems, which become the pivot of their interaction. Many parliaments are already using advanced information system to support their internal activities, as well as the connections with the political and social environment, as you can see in Fig. 1.2.

1.4 Legislative Information Systems

The importance of legislative information systems has vastly increased in the last years, since the advent of the Internet has dramatically changed the ways in which all information is produced and communicated. Nowadays the Internet has become the principal source of legal cognition for citizens, and it is rapidly becoming the main source of information also for professional lawyers, as previously existing legal sources are moving into the Web and new electronic sources of legal information are emerging.

The law has indeed massively entered into the so called *knowledge soup*, namely, the mass of information which is available on the web: the law constitutes an important subset of the web, a subset distinguished not only by its particular (legal) content, but also by the fact of being densely interconnected (since legal documents so often refer one to the other, while having fewer links to non legal materials). Consequently we can possibly say that a *legal web* is emerging, as a distinct subset of the broader world-wide web.

Besides being the source of legal information, the web is increasingly becoming the place of political and legal interactions. It is the place where political debate occurs (consider for instance the many web-sites and forums devoted to electoral campaigns), citizen interact with institutions and with their representatives (in the many institutional sites now provided by public administrations, and in particular by parliaments and other elective assemblies), legal transactions are performed (through on-line e-government and e-commerce applications), legal decisions are commented and criticised (in the many legal fora, blogs, web-pages devoted to controversial legal issues, such as the patentability of software or censorship over the Internet). We have indeed entered the era of the so called Web 2.0, where user-generated contents play an ever increasing role. This does not concern only entertainment or personal interaction, but includes political and legal communication.

In the Internet era parliamentary information systems need to have a Janus-like double face: one face must look at the internal side of the parliament and support all parliamentary activities, the other face must look outside, and provide citizens with information on parliament's activities and outputs, as well as opportunities to participate in parliamentary processes.

These two faces need not be sharply divided as far as technologies are concerned: increasingly the same protocols, models, languages, and tools can be used both inside an organisation and for its relations with the external world. Following the trend already existing in many domains, each parliament can exploit Internet technologies for building its Intranet, namely, its private version of the Internet, whose access is limited to MPs and staff, and which offers them not only various computer applications but also new ways of communicating and cooperating. The same technologies and protocols used in the parliamentary Intranet can be employed for giving citizens (as well as their associations and economic and social organisations) access to information and applications existing within the parliament, and ways of participating in parliamentary activities.

A moving and flexible border separates information accessible only though the parliamentary Intranet from information externally distributed, a border depending on changing political and organisational choices, as well as on the passage of time (what is now internal, like a proposal discussed in a committee, may and should become public tomorrow, when the proposal is approved and subject to public debate). Thus such information must, from the start, be encoded in such a form as to enable its future use and distribution (while adopting all technological and organisational measure to maintain its confidentiality, when this is needed and is consistent with transparency requirements).

Parliaments need not be the only providers of parliamentary information. In pluralistic and democratic societies such information may indeed be distributed—organised and presented in different ways, and possibly enriched with additional information—by other actors, private or public, profit or no-profit (see Sections 2.1.6 and 3.1.4). These further activities can indeed contribute to the achievement of the purposes of legislative information systems, namely, supporting the best use of parliamentary information and facilitating citizen's involvement and participation. Such purposes can be indeed achieved not only through direct provision of information services to the internal or external actors, but also by making available to third parties, in appropriate electronic formats, all relevant parliamentary data.

The link between parliamentarian democracy and ICTs is further enhanced by considering that the emergence of a global society (constituted by a network of networks of global, national and local social system, based upon ICT-based communication) can be matched by a network of networks of democratic legislative authorities, using a distributed shared set of documents and information. Sharing information not only enables each one to learn from others' experience so that best practices can spread; it may also induce national legislators to take into account the needs of others countries, so that they move beyond a narrow focus on their national interests.

1.5 Legal and Legislative Informatics

In the present section we shall shortly introduce legal informatics, presenting its evolution and its main objectives. We shall then delimit the area which is relevant to our concerns, namely, *legislative informatics*.

1.5.1 A Short History of Legal Informatics

Legal informatics is the discipline dealing with the use of ICT to process legal information and support legal activities, namely, the creation, the cognition and the application of the law. As automatic processing of information has been expanding from mathematics calculations, to data management, to office automation, to telecommunications, to the global knowledge infrastructure, so has been expanding the domain of legal informatics.

The first realisation of legislative informatics goes back to the 1960s when the first databases of legal documents were started.

The 1970s saw the growth of informatics within the public administration, where large databases where constructed with various administrative data (e.g. population data, fiscal data, etc.).

The 1980s were the era of personal computers, which enabled the decentralised use of information technology by individual users. Through office automation, computers entered most legal and administrative offices (both in the public and the private domain), accompanied by suites of user-friendly applications (though the use of information technologies was generally limited to single-user mundane applications, like text processing, archiving data, accounting, etc.).

In 1990s computerised information systems were created supporting legal organisation (parliaments, judicial offices, administrations, etc.). Automation within legal organisations started being conceived as a comprehensive project: not only different computer applications had to be viewed as compatible and coherent aspects of an integrated architecture, but the provision of ICTs has become the occasion for reengineering processes and rationalising workflows, so as to enhance the capabilities of the concerned organisations.

At the same time research in legal informatics has started to achieve scientific significance, contributing to both legal theory and computing. A scientific community has emerged in legal informatics, having recurrent meetings such as the biannual International conference on Artificial intelligence and Law (ICAIL), and the annual Conference on legal information Systems (Jurix). Computationally oriented analyses of legal reasoning and knowledge have had a strong an impact on legal theory, providing innovative analyses of legal reasoning, norms, normative systems, and normative concepts. Models developed within legal informatics have influenced computer science, in areas such as belief revision, defeasible reasoning, agent-based models and argumentation.

Since the second half of the 1990s, legal informatics has made use of the Internet, addressing communications between legal organisations and their public, namely, citizens, economic units, and their consultants (lawyers, accountants, etc.). In this way, it has become a significant aspect of, and an important resource for, *e-government*, which in general terms, may be viewed as

> the public sector's use of ICTs with the aim of improving information and service delivery, encouraging participation and making government more accountable, transparent and effective.

This is the definition we can find in the UNESCO's web site, `http://portal.unesco.org`, which provides the following description of the main sectors of e-government:

- e-administration- refers to improving of government processes and of the internal workings of the public sector with new ICT-executed information processes;
- e-services- refers to improved delivery of public services to citizens (e.g. requests for public documents, requests for legal documents and certificates, issuing permits and licenses);
- e-democracy- implies greater and more active citizen participation and involvement enabled by ICTs in the decision-making processes;

As the law is at the core of government, so legal informatics is at the core of e-government, its applications cover legislation, justice, administration, as well as legal professions. In all of these areas ICTs can contribute to the efficiency of legal processes and to their rationalisation, but also to the advancement of legal values such as transparency and controllability (providing comprehensive and accurate information on political, legal and administrative processes), reasoned deliberation (enhancing the possibility of addressing communal issues though informed and reasoned debate), democracy (providing all citizens with information about social problems and their legislative and legal regulation, and new way to discuss such problems and to interact with representative bodies and with their members).

1.5.2 From Legal to Legislative Informatics

Though the scope of legal informatics is not limited to the legislative process or to the provision of legislative information (applications for the judiciary, for administration or for private practitioners are also important), legislative informatics has a particular significance within legal informatics, as legislation has a prominent importance among the sources of the law.

Legislative informatics achieves its general goal of supporting the legislative process by realising the following functions:

- providing information to all actors involved in the legislative process (legislators, citizens, experts, political parties, associations, organisations, lobbies, etc.);
- enabling cooperation among such actors, so that all can contribute to the process, according to their role;
- ensuring efficiency, transparency, and control;
- enabling access to the outcomes of each phase of the legislative process, and contributions to the next phase (managing the workflow);
- ensuring the quality of the legislative outputs;
- ensuring knowledge of the produced law texts and preliminary documents.

Though legislative informatics still is a young discipline, it has achieved in the recent years a number of significant results in different areas.

In the domain of legislative documentation, the first one where computer systems were used, legislative informatics can and indeed does already make a difference. Nowadays not only legislation is available in electronic format, but is also often made freely accessible to the public, through the Internet. Additional retrieval functionalities are sometimes provided, such as access to legislative acts in their amended versions (with regard to any points in time), or retrieval through various advanced techniques (thesauri, ontologies, linguistic resources, methods for indexing and ranking documents, etc.).

Some results are also available in managing of legislative processes (work-flows). A vast amount of information concerning legislative activities is now stored in electronic format (bills, reports, comments, queries, proposals for amendment, etc.) and is made available to legislators, officers, stake holders and common citizens. Such information is (at least partially) collected and used by work-flow systems that monitor and support the legislative process, providing information about the past steps as well as indications on mandatory and optional further steps, and facilitating the respect of deadlines and other formal requirements. Tools are provided for legislative drafting and in particular for embedding amendments into bills.

Increasingly ICTs support information and communication in the legislative process. On the one had they provide access to knowledge sources relevant to legislative decisions-making, on the other hand they support multiple interactions, involving members of parliaments, officers, other institutions, organised stake-holders, as well as individual citizens (from simple e-mail exchanges, to the organisation of on-line debates, argumentation environments, and other architectures for e-participation).

Legislative informatics is also starting to profit from research in the construction of computable models of legislative knowledge: computable models are built of legislative and legal concepts, future laws are tested with regard to sets of possible future cases, and social impacts are modelled (by using different techniques, from ontologies to knowledge-based systems, statistical analyses and agent-based models).

As we shall see in Chapters 3, 4, 5, 6, 7 and 8 of the present volume, legislative informatics has achieved considerable results in the area of legislative standards (concerning, as we observed above, ways of enriching legal text with machine-processable structural or semantic information). Nowadays in various countries standards are used for marking the structure of legal acts, legislative references, and sometimes also textual modifications. Standards have also been defined for the preliminary materials produced along the legislative process. A few standard-compliant software programs have been developed for supporting legislative drafting.

Using shared standard brings with it considerable advantages: the possibility of enabling communication and dialogue (vital aspects for deliberative democracy) at all levels; improving the quality and accessibility of legal information in different legal systems; promoting the interoperability among applications and information systems managing legal information; providing high quality integrated services for both policy makers and citizens.

For legislation to cope with the formidable challenge of providing a suitable regulatory framework for the information society it is necessary that legislative authorities are able to make the best use of the many models and tools provided by legislative informatics. Thus, a stricter connection would be desirable between academic research and the construction of computer infrastructure and tools: too often academic research does not pay attention to user needs and development initiatives do not pay attention to research (and are not even made known to the scientific community). Fortunately, there are recent signs that a stricter co-operation between researcher, users and developers is underway. While research in legislative informatics is producing usable results some operational ICT projects within legislative bodies show awareness of academic results.

References

1. Commission of the European Communities. 2002. Better Lawmaking 2002. A shared Responsibility, Commission Report to the European Council, COM(1998) 715 final.
2. Commission of the European Communities. 2006. A strategic review of Better Regulation in the European Union Commission communication -COM(2006)689 (14 November 2006).
3. OCDE. 1994. Improving the quality of laws and regulations: Economic, legal and managerial techniques. OCDE/GD(94)59. Technical report.
4. OCDE. 1997. *Regulatory impact analysis: Best practice in OECD countries*. Paris: OECD.

Chapter 2
Legislative Information and the Web

Giovanni Sartor

2.1 Trends in the Provision of Legal Information

The ways in which legal information is provided have changed enormously in the last years, in connection with the evolution of ICT and in particular with developments in legal informatics. In the following pages I shall present the main trends in this rapid and still ongoing transformation.

2.1.1 The Digitalisation of Legal Information

The first, and most basic, trend is the rapidly progressing digitalisation of legal information. An increasingly larger amount of law texts and data is available in electronic formats: legislation, regulations, administrative decisions, case law, contracts, fiscal data, files concerning court proceedings, and so on.

The push towards digitalisation is favoured by the integration between the computer-supported drafting of documents and their electronic distribution, and also by the availability of reliable technologies for ensuring authenticity and integrity of electronic documents (e.g., electronic signatures). Electronic legal documents rather than being a copy of pre-existing original paper documents tend to become official legal texts. The production of private contracts and administrative acts in electronic formats, to be preserved in computerised databases, is today common in many countries.

This trend is being encouraged by the expansion of e-commerce and e-government: exchange agreements concluded over telecommunication networks are naturally recorded in electronic documents, and so are administrative decisions resulting from electronic interactions between offices, and between offices and citizens. An important development of e-government is represented by on-line judicial proceedings, that is, by two-ways document interchange and application

G. Sartor (✉)
Faculty of Law CIRSFID, University of Bologna, 40126 Bologna, Italy;
European University Institute, Department of Law, 50016 Fiesole, Florence, Italy
e-mail: giovanni.sartor@eui.eu; giovanni.sartor@gmail.com

G. Sartor et al. (eds.), *Legislative XML for the Semantic Web*, Law, Governance and Technology Series 4, DOI 10.1007/978-94-007-1887-6_2,
© Springer Science+Business Media B.V. 2011

interoperability between all the Courts' internal users (clerks, judges, etc.) and all their external users (lawyers, expert witnesses, etc.). When this idea will be fully implemented, all judicial decisions, in all degrees of jurisdiction, will be in electronic form, and so will be all acts by the parties, the files of each process, the records of the proceedings, all data kept by the clerk's offices. Finally, there are a few experiences concerning electronic promulgation of law texts, so that even the original statutory instruments are going to be electronic files, authenticated by an electronic signature of the competent authority (for instance, the Head of State).

2.1.2 The Law on the Internet

The second trend, which is synergetic to the first one, consists in the law moving into the Internet. Digitalised legal information, free from its traditional paper hardware, can be processed by computer and transmitted over computer networks: it can inhabit the expanding virtual word of the so-called cyberspace. The Internet already contains many legal sources, and already is, in many domains, the main source of legal information for lawyers and citizens. One can find over the word-wide-web many statutory texts, a vast amount of case law, and also many comments on laws and cases (there is an emerging vast amount of digitalised legal doctrine): the web not only is a huge repository of legal information, but is also becoming the open forum where legal issues are debated, where legal reasoning is publicly deployed.

The Internet (in combination with computer nets internal to public administrations), moreover, is the place where legally relevant information is exchanged, and where, as a result of such exchanges, legally binding texts are produced. As legally relevant procedures are taking place through communication exchanges over the Internet (or Intranets)—in all kinds of legislative, administrative or judicial procedures—the legal relevance of the cyberspace changes: the Internet not only contains information about legally relevant facts happening in the real word (enactments, judicial decisions, contracts, etc.), it has also become the virtual location where certain legally relevant events primarily take place.

2.1.3 The Standardisation of Formats for Legal Information

The third trend concerns standardisation of document models for textual legal information. As everybody knows, the strength of the Internet is its inclusiveness and openness: one accesses whatever information is available, and one provides (within general legal constrains) whatever information one can upload to a connected computer. For the network to grow, a central authority is not required: growth is governed by the decentralised decisions of users and providers. However, in order that information can be accessed and appropriately processed by decentralised users, it is necessary that it is coded and decoded according to shared machine-readable standards or protocols.

Standards can concern different aspects of legal information, at different levels: the communication protocols that are required for information to be made accessible over the web; the ways of specifying the typographical appearance of the documents; the links to other documents; the structure of the documents (their division in component units, like sections and subsections); the description of their content, at different levels. The determination of machine-processable standards is a crucial issue for public policy in the information society.

On the one hand standardisation involves some dangers: (a) standards, once they are established, tend to spread regardless of their merit since the need to participate in communication pushes everyone towards the standards already in place; (b) privately determined standards, or the related algorithms, can be disclosed to others only under specific conditions or can even be the object of intellectual property so that competition can be hindered; (c) the need to respect standards may limit innovation and diversity. On the other hand the shared adoption of appropriate open standard greatly facilitates technological progress, cooperation and competition in the framework of the knowledge society. Such standards, besides having a high technical quality, must be non-proprietary, i.e., free from exclusive intellectual property rights, generally accessible, and managed by impartial bodies.

2.1.4 The Law in the Semantic Web

The fourth trend is the move from the present, text-based web, into the so-called semantic-web. This means that the legal information available over the Internet is increasingly processed according to its content (or meaning), and not only as a pure text (as a sequence of words, to be read by a human). This result is usually achieved by embedding in the natural language text special computer readable specifications, which can be processed in various ways: for retrieving the document, for accessing related information, for determining the legally binding content of the document, for applying the rules it includes, and so on. XML tagging is normally used to embed such meta-textual information in legal documents, supplemented with languages like OWL for specifying conceptual structures, and logical extensions, like RULE-XML for capturing the logical structures of legal rules.

Ways of specifying derogations and modifications in legal documents have been devised, which allow legal texts currently in force to be automatically constructed. Further meta-information is embedded in legal texts available through the Internet for the purpose of conceptual information retrieval. In particular, documents are indexed according to conceptual analyses (ontologies) of the concerned legal domains.

2.1.5 The Executable Representation of Legal Information

The fifth trend, just at its beginning, concerns the executable representation of legal regulations. This means that computer systems not only help humans in accessing legal texts, but they directly apply the legal regulations embedded in (or linked to) such texts, or support humans in this task. This is happening in two areas.

Firstly, advanced systems are being developed for automatic contracting, within e-commerce. These systems establish the content of binding contracts for the delivery of goods and services, according to the agreed result of negotiations (this takes place particularly in digital-rights-management environments). For such systems to be able to interact meaningfully and correctly both with humans and with other similar systems, it is necessary that they share the same way of representing normative positions (rights and duties) and other legal qualifications.

Secondly, some large-scale rule-based systems have been developed for public administration. Such systems assist employees and citizens in applying legal rules, by performing automatically the corresponding inferences (determining taxes, assessing entitlements, and so on). Both systems for automatic contracting and rule-based systems for public administration often make use of proprietary languages for representing normative information, languages that are usually not translatable one into the other. The use of such languages (without their interoperability being ensured and a shared standard being available) may hinder the development of new applications, prevent communication between different systems, and in general reduce competition.

2.1.6 An Increasing Diversity in Information Providers

The sixth trend is the increasing diversity in the provision of legal information. In Europe we have seen at first, in the 1970s, the emergence of national public systems for the on-line provision of legal information, while in the US private companies have played from the start a major role. Then, in the 1980s we have witnessed the crisis of public systems (with a few exceptions), and the increasing provision of electronic legal information by private publishers (often using compact disks for distribution). In the 1990s public providers have come back, exploiting the fact that law text are available to them in digital format (since they are typeset through computer systems by the public bodies producing the law, such as legislatures and courts), and that the Internet allows such texts to be distributed at low cost. At the same time, thanks to the Internet, a number of new actors have emerged in the provision of legal information. Legal information institutes, educational institutions, professional associations, law firms, and individual researchers and activists are providing large amount of freely-accessible on-line legal information (there are even portals which have the specific purpose of providing access to on-line legal resources).

There is the need to define a new framework for the provision of legal information, which ensures that different information needs (of citizens, public authorities, and professional lawyers) can be satisfied in the best way, through the cooperation and competition of different providers. In particular, it is urgent to redefine the tasks of public authorities, namely the way in which they should accomplish their duty to ensure knowledge of the law in this complex multi-actor environment (for instance, it has been argued that such authorities do not fulfil their duty by only providing raw texts; they must also structure such texts and enrich them with machine readable meta-textual information, according to the best available standards).

2.1.7 An Increasing Integration Between Legal Theory and Legal Informatics

The seventh trend is the two-ways integration of legal theory and legal informatics. On the one hand results provided by legal theory—with regard to aspects such as legal logic, the theory of norms and normative positions, models of legal reasoning—are translated into computable models. On the other hand legal informatics is providing new models of legal reasoning to legal theory, taking into account the achievements in cognitive science and artificial intelligence.

By integrating these two domains of research it is possible to obtain different valuable results: a better understanding of the law, a better specification for legal information systems, a critical approach to the computerisation of the law, the identification of new ways of processing legal information. The contribution of legal theory is particularly important with regard to standards for legal information, which must correspond to the nature of the law, to its social functions, and to the needs of institutions and citizens, so that they may appear rational and acceptable to both the providers and the receivers of legal information.

2.2 Focus on the Semantic Web

With regard to the management of parliamentary information the move toward the semantic web (already mentioned in Section 2.1.4) is particularly significant. In the present section I will first shortly introduce the basic idea of the semantic web and then consider its relevance for legislative information.

2.2.1 The Semantic Web

The emergence of the semantic web results from embedding in the world-wide web (the system of interconnected document today available over the Internet, thanks to the use of the HTTP protocol) information that is machine understandable and can be processed through advanced technologies. This represent a significant advancement with regard to the present situation, where web documents (web pages) mostly contain natural language texts or multimedia files.

The promotion of the semantic way is the leading idea of World Wide Web Consortium (W3C, see `http://www.w3.org/`), whose overarching goal is that of achieving a *one-World-Wide-Web*, shortened into one-Web, namely, an open platform where an increasing amount of information and services can be made universally available. According to the same consortium, the achievement of the one-Web goal depends on the realisation of the following long-term sub-goals:

- web for everyone, i.e., enabling everyone to get the benefits of the web, consisting in the fact that it enables human communication, commerce, and opportunities to share knowledge;
- web on everything, i.e., enabling every kind of device (including phones, television systems, etc.) to access the web;
- knowledge base, i.e., enabling the web to be used not only by humans but also by computer, namely, embedding in it machine-processable information;
- trust and confidence, i.e., enabling accountable, secure and confidential transactions.

The main way in which W3C has contributed to the one-Web goal consists in providing standards for technologies. Here is how the W3C characterises this objective (`http://www.w3.org/`)

> Specifications for the web's formats and protocols must be compatible with one another and allow (any) hardware and software used to access the web to work together. W3C designs and promotes interoperable open (non-proprietary) formats and protocols to avoid the market fragmentation of the past.
>
> Since 1994, W3C has produced more than ninety web standards, called "W3C Recommendations." A W3C Recommendation is the equivalent of a web standard, indicating that this W3C-developed specification is stable, contributes to web interoperability, and has been reviewed by the W3C Membership, who favors its adoption by the industry.

As we have just observed, the W3C, as indicated by the knowledge-base aspect of its vision, is leading toward the realisation of the semantic web, namely, a web where not only information is be made accessible on line, but where this information is increasingly machine-processable. This idea has lead to the design and progressive implementation of the pyramid of technologies you can see in Fig. 2.1, whose layered structure can be described as follows:

- The basic layers is constituted by two standards:
  - the Unicode standard, providing an agreed computer representation (a unique binary number) for any character in any human alphabet;
  - the URI (uniform resource identifiers) standard, providing an agreed unambiguous way of naming the entities which are accessible on the web (the resources).
- XML provides a metalanguage enabling individuals and communities to define tags for expressing the structure of documents, and for including further information (metadata) in the documents, so that they can be automatically processed according to such structure and additional information.
- RDF enables us to include in the documents machine understandable statements on relevant objects and their properties.
- Ontologies enable us to specify concepts and conceptual relations and to make conceptual inferences.

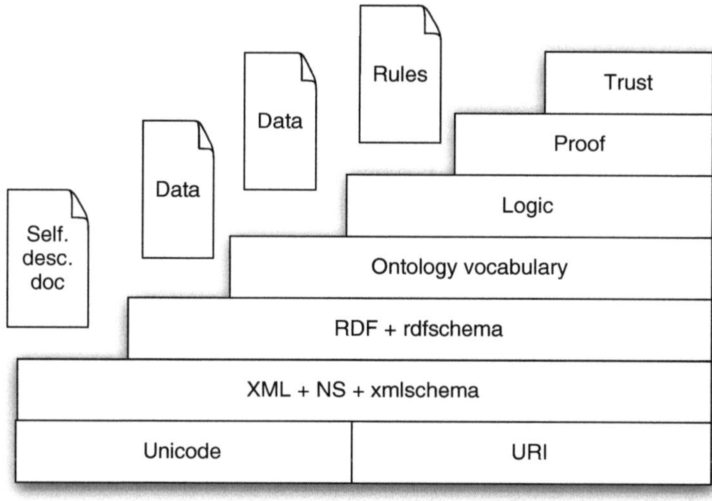

Fig. 2.1 Levels of the semantic web

- Logic permits us to express complex information in formal structures.
- The proofs layer concerns the use of logical information in inferences and arguments.
- The trust layer includes ways to ensure confidentiality, authenticity, integrity and reliability (such as cryptography and digital signatures).

The realisation of the semantic web will enable us to overcome the limits of the current web, facilitating access to information, as well as various activities over the web (from e-commerce to e-government). On the one hand semantically enriched documents can be automatically adapted to the needs of their user on the basis of the machine-processable information they contain (e.g. a legislative text can be presented in the preferred format, it can be visualised in the version now in force, or in a previous version, etc.); on the other hand such documents can embed the information required for e-commerce or e-government, and this information that can be used by the relevant applications (e.g. names or authors and addressees of a legal act can be identified, times when the legal acts become effective can be detected, deadlines concerning consequential activities can be signalled, etc.).

2.2.2 The Legal Semantic Web

Within the emerging reality of the semantic web we can distinguish a subset of it, which we can call the *legal semantic web*, which is constituted by the legal contents available in the web, content that are (or at least may be) enriched with machine-processable information. Thus the "one web" vision can be translated into a "one legal-web" vision, namely into a vision where everyone, on any kind of device will be able to obtain reliable legal information, and where legal information will be enriched with machine-processable data, so that accessing information and performing legal transactions are facilitated by computer support.

Indeed we can discern the progressive emergence of such a legal semantic web, where electronic legal documents are made available on the web together with machine processable information. The pyramid of web technologies of Fig. 2.1 is indeed being transferred into the legal semantic web, originating the layered pyramid of Fig. 2.2:

- standards are being defined for identifying legal resources, so that each legal document, produced by any legal authority, can be univocally identified (and consequently retrieved);
- standards are being defined for structuring legal documents, of any kind, according to well-specified XML definitions;
- standards are being defined for making assertions on legal documents;
- legal ontologies are being created (and linked to general ontologies);
- ways of formally representing legal norms are being devised.

The coherent implementation of such a technological model has so far been accomplished only to a very limited extent. Thus, even though a huge amount of legislative information is nowadays available on the web, its utility is limited since this information has the following features: it is stored in different formats (word, pdf, html, xml, etc.); it is searchable through search engines (good recall, but a lot of noise, little reliability); only single pages are retrieved (no integration of data contained in different pages); the data within pages are not automatically processable. Through the realisation of legal semantic web it will be possible to improve substantially the usability of such information, by enabling the automatic retrieval of relevant

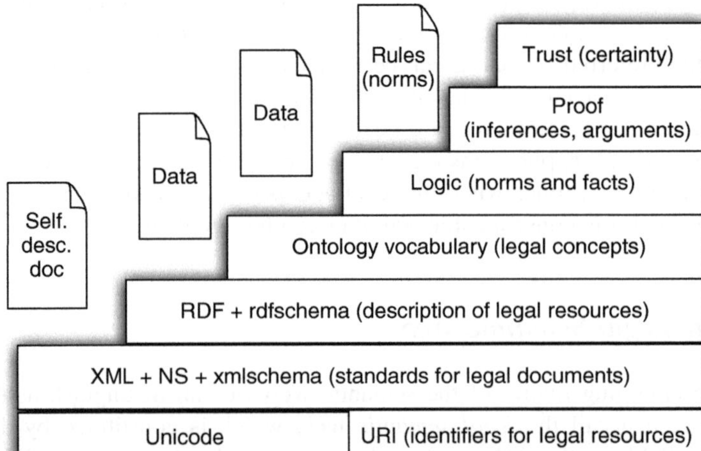

Fig. 2.2 Levels of the legal semantic web

legal information, opportunely selected and integrated, and the automatic processing of legal information embedded in web documents for many different purposes (e.g. generate the law in force, control deadlines, apply rules, etc.)

In the future all actors in the legal world, when looking for legal information, will search the legal semantic web, and will be provided with legal information which has been, at least partly, shaped by ICT processes (see Fig. 2.3). This information will be automatically presented in different ways, according to the different issues at stake and the different roles of its users (legislators, judges, administrations, parties in economic or other transactions).

The realisation of the legal semantic web, focusing on the addition of machine-processable information to legal documents, according to shared standards, facilitates the integration between on the one hand the production of documents and the management of their workflow, and on the other hand the distribution of the documents to the public (possibly integrated with additional related information). During the production phases machine processable data can be added to the documents in order to facilitate the subsequent use of such documents and to keep track of their workflow. These same data (for instance the specification of the structure of a document, its authors, its life-cycle, etc.) can enrich the documents when they are provided externally, and can provide information concerning the procedure through which the documents were produced.

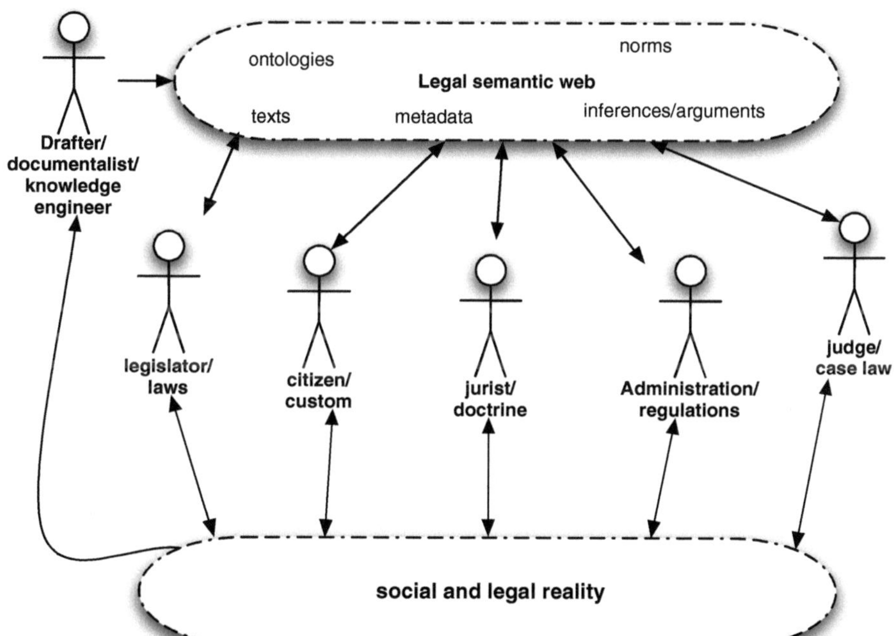

Fig. 2.3 The law between virtuality and reality

The semantic web represents an opportunity for legislation, facilitating production-processes internal to parliaments (legal drafting, maintenance of legal sources and management of legislative workflows and procedures), and enhancing interactions with external actors (publicity of procedures and information, communication with citizens, dialogue with sub-national, national, and international institutions). The definition of appropriate standards for legislative documents can indeed provide the link between the production of legislation and its use in the legal community.

Chapter 3
ICT-Based Management of Legislative Documents

Giovanni Sartor

We shall now narrow our focus, moving from legal informatics in general to the most specific topic of the present report, namely, the management of legislative documents.

The issue of the management of legislative documents involves both aspects of Parliamentary information systems I have considered above: the "Intranet" aspect, concerning computerisation within Parliaments and the "Extranet" aspect, concerning the provision of legal information (and of various services) to external actors, since most documents produced during the legislative process will both be used internally and provided externally (as required by democracy and transparency).

Moreover, the discussion of the management of legislative document cannot be limited to parliamentary information systems. As we shall see in the following, legislative document are (and should be) stored and processed also outside Parliaments. Thus, legislative informatics is not limited to the study and development of computer applications for Parliaments. It also includes orchestrating, for the benefit of legislation, activities, applications and systems existing within Parliaments and outside of them (in other branches of public administration, or in the private sector, both profit and no-profit).

This is even more relevant today, in the age of web services, i.e., software system designed to support interoperable machine-to-machine interaction over a network, according to the definition in [3]. Thanks to web services, complex functions—rather then being executed by an integrated system covering all aspects of them—will be provided by combining the performances of separate heterogeneous systems (agents) interacting according to shared protocols. In particular, as I shall emphasise in the following, the issue of the management of legislative document is not reduced to the issue of their storage and processing within Parliaments, but includes the discussion of how such documents, after being produced by Parliaments, can become shared resources, whose decentralised and autonomous reuse contributes to the ideal of an open Parliamentarian democracy.

G. Sartor (✉)
Faculty of Law CIRSFID, University of Bologna, 40126 Bologna, Italy;
European University Institute, Department of Law, 50016 Fiesole, Florence, Italy
e-mail: giovanni.sartor@eui.eu; giovanni.sartor@gmail.com

G. Sartor et al. (eds.), *Legislative XML for the Semantic Web*, Law, Governance and Technology Series 4, DOI 10.1007/978-94-007-1887-6_3,

© Springer Science+Business Media B.V. 2011

The following pages will be devoted to the analysis of the evolution of legal information systems. Firstly, in Section 3.1 I shall describe the achievements of the past, and then, in Section 3.2 I shall consider the currently emerging trends.

3.1 A Short History of Legal Information Systems

I shall describe the evolution of legal information systems in the past century, from its beginnings in the 1950s until the emergence of the Internet in the 1990s, focusing on the issue of documents management. Then I shall consider current approaches, and discern emerging trends.

3.1.1 The Beginnings

The history of systems for dealing with legal information starts in the second half the 1950s when the first applications of computers in the legal domain were developed. At that time, obviously, what could be asked was just a printout of the texts containing the specified search terms. The documents were collected through a sequential search of the tape where they were stored. No real time answer (and adjustment of the query) was possible.

During the 1960s, a number of information retrieval systems for legal sources were created, both in Europe and in North America. In the US such systems were mainly developed by private firms, while in Europe initiatives was mainly taken by public bodies, in particular within public administrations. The motivation behind such initiatives was the idea that legal sources had grown so much in quantity (in particular since the welfare state had started to regulate minutely social benefits as well as economic activities) and were changing so quickly that only computers could effectively provide knowledge of the law. Technological developments taking place between the 1960s and the 1970s provided the basis for the successful deployment of legal information services: disk mass memories allowed much quicker access (and consequently enabled real time responses), and the integration of telecommunications with computing provided remote access to information system (through telephone lines).

In these years various legal information systems were constructed in Europe. For instance in Italy in 1963–1964 the Court of Cassation (Corte di Cassazione), the highest judge in matters dealing with civil and criminal cases, started a database of abstracts ("massime") of its own decisions. This database progressively expanded its coverage, including state laws, regional laws, administrative regulation, etc. It still is the most extensive information system available in Italy.

Similar initiatives where taken by in France by the Conseil d'Etat (the supreme judge in administrative cases), in Germany by the Ministry of Justice, in Sweden by the Directorat of Court administration, in Finland by the Supreme administrative court, in the EU by the legal service of the European commission. In general the initiative for building such systems did not come from the legislature, but rather from the public bodies applying the law, namely, courts and public administrations.

Though such systems started with a limited coverage (usually certain decisions of a supreme court, or acts of a legislature), they tended to expand with further contents, and in particular with further judicial decisions and regulations. The emerging vision was indeed that of a single national legal information system, where all legal sources (legislation, precedents, regulations, treaties, etc.) would be electronically stored and made available for retrieval. This vision underlies the main efforts of the 1970s, it express a *thesis* that would soon be challenged by technological evolution (I will describe the evolution of legal information systems as a sequence of theses, antitheses and synthesis, following the triadic pattern which characterises Hegel's philosophy, though just as a pattern for presentation, without any philosophical commitment).

At that time computers were not used yet during document drafting (word-processing was not yet commonly available, so that the original documents were written on paper). Consequently, there was a complete separation between the preparation of legal documents and their subsequent storage in an information system; documents had to be retyped in order to be made electronically available. Thus Parliaments used such systems only for information retrieval. They resided in big and costly computers, the so-called mainframes, remotely accessible through dedicated terminals. Parliamentary staff would make use of legal databases during the drafting phase, in order to access the relevant pieces of pre-existing legislation. It was possible to scroll the retrieved documents and to print them, but not to reuse the electronic materials. In general, the only users of such systems were legal professional (judges, civil servants, lawyers and their assistants), while citizens could access electronic legal texts only in very limited exceptional cases.

The systems just described had a mixed history of success or failure, and only a few of them have survived until our days. In the USA the publicly owned systems FLITE and JURIS died out, while the private providers Westlaw and Lexis have prospered and even expanded to other countries. In particular, Westlaw has become part of Thompson, a huge media company, who has also acquired Lawtel, the legal information system available on Prestel (pre-Internet British system for delivering on-line legal information). Similarly the privately owned systems existing in England or Australia did not survive until our days. On the other hand certain systems, such as the Italian public service Italgiure-Find or the Norwegian System Noris (managed by Lovdata, a private foundation established by the Ministry of Justice and the University of Olso) have continued until our days, increasing progressively their contents and their services.

3.1.2 The Antithesis: The Multiple Isolated Systems of the 1980s

The personal computer (PC) was the biggest ICT invention of 1980s, leading all of us into the information society. It enabled computing to enter all economical and social activities, and also all legal activities: public administration, the judiciary, parliaments, regulatory bodies, private law practices. In the legal domain personal computers started being used mainly for word-processing, but this was soon followed by further applications, like account-keeping, filing, and information-retrieval. Though PCs could access remote databanks through the telephone lines, the emphasis moved to applications directly available on the PC, whose facility of use lawyers and paralegal had learned to appreciate, and which was not subjected to the costs and the delays of remote telephone service.

Consequently, legal documentation moved to the PC, where it could be independently used by individual users, thanks to the storage of legal databases on a new high capacity storage medium, the Compact Disk, which would be accessed through retrieval software residing on the PC. This technological change enabled new actors to enter the market of electronic legal information, namely, private publishers. They could sell legal databases through the existing channels available for the sale of books and journals (since legal databases were embodied in an easily tradable physical object, namely, the CD). In comparison to remote databanks, CDs were inferior with regard to the breadth of their coverage and the frequency of update (which required purchasing a new edition of the CD), but they were highly superior with regard to ease of use and integration with further legal materials. In fact, many publishers provided CDs merging the various materials at their disposal, and in particular combining official texts (legislation and judicial decisions) and copyrighted doctrinal contributions. This anticipated the combination of different sources of legal knowledge now taking place over the Internet.

One important implication of the office-automation revolution of the 1980s was the computerisation of legal drafting. At the most modest levels this just involved using computers as advanced typewriters, but had the effect that an electronic version of legal texts was available at the very time when the texts were produced, without additional costs. Moreover, not only the final documents were available in electronic form, but also the *travaux preparatoires* in a broad sense, i.e., the various studies, reports, drafts, comments, amendment proposals produced during the legislative process (or the various documents produced by the parties of a case and by the judge during a judicial procedure).

The use of computers in the production of legal documents had various impacts on their electronic distribution:

- It enlarged the range or documents which could made available to the public; non only the final, legally binding acts, but also the texts delivered at earlier stages.
- It enabled a strict connection between the procedures aimed at producing new law and the legal information systems; the procedure itself could deliver electronic documents, which were used within the same procedure (for its further steps) but also could be made available outside of it.
- It strengthened the role of legal authorities, as the providers of the original legal texts; they could distribute electronically their own outputs, without the intermediation of professional publishers.

Since legal authorities could themselves, with little additional cost, make the legal texts they produced accessible to the public, professional providers of electronic legal information (in particular private publisher) had to change their mission. They could no longer limit themselves to the provision of the bare legal sources, but they needed to provide added value to legal documents (comments, notes, doctrine, etc.), if they wanted to continue to play a significant (and economically rewarding) role in legal documentation.

3.1.3 The Synthesis: The Universally Accessible But Plural Systems of the 1990s

The synthesis between the thesis of the 1970s (the construction of a unitary National legal information systems, including all legal sources and remotely accessibly by all) and the antithesis of the 1980s (the distribution of multiple instances of multiple databanks, to be used on individually accessible personal computers), was achieved in the 1990s through the Internet revolution, and in particular through the WWW. Internet resulted from (and contributed to) the integration of computing and telecommunications: by making distances irrelevant it enabled the virtual integration of resources resident on different computers; by supporting the seamless interaction of systems and application it enabled merging services of different applications, interacting with different resources, into complex functionalities; by making systems communicate it enabled conversation between their users.

We can say that the Internet provided a synthesis between the unifying approach of the 1970s and the separating approach of the 1980, since it allowed each one to access from a single point (name the Internet itself) all legal information, while preserving (and even increasing) the diversity of such information.

One of the major effects of the Internet has indeed been the empowerment of individuals and groups. By drastically reducing the costs of producing and publicly distributing information, the Internet has enabled individuals and groups to participate in information processes, rather than being merely passive users.

With regard to legal information we have assisted in last years to an impressive, both in quantity and diversity, richness of initiatives. As [1] observes, there has been "a profusion of initiatives ... each court, each agency, each institution presented their own site to the public." This increased offer of legal information involves a tendency toward fragmentation: not only legal information is provided by different agencies and is split in different sites, but "these sites often do not have standards for updating, response, document design, retrieval strategies etc."

Such puzzling diversity has been increased by the fact that not only institutions have been providing legal information; private law firms too have uploaded legal information into the web as a way to lure possible clients to their web sites. Similarly non-profit organisation have begun to provide on-line legal information related to their activities (see for instance the various legal sources on human rights at `http://web.amnesty.org/`). So, multiple copies are now available on line of many legislative acts (especially those more frequently used, such as regulations on privacy, contracts, intellectual property, rents, product liability, etc.), in a plurality of sites, and in different formats.

Nor has the provision of legal information been limited to the reproduction of legal sources, or anyway of documents produced by public authorities; it has been extended to comments on legal sources (news reports, political evaluations, academic analyses), and more generally, legal doctrine. One of the richest sources of doctrinal information is nowadays the Social Science Research Network (`http://www.ssrn.com`), whose eLibrary consists of two parts: an Abstract Database containing abstracts on over 162,600 scholarly working papers and forthcoming papers and an Electronic Paper Collection currently containing about 130,000 downloadable full text documents in Adobe Acrobat pdf format, a large section of which is constituted by doctrinal contributions.

In addition, we must consider the domain of legal blogs, which have rapidly become one of the richest sources of doctrinal information (see for instance `http://www.becker- posner-blog.com` where two leading legal academics address current legal and political issues). The are also many discussion groups devoted to legal issues and even websites devoted to the presentation-discussion-advocation of important legal topics (see for instance `http://www.nosoftwarepatents.com/en/m/intro/index.html`).

The Internet's synthesis has lead to an enormous growth of the body of legal information available to all—the shared *Jurisphere*—an expansion that has benefitted not only legal researchers but also many practitioners. However, it is no easy task to find in the Jurisphere the information we need: such information is to be extracted from a huge and diverse collection of materials, dispersed in multiple sites, having different document designs, retrieval strategies, kinds of material, levels of accuracy, update strategies. Typically we use one of the generally available search engines to retrieve all texts containing certain words or combinations of words, ordered according to their relevance (on the basis of the relevance algorithm used by the search engine). The output is usually a very big set of documents, but such a result usually just represents the beginning of our inquiry: to complete our inquiry we have to browse through the retrieved documents, checking for their pertinence with regard to our objective, and for the reliability of their source.

Even after solving the problem of noise (false positives, namely the retrieval of irrelevant documents), we would have to solve the problem of silence (false negatives, namely, failure to retrieve relevant document), which is only partially addressed by the richness of the documentation available. In fact the documents we have automatically retrieved are only those containing the words in our query; we fail to retrieve the relevant documents expressing the same concepts through different words. For addressing this problem we need advanced search tools, able to map the user-query into the documents that, using whatever linguist form, express information relevant to the user. Moreover, further documents may be relevant, in virtue of their relation to documents pertaining to the users query (consider for instance laws modifying, abrogating or suspending the documents dealing with the users' interests).

Finally, even when users retrieve the documents most relevant to their interests, unless they are assisted by advanced legal information systems, they still have to combine the different bits of information (possibly contained in different documents) pertinent to their problem (for instance, they would have to construct the law in force by mentally performing all the required textual modifications).

3.1.4 Legal Information Institutes

The Internet, besides enabling anyone to add his or her bit of information to the available "legal-knowledge soup"—by republishing existing sources (possibly in new combinations), producing new versions of them (for instance consolidated texts), or adding original comments or doctrinal contributions—has also enabled new actors to engage in the construction of broadly scoped legal information systems. This is the case in particular for Legal Information Institutes (LII), namely, independent bodies aimed at providing free access on a non-profit basis to multiple sources of legal information, originating from multiple public bodies (see `http://www.worldlii.org/`).

The activity of such institutes is based upon their idea that all legal limits to the duplication of legal information (as deriving in particular from the so called Crown Copyright of Commonwealth states over their official documents), should be overcome, as it is affirmed in the joint "Declaration on Free Access to Law", which states the following principles:

- Public legal information from all countries and international institutions is part of the common heritage of humanity. Maximising access to this information promotes justice and the rule of law.
- Public legal information is digital common property and should be accessible to all on a non-profit basis and free of charge.
- Independent non-profit organisations have the right to publish public legal information and the government bodies that create or control that information should provide access to it so that it can be published.

According to the same declaration, public legal information is defined as follows:

> Public legal information means legal information produced by public bodies that have a duty to produce law and make it public. It includes primary sources of law, such as legislation, case law and treaties, as well as various secondary (interpretative) public sources, such as reports on preparatory work and law reform, and resulting from boards of inquiry. It also includes legal documents created as a result of public funding.

The experience of the legal information institutes started in 1992, when the legal information Institute of Cornell Law School (`http://www.law.cornell.edu` was launched by Peter Martin and Tom Bruce. One aspect of vision of Legal research institutes, which strongly distinguishes them from previous initiative in legal documentation, consists in the purpose of extending electronic access to the law also outside professional users. As Peter Martin puts it:

> One of our powerful early discoveries was how much demand outside those professional sectors there was, ordinary citizens trying to make sense of laws that impinge on their lives (cited from [1]).

Cornell's initiative (which covers now codes, federal laws, decisions by the Supreme court and by the New York Court of appeal, and many further collections of legal materials) was followed by the creation of other similar institutes in many countries. In particular, the Australasian legal information institute (`http://www.austlii.edu.au`) has been particularly successful and has represented the model for further initiative in various countries, like Canada, UK and South Africa. A World legal information Institute has also been established, which provides an access point to the collections of various legal information Institutes, containing 865 databases from 123 countries and territories.

Jon Bing [1] observes that legal information institutes provide a useful service in contributing to make original legal sources available to both legal professionals and lay citizens, as required by the idea of *publicatio legis* (the idea that the law should become binding only after being made available to all) an idea which is related to fundamental principles such as those of legal certainty and democracy. However, according to Bing, such institutes are now facing two problems. Firstly it may be doubted that knowledge of the law can be effectively ensured by providing citizens with original texts. Lay citizens would rather need "a problem-oriented gateway to the material, where the authentic instruments are commented and explained". Secondly, as I have observed above, the function of providing the original sources tends to be assumed directly by public bodies. Such bodies can today build their electronic repositories as a (almost) costlessly by-product of using ICT for the purposes of drafting and workflow-management. This enables them to increasingly provide free generalised access to their sources without the mediation of a third party.

3.2 The Dialectics of Current Approaches

Different trends and different models can be anticipated for legal information systems in the framework of the Internet synthesis I described in Section 3.1.3. I will distinguish two main approaches, again a thesis and an antithesis:

- the thesis (presented in the next section) consist in a newly-conceived centralised and comprehensive public legal-information system, integrated with the management of legislative (and judicial) procedures, and using the Internet for dissemination;
- the antithesis (presented in the Section 3.2.2) consists in the decentralised non-governmental development of legal information systems and services on the basis of the public availability of electronic legal documents.

I shall than argue (in Section 3.2.3) that a synthesis of these two model is also possible, where legislative information is unified through the use of shared standards.

3.2.1 *A New Thesis: A Centralised Legal Information System for the Internet Age*

This thesis is clearly presented by Jon Bing, who argues that the way ahead in legal documentations is represented by the move from retrieval into *regulatory management*. This requires adopting a different view of the services to be provided by legal information systems, a view that is not restricted to their use in legal research (for retrieving stored documents), but which also includes the preparation of new regulations (drafting, reviewing, amending, etc.) and the application of such regulations (by judges and administration).

This approach, he argues, is mostly appropriate for developing countries, which are not—like the North-American or European jurisdictions—"seeped in traditions and established arrangements, where the new computerised service has to find its place among legal publishers of primary and secondary sources, legal gazettes, and other well established practises." An integrated system for regulatory management should cater for the need of different users: the legislator, the administration, the judiciary and private lawyers, as well as the common citizen (to the extent to which the latter may be content with the original legal sources).

According to Bing's vision, the core of such a system should consist of a mother-database, containing all documents, coherently marked using to the same markup language. Such a database should be prepared and updated through a centralised editorial process which controls the input documents, normalises them, and gives them the appropriate format (see Fig. 3.1).

From the mother-database different outputs in different formats should be produced (see Fig. 3.2). In particular, the mother-database should deliver the following outputs: a *status* database (a database that provides the law in force, and offers high performances to professional users), a legal gazette with the new legislation, compilations of the law in force, and freely accessible text for Internet browsing.

Note that in many jurisdictions a gazette in electronic form is already published together with the gazette in paper form. Given that electronic texts can be delivered

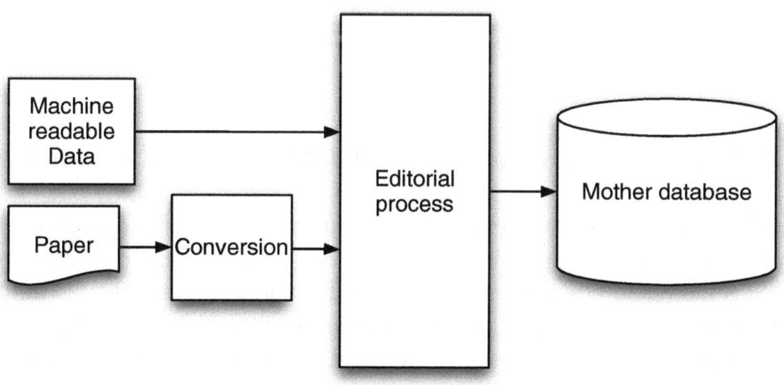

Fig. 3.1 Jon Bing: the production of a mother-database

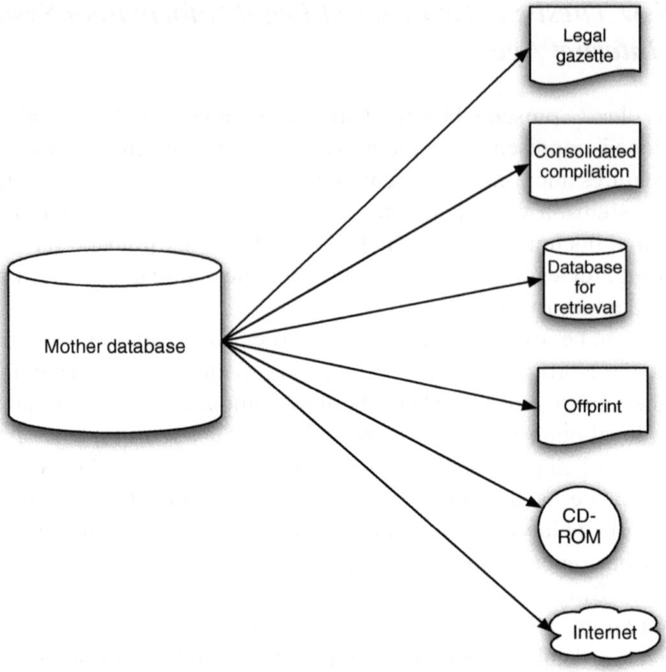

Fig. 3.2 Jon Bing: the outputs of the mother-database

immediately and costless, the electronic gazette is gradually substituting the paper version as the main reference for professional lawyers and for ordinary citizens. This fact has been officially recognised in some countries, like Norway or Austria, where the electronic publication of a law already represents the original official legal text. In Austria, in particular, the federal Constitution has been changed in order that the official gazette be constituted by the document published on line in the Austrian legal information system (at the web sit: `http://ris1.bka.gv.at/authentic/index.aspx`), which is digitally signed by the Federal Chancellery.

3.2.2 A New Antithesis: Access to Distributed Legal Resources

The antithesis to Bing's centralised solution (universal access to a central official legal database) consists in providing an universal access point to distributed legal resources. Such resources will reside in the information systems of the authorities creating the stored legal texts, but different content providers (public or private, profit of no-profit) will provide access to them, either by just building an index to such resources or also by copying them to a central repository. In this model the Internet provides both the channels through which information is extracted from the

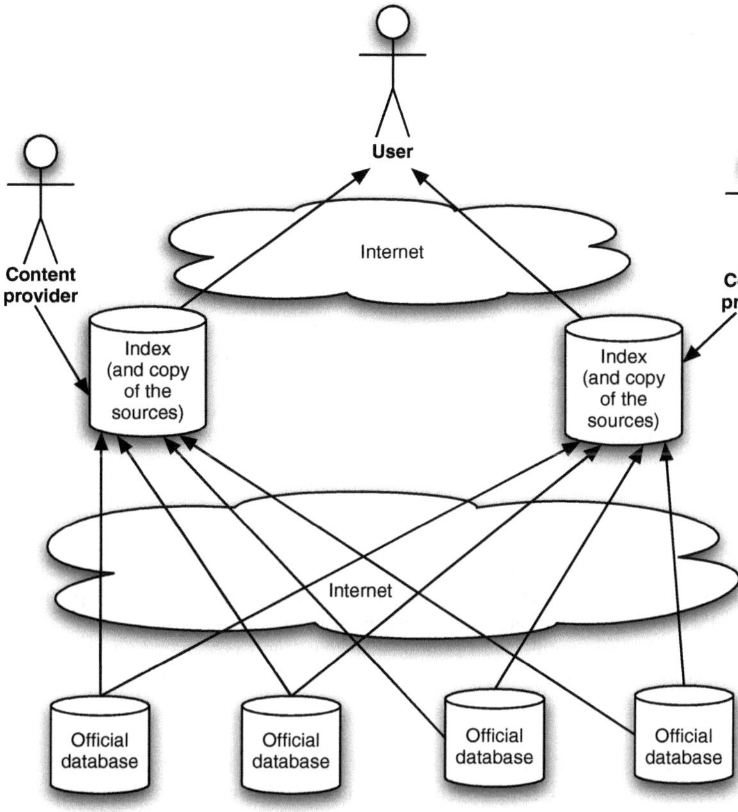

Fig. 3.3 Providing information from distributed legal databases

distributed original databases and the channel through which the user accesses such information, as you can see in Fig. 3.3.

The latter view is advocated by Graham Greenleaf, according whom the centralised solution proposed by Bing may be adequate to certain context (small countries, like the Scandinavian ones, having an efficient, homogeneous and integrated public system), but it is not appropriate for coping with large, heterogeneous and diversified legal environments. For legal systems fitting within the latter profile (and for integrating different legal systems), only a decentralised architecture can work.

Greenleaf argues that for achieving an adequate provision of legal information it is not necessary that public authorities directly provide a legal information service covering all possible needs: such needs can be met in different ways, by different providers, among which an important role can be vested by the legal information Institutes. Public authorities are rather required to comply with the obligation to provide "full free access to the law", by which he means "free access to the computerised sources of legal data to those who wish to publish it" [2]. Such an obligation would fall upon of the legislature as on any other producer of legally binding documents. More exactly, according to the philosophy of the legal information Institutes, legal authorities have the obligation to make legal information available in such a way the its provision satisfies the following requirements:

- Provision in a completed form, including additional information best provided at source, such as the consolidation of legislation, and the addition of catch words (index terms) or even summaries to cases.
- Provision in an authoritative form, such as use or court-designated citations for cases and (eventually) use of digital signature to authenticate the versions distributed.
- Provision in the form best facilitating dissemination, which should always now mean in electronic form, should in most cases be possible by e-mail or more sophisticated form of data delivery, and should be possible in a form facilitating conversion.
- Provision on a marginal-cost-recovery basis to anyone, so that governments do not attempt to profit from the sale of public legal information, thereby creating artificial barriers to access to law.
- Provision with no re-use restrictions or licence fees, subject only to such minimal restrictions as are necessary to preserve the integrity of published data.
- Preservation of a copy in the care of the public authority, so that an archive of the data is preserved to enable greater competition whenever a new entrant wishes to publish the date and whether or not the public authority publishes the data itself.
- Non-discriminatory recognition of citations, so that Court-designated citations are not removed from "reported" cases, ending the privileged status of citations of "official" reports [2, page 69].

Once public authorities have made legal content accessible in this way, they can rely on non-governmental actors for distributing and enriching legal information (or can intervene by supporting and regulating the operation of such actors, through funding or other incentives).

Greenleaf also observes that nowadays the task of collecting different sources into a distributed unique database does not necessary require an editorial process, since the collection can be performed automatically by spiders or web-robot (also called crawlers) which can peruse the web, indexing all relevant sites. He also observes that noise and redundancy in search results can be reduced by using relevance ranking, as performed by leading web-search engines such as Google's.

3.2.3 A New Synthesis: Standard-Based Legal Information in the Jurisphere

Both approaches just described present significant advantages. The model of the unique official mother-database is based upon the idea that all legal sources should be stored a uniform format, according to a consistent editing procedure, and that such sources should include all machine-processable information needed to support subsequent multiple uses. Consequently, it seem capable of providing significant advantages:

- Reliability of (and consequently trust on) legal information would be ensured, since such information would always be extracted from the official database.
- Formal coherence of the different legal sources and formats would be achieved (for instance, in the way of expressing references), since all sources would result from the same repository.
- Noise in information retrieval would be reduced, since users could choose to search only the official database (rather than the multiple overlapping pages and repositories now available over the Internet).
- No strong technological requirements would be imposed on legal drafters, who could just use ordinary word-processing tools, since the texts would be structured and enriched with metadata only at the moment of their transfer into the mother-database.

Also the idea of extracting information from distributed legal database—and more generally, from distributed repositories of legal sources, possibly managed by the same authorities who have adopted the stored normative acts—has distinctive advantages:

- It would enable a diversified and competitive provision of legal documents.
- It would facilitate the integration between legal procedures and the provision of legal information (each producer of legal sources would deliver to the public the documents in the same electronic form they had when resulting from the procedure leading to their adoption).
- It would provide decentralisation and autonomy, since each (kind of) authority would be able to organise its document management-system according to its needs, possibly enriching it with additional services (e.g. workflow management), and tailoring it to the needs of its users.

Fortunately we are not facing here a tragic choice between the two approaches just presented, namely, a choice where the adoption of one approach would entail loosing the advantages of the other: in the last years a synthesis has emerged that is able to preserve the advantages of both.

This synthesis is based on the decentralised production of electronic legal (and in particular, legislative) documents according to shared XML standards. Thus, the unifying aspect no longer consists in the creation of a unique database, or in a uniform editorial activity, but rather in the adoption of a common standard specifying how legislative and other legal document are to be given unique names, and how they can be enriched with machine processable data specifying their structure, indicating their links, and describing their content. The shared standard should provide ways of expressing non only the structural elements of the text (articles/sections, subsection, chapters, titles, etc.) but also the references and textual modifications. In this way, both hypertextual navigation and the construction of the law in force could be automatically delivered. The standard should be extensible so that further components can be accommodated in it, if required by further applications (e.g. for checking the logical consistency of the norms expressed by a legal document, analysing the ontology of its concepts, expressing its rules, and so on).

According to this vision, standard-compliant legal documents can be drafted and processed using standard-compliant software tools. They can be stored in distributed databases or in centralised ones. They can be delivered to the public in their original document model (including the standard-based markup), but can also be split into articles or commas and fed into a traditional relational database (for the purpose of efficient information retrieval) or merged into electronic books (for distribution to the public).

Documents including the original markup can be reused by any person or system knowledgeable of the standard, and can be enriched by adding further information and ways of processing it. In this way users could be provided with various "derived legislative works", constructed by the Parliamentary offices or by third parties. For instance, texts can be expanded with doctrinal comments or semantic metadata, or even with a machine-processable representation of concepts and norms (which could then be applied with the support of knowledge-based systems). However, the official instances of such documents will remain distinguishable from the such derived works, and all content (both the text and the originally added machine-processable information) will be controllable and reliable.

As we shall see in Chapter 10, various countries are adopting XML standards for legal documents. Besides national projects some international initiatives (such as the AKOMA-NTOSOand METAlex projects) have been undertaken. By delivering internationally agreed standards, such initiatives facilitate the development of national XML standards (which may rely on the international standards or develop adaptations of them), the exchange of legal information at a transnational level, and the emergence of a competitive transnational market for standard-based software products.

References

1. Bing, J. 2003. The Policies of Legal Information Services: A Perspective of Three Decades. In *Yulex 2003*, ed. L.A. Bygrave, 37–55. Oslo: Norwegian Research Centre for Computers and Law.
2. Greenleaf, G. 2004. Jon Bing and the history of computerised legal research: Some missing links. In *Et tilbakeblikk pa Fremtiden*, eds. O. Torvund and L.A. Bygrave, 61–75. Institutt for rettsinformatikk.
3. W3C. 2004. Web Services Glossary: W3C Working Group Note 11 February 2004.

Chapter 4
A Standard-Based Approach for the Management of Legislative Documents

Fabio Vitali

This section will present the emerging standard-based approach to the management of legislative documents, an approach that best fits the needs of a Parliamentarian democracy in the Internet age.

As we have already observed, this approach focuses on a definition of the ways in which machine readable information is to be added to the official text of legislative documents. On the basis of this definition two kinds of software tools can be developed: tools supporting the preparation of standard-compliant documents (by helping the drafter to embed the machine-processable information in the document) and tools managing the documents compliant with standard (on the basis of the machine-processable information embedded in them). In this way a seamless integration between the production of legislative documents and their subsequent use is enabled.

For *open access* to be ensured, such a standard should be *open* in multiple senses:

- its use should not be limited by intellectual property rights (see the W3C patent policy on `http://www.w3.org/Consortium/Patent-Policy-2004-0205`);
- its definition should be publicly accessible and understandable to all (having the required technical competence), being expressed in a publicly known format (metalanguage);
- the machine-processable information added to the document should also be accessible and understandable (self-explanatoriness);
- the standard should allow extensions and adaptations to match specific present and future needs (extensibility);
- the development of the standard should be entrusted to a body open to the participation of all interests on which the standard impacts and on all capacities which are useful for its development.

In the following we will first present the purpose and the scope of a standard for legislative documents, and then we will identify the user of standard-compliant documents, and finally we shall consider the different software tools needed for

---

F. Vitali (✉)
Department of Computer Science, University of Bologna, 40127 Bologna, Italy
e-mail: fabio@cs.unibo.it

G. Sartor et al. (eds.), *Legislative XML for the Semantic Web*, Law, Governance and Technology Series 4, DOI 10.1007/978-94-007-1887-6_4,
© Springer Science+Business Media B.V. 2011

a standard-based management of legislative documents. Our model will be strongly be based on the ideas characterising the project Akoma-Ntoso (as described in [1]), which, among the initiatives so far developed, mostly embodies the principles of a standard-based management of legislative documents.

4.1 The Objective of a Standard for Legal Documents

Good standards for legislative documents define a set of simple, technology-neutral representations of Parliamentary documents for e-Parliament services and provide an enabling framework for the effective exchange of "machine readable" Parliamentary documents such as legislation, debate record, minutes, etc.

Providing access to primary legal materials and Parliamentary documents is not just a matter of giving physical or on-line access to them. As we have observed above, "Open access" requires the information to be described and classified in a uniform and organized way so that content is structured into meaningful elements that can be read/understood by software applications, and the content is made "machine readable".

4.1.1 A rationale for Shared Standards

A standard for Parliamentary documents contributes to fulfil the citizens' right to access Parliamentary proceedings and legislation by providing "open access" and advanced functionalities like "point-in-time" legislation through standardised representations of data and metadata in the Parliamentary domain and mechanisms for citations and cross referencing of legal documents.

Regardless of the processes that generate and use Parliamentary documents, regardless of the cultural and historical factors that give shape and substance to Parliamentary documents, and regardless of the human languages in which these documents are written, there are undeniable relationships that connect documents of the same type, of different types. There are also similarities among documents of different countries. One of the main objectives of a standard for legislative documents is to be able to capture and describe these similarities so as to unify and streamline, wherever possible and as far as possible, the processes and formats and tools related to Parliamentary documentation. This lends itself to reducing investments in tools and systems, helping open access, and enhancing cooperation and integration of governmental bodies both within the individual countries and between them. A standard would define a model for open access focused on the following issues:

- generation of documents: it should be possible to use the same tools for creating the documents, regardless of the type, country, language, and generation process of the document.

- presentation of documents: it should be possible to use the same tools to show on screen and print on paper all documents, regardless of their type, country, language and generation process.
- accessibility of documents: it should be possible to reference and access documents across types, languages, countries, etc., implementing the network of explicit references among texts into a web of hypertext links that allow the reader to navigate easily and immediately across them.
- description of documents: it should be possible to describe all documents, regardless of their types, languages, countries, etc., so as to make it possible to create repositories, search engines, analysis tools, comparison tools, etc.

At the same time, a good model considers the differences that exist in individual document types, that are derived from using different human languages, and that are implicit in the legislative culture of each country. Therefore the common open access model needs to be designed to be flexible, support exceptions, and allow extensions far enough to provide support for all peculiarities that can be found in the complete document set.

4.1.2 National and Transnational Standards

A standard for legislative documents can aim only at being shared within a particular national jurisdiction, or also at being shared by different national jurisdiction.

Sharing a legislative standard within a single jurisdiction means that the standard can (and should) be used by all normative authorities in that jurisdiction (not only Parliaments, but also regional assemblies, regulatory bodies, local authorities, etc.), when producing and disseminating the documents. Moreover, it means that such a standard will be used by other authorities, private publishers, citizens, when accessing or reusing such documents. Finally the standard will be used by software developers, in order to produce software meant to support the preparation, the distribution, the use, the reuse of legislative information.

Sharing a legislative standard within a single jurisdiction will contribute to leveraging modern information and communications technologies to radically improve the usability of Parliamentary information as a strategic resource both insider and outside Parliaments. In particular, improved access to documents regarding Parliamentary activities will enable citizens to hold Parliaments accountable, stimulate greater efficiency and enhance democracy. We can consider Parliaments as major producers of data and information that are vital for the democratic well being of a country and the lifeblood of political participation. The lack of a standardised way for Parliaments to classify and structure their data resources, information technology and business processes stands in the way of increased integration of information exchange and this in turn limits the efficiency and effectiveness of Parliamentary activities.

Sharing a single jurisdiction-wide standard for legislative information fosters greater co-operation between different institutions, administrations and Parliaments using common open standards that avoid vendor lock-in and allow for greater public access to information.

Further increased and additional advantages can be obtained when a standard is shared not only within a single jurisdiction, but also by different jurisdiction, in the framework of a transnational cooperation. Parliaments are now endeavouring to promote collaboration and co-operation with Parliaments of other countries. A transnationally shared standard would represent a significant contribution to overcome the present state, where most interactions within and among Parliaments require numerous disparate transactions across multiple departments/Parliaments and there is very limited consolidation and aggregation across national Parliaments' boundaries.

Connecting Parliaments has many benefits: in addition to its value as a knowledge transfer mechanism, where one Parliament can learn from the other, it also can be a tremendous boost to Parliamentary positive imitation. By seeing what others are doing, a Parliamentarian can discover the possibility of doing the same in his or her Parliament.

The explosion of Internet-based systems have increased the possibilities and range of such dialogue but this can be achieved and exploited only if common standards to produce, classify and share Parliamentary and legislative electronic documents are agreed and used by the Parliaments themselves.

4.1.3 Interoperability

Although each Parliament has its unique characteristics, all Parliamentary democracies have a number of characteristics in common: Actors, Structures, Procedures, Acts and Information. A good standard defines common building blocks in a single model that can be applied to each (or at least most) Parliamentary documents.

A good standard defines a set of recommendations and guidelines for e-Parliament services in an international context. The framework will be an essential prerequisite for interlinking and web-enabling Parliaments. It will address information content and recommend technical policies and specifications for connecting Parliament information systems across countries. It needs to be based on open standards.

Country Parliaments should use the guidance provided to supplement their national e-Government Interoperability Frameworks with an international dimension and thus enable international interoperability of Parliaments. So a good standard is meant to supplement, rather than replace, national interoperability guidelines that may exist by adding the interoperability dimension. Any such initiative will enable open access by focussing on both *semantic* and *technical* interoperability.

- Semantic interoperability is concerned with ensuring that the precise meaning of exchanged information is understandable by any person or application receiving the data.
- Technical interoperability is aimed at ensuring that all applications, systems and interfaces for e-Parliamentary services are based on a shared core of technologies,

languages and technical assumptions easing data interchange, data access and reuse of acquired competencies and tools. A good standard ensures technical interoperability by enforcing the use of open standards and open document formats, such as those based on the XML (eXtensible Markup Language) language, whose specifications are a worldwide standard and for which numerous tools and applications have been developed and are widely available.

By adopting such specifications, Parliamentary system designers (and more generally, the designers or information systems for any system meant to support production, access and reuse of normative information) can ensure interoperability between systems while at the same time enjoy the flexibility to select different hardware, and systems and application software to implement solutions.

4.1.4 Presentation, Structure and Semantics

There are three aspects to any Parliamentary document: (1) Presentation—how the information looks e.g. the colour of the text used in the document, the headings and other such formatting issues; (2) Structure—how the information is organized; (3) Semantics—what the information represents or means.

Online publishing of Parliamentary documents has long been confined to presentation issues. Documents have been put on line trying to replicate as much as possible the layout and formatting of paper. The way a document looks is very important to the "human reader" but does not really provide much useful information to the computer to actually "read" a document as a knowledgeable human being could do. The development of descriptive markup meta-languages such as XML allows to add information to any document that would make both the structure and the semantic of a document "readable" by a computer. Computer do not have the kind of experience and knowledge that allow professional human being to be able to deduct structure and semantics from a document unless this document has been previously "marked up" to make it "machine readable". More specifically:

- Semantic markup—semantically identifies parts of the document (e.g., headings, names, references, provisions, In this way the "meaning" of the different parts can then be "understood" by machines as well, in the sense that a machine will be able to distinguish such parts and consequently to process them accordingly.
- Structural markup—this refers to the categorisation of different parts of a document based on their functionality e.g. In a Parliamentary document you may want to indicate that a certain section of the document is the Preamble, Question, Motions etc.

A good legislative standard may provide a way to move digital documents from the presentation era into a more semantic-oriented generation, in which digital Parliamentary documents are not just displayed online, but are "understood" by software applications (according to the ideas of the semantic web, see Section 2.2. Both the "meaning" and "structure" of every element in a Parliamentary document is available for all machines to access, thus providing the unprecedented opportunity to exploit the speed and accuracy of ICTs to manage, access and distribute such documents.

4.2 Scope of a Standard for Legislative Documents

Parliaments function through the medium of documents. Debate in Parliamentary chambers is recorded as documents. Legislation is passed through the voting process via a combination of documents; the proposed legislation itself, proposed amendments, committee working papers and so on. Given that the process is document-centric, the key enabler of streamlined Information Technology in Parliaments will be the use of open document formats for the principal types of documents. Such open document formats will allow easy exchange and aggregation of Parliamentary information, in addition to reducing the time required to make the information accessible via different electronic publishing media.

In the following section we will consider the main conventions which concur in providing a standard for legislation, namely, a structural convention (concerning ways to partition and organise of the documents), a metadata convention (concerning ways to add information to the document), a naming convention (concerning ways to name documents and their parts and reference them),

4.2.1 A Structural Convention

A good standard needs to include a comprehensive set of XML-based Parliamentary Open Document Formats. Document standards makes use of industry standard XML (eXtensible Markup Language) to define open document formats. Parliaments work with a number of distinct types of documents such as legislation, debate record, Parliamentary questions etc. Thus, comprehensive set of XML-based Parliamentary open document formats would cover all of the following categories:

- Primary legislation—covering the lifecycle of a piece of legislation
- Parliamentary Debates
- Amendment lists
- Committee briefs
- Journals

The standard should define a distinct document type for each major type of document. The definition takes the form of human and machine-readable document models, one for each document type. All document types would share the same basic structures, provide support for metadata, addressing and references, and differentiate common structure and national peculiarities and extensions. All documents can be produced by the same set of tools (although specialized tools may provide more detailed and specific help in specific situations), need the same tools to be displayed or printed (although specialized tools can provide more sophisticated and individual presentations), can reference each other in an unambiguous and machine-processable way, and can be described by a common set of metadata that helps in indexing, analysing and storing all documents.

4.2.2 A Metadata Convention and a Shared Ontology

Metadata is structured information about a resource. metadata records information about a document that does not actually belong to it, but is necessary to examine in order to deal with it (for instance, information about its publication, lifecycle, etc.). metadata also enables a resource to be found by indicating what the resource is about and how it can be accessed. Furthermore, metadata facilitates the discovery and use of online resources by providing information that aids and increases the ease with which information can be located by search engines that index metadata. Metadata values are labelled and collected according to a common ontology, i.e. an organized description of the metadata values that describe the resources. A common ontology is fundamental to provide a way for managing, organizing and comparing metadata.

The Parliamentary Ontology is concerned particularly with records management and resource management, and covers the core set of elements that contain data needed for the effective management and retrieval of official Parliamentary information. The aim of the Parliamentary Ontology is to provide a universal container for all the information about a resource that is available to the owner of the resource, does not belong to the recourse itself, and might be needed for management or searching. The Parliamentary Ontology needs to be designed to be extensible so that those Parliaments with different, or more specific, metadata needs may add extra elements and qualifiers to meet their own requirements.

4.2.3 A Naming Convention

The Parliamentary Naming Convention and the reference mechanism are intended to enable a persistent, location-independent, resource identification mechanism. The adoption of a scheme based on this Naming Convention will allow the full automation of distributed hypertext. The reference mechanism, based on a shared naming convention, allows the automated generation of hypertext links and access to resources explicitly cited in legislative documents. This automation can cater for:

- the availability, at a certain time, of more than one resource corresponding to the document referred to;
- the possibility that references to resources not yet published on the web are present.

Official documents, bills, laws and acts contain numerous references to other official documents, bills, laws and acts. The whole Parliamentary corpus of documents can be seen as a network, in which each document is a node linking, and linked by, several other nodes through natural language expressions. The adoption of a common naming convention and a reference mechanism to connect a distributed document corpus, like the one embodied by the Parliaments, will greatly enhance the accessibility and richness of cross references. It will enable comprehensive cross referencing and hyperlinking, so vital to any Parliamentary corpus, from:

- debate record into legislation
- section of legislation to section of legislation in the same act
- section of legislation to section of legislation in another act of the same Parliament or of other international institutions.

4.3 The Users of a Standard for Legislative Documents

A good legislative standard aims at providing support for a large number of tasks and users spread throughout time, space and competencies. The types of potential users that might end up using or benefiting from such standard can be grouped in the following categories:

4.3.1 The Legislator

The legislator is either a member of a Parliament, or a personal assistant of a member of the Parliament. He is currently drafting a new piece of legislation, due to be discussed and, maybe, approved in a future session of the Parliament. "The legislator" is not aware of the existence of legislative standards, XML, or any such technicality. He/she might, or might not, be aware of the existence of guidelines in the formal drafting of law, he/she does not know what XML is, and does not care. He/she wants be able retrieve bills and acts effectively, to be able to access explicit references to other laws made in a bill or act, et. The legislators want to be able to access "point-in-time" consolidations of laws that provide a consolidation of the original act and the subsequent amendments up to a specific point in time, the legislator wants easy and effective tools to find and retrieve bills and acts to carry out their duties more effectively.

4.3.2 The Legal Drafter

The legal drafter is a member of the office supporting the process of legal drafting. During the discussion phase in Parliament, "the legal drafter" receives all proposed text modifications to a bill being discussed, and generates any of a number of documents used by members of the Parliaments (such as summaries, synoptic views of amendments, etc.). When the proposed bill is finally approved, he/she creates the final version of the bill; either directly in XML or in a word processing file that is then translated into XML by some downstream process phase. "The legal drafter" is an expert in the matters of law, and has some computing experience, but he/she is no lawyer and definitely no computer scientist. He/she knows something about legislative standards and XML, but not much.

4.3.3 The Toolmaker

The toolmaker works for a ICT company who has a contract for creating specialized software for a Parliament. The toolmaker decides to create a specialized editing tool by customizing a well-known Word Processor (such as MS Word or OpenOffice) and a conversion tools that creates valid documents recognizing formatting characteristics of the input texts. He has the goals of making the tools usable by the legal drafter and his/her colleagues, and at the same time compatible with the rules of the standard. Differently from the "legal drafter", "the tool-maker" has full access to the standard's documentation, and can talk to his users to understand together what each part of it really is relevant to their task and how to proceed.

4.3.4 The Citizen

"The citizen" of a country where the system based on the good standard is being used, might be a lawyer, a judge, a public employee, or just any ordinary citizen needing fast and easy access to laws and legislation for his/her own purposes. "The citizen" main objective is searching for laws either through an explicit reference (e.g. section 36(2)(c)(ii) of Act 2-1999) or via a search interface (either textual or exploiting vocabularies and ontologies specified through the legislative metadata). "The citizen" doesn't know what the standard is about, nor what XML is, and does not care. He/she wants his/her web browser to display the text of law searched, he/she wants all explicit references to other laws to be hypertext links, and a reasonable interface that lets his/her read the text on the screen and, when necessary, print it on paper.

4.3.5 The Future Toolmaker

"The future toolmaker" is 10 years old now. He is playing with his school friends and does not know anything about legislative standards and does not care. Yet. He/she is in this list because in 15 years, when turning 25, he/she will be a professional computer programmer and will have to create new tools for the Parliament. The key difference between "the toolmaker" and "the future toolmaker" is that "the future toolmaker" may not have access to complete documentation, lost through time after internal evolutions of the standard as well as the workflow of the Parliamentary systems. He/she will only have sparse documentation of the actual requirements of the system he/she is working on. Furthermore, he/she will have to deal with a fairly stratified situation where the basic ideas (on which "the tool-maker" has worked) have evolved, modified, expanded and changed emphasis. Furthermore, more often than not these changes have happened slowly and without documentation. The only sure thing that "the future toolmaker" has to work on is more than 15 years of legislation available in XML format, whose documentation is introductory for certain, but far from complete and sufficient. Fortunately the early decisions have been to have the XML format be as self-explanatory as possible, so that "the future toolmaker" can, in principle, deduce all undocumented facts about the standard by simply examining a few relevant XML instances of the legislation and discovering there how it should work. In a sense, "the future toolmaker" is more a key user for our system than "the toolmaker", and the possibility for "the future toolmaker" to deduce fundamental properties of the standard from the visual examination of XML documents will make us sure of long-term existence and usefulness of the e-legislative system itself.

4.4 The Tools for the Standard-Based Management of Legislative Documents

Just as many are the users (some of whom are not even aware of the fact they are using or relying on XML-enabled systems), many also are the tools that need to be created around the standard document model. Some of them are basic tools that are necessary for the system to work at all. Others are additional applications that will be created once the basic tasks have been catered for. A brief list of the main categories may help in explaining the breadth and variety of scope of such a standard, and the number of issues that need to be considered in the development of the data formats.

4.4.1 The Editor

The editor is the fundamental tool for the generation of XML versions of legislation. Although not all drafting needs to be actually done on a specialized editor (much less an XML editor) in any real life scenario, there will be situations in which that will be possible and actually necessary (as examples of editors for generating standard-based legislative documents, see [2–4]). The editor will be used in three different scenarios:

- As an interface to activate, control and verify the automatic conversion tool previously described. Through the editor "the legal drafter" will be able to verify the correctness of the conversion, and change and add whatever the conversion engine has forgot or misidentified.

- As a tool to manually mark-up a document provided in a different format. Depending on the sophistication of the conversion engine, this scenario will most probably blend naturally with the first one. Surely the editor will provide for functionalities to edit and add any kind of conformant markup, and will be able to check validity of the intermediate result.
- As an application for direct insertion of both text and markup, starting off an empty document: this will probably be the rarest scenario of use, as the drafting offices will most usually work off an existing document in some other format.

4.4.2 The Converter

It is the converter, with the editor, the most fundamental tool for bootstrapping a standard-based management of legislative information. It will take some convincing for "the legal drafter" to switch from her old faithful word processor and her manual system of handling amendments through a combination of glue and scissors, to use any kind of strange text editor. In the meantime, one of the most important tools will be the converter (for an example of a converter, see [5]).

The converter has the double purpose of converting into XML structures the documents that "the legal drafter" is still producing traditionally, and, most importantly of all, of converting into XML structures the legacy documents, the already approved bills and acts that form the current legislative situation of the country, and whose conversion to XML is needed for any hypertext web of references to work at all. Since legacy documents are, by definition, in any old format, and since "the legal drafter" is not interested in converting them into XML using an editor, "the toolmaker" will have to create an automatic mechanism for the task anyway.

The converter is based on the idea of semi-automatic conversion, i.e., it has automatic processes to determine as correctly as possible the actual interesting structures, and has a manual process to confirm (or, if there is an error, to edit) the inferences made by the automatic process. In fact, this application could even be one of the modules of the editor, and use the editor itself for corrections to the automatic inferences of the converter. Of course, the amount of human editing is inversely proportional to the sophistication of the converter, and in theory large quantities of documents could be processed automatically with little or no manual intervention.

The converter works by examining the typographical and textual regularities of the document, and inferring a structural or semantic role for each text fragment. For every fragment that has no deducible structural or semantic role, the presentation characteristics will be recorded instead and it will be left to the human user to infer the structural or semantic role (if any) needs to be associated to the fragment.

Experience with existing legislative systems show that the basic structure of a legislative act (sections, subsections, clauses, preambles, conclusions, attachments, etc.) can be inferred automatically with great precision and few errors. The most important semantic elements, references and dates, can also be deduced automatically with great precision as long as the human-readable text used for them uses one of a limited number of acceptable forms. More complex structural elements (explicit modifications, specialized terms, people, etc.) might be difficult to catch automatically, but not impossible.

4.4.3 Name Resolvers

In Internet-based framework, legislative documents will be stored on networked computers and will be accessible by specifying their addresses. Yet these addresses are extremely dependent on the specificities of the architecture that will be in vogue or appropriate for the economic and technical context of the moment. It is extremely inappropriate, therefore, that any content or structure that is planned to last for more than a short period of time is given direct access to the physical address of the document in the form that will be eventually used for display.

As we have seen in Section 4.2.3, an essential component of a standard for legislative document is a Naming Convention, namely, a mechanism for creating identifiers of documents that can be used for accessing content and metadata regardless of storage options and architecture. However, a Name-convention needs not (and should not) be used directly for accessing these structures, since it should specify an architecture-independent URI address for all relevant structures of the concerned standard. Thus a naming convention needs be combined with a Name resolver. A Name resolver is a software tool that can, given an architecture-independent URI, identify the resource being sought and provide the current architecture-dependent address that needs to be used at any given time for actual access. Name resolvers are either indirect (in that they redirect the client application to the current address of the requested document) or direct (in that they immediately provide the requested document by generating the actual address and requesting the document as a proxy for the initial client application).

4.4.4 Validations Tools

The "legal drafter", as soon as editing is finished, needs validation tools to check that the document complies with all requirements:

- A content and structure validator that checks the correctness of the document instance with regard to the XML-schema and other rules applicable to it.
- A reference validator that checks whether all references contained in the document already belong to the document collection and are correctly referenced.
- A metadata validator that checks whether the metadata stored with the document are correct and complete.

4.4.5 Document-Management and Other Post-editing Tools

To take full advantage of the information encoded in standard-compliant texts, an advanced document management system is required, with search engines, hypertext functionalities, visualisations and versioning facilities. Such a system will provide the standard-compliant documents to a number of browsers and applications which will increase and get more sophisticated in time. Among such application we can mention the following:

- retrieval facilities, from general search engines, to legally specialised search agents;
- workflow managers, using the information inside the texts to direct the Parliamentarian procedures concerning such texts;
- publishing system, providing the texts in different media and formats;
- knowledge-based systems, using the text for providing explanation and advanced metadata (concepts and rules) associated to it for performing inference.

Such a list is certainly not exhaustive, since, as it has always happened with the Internet, once certain information is made available, multiple unpredictable ways of using it will be discovered by developers and users.

References

1. Africa i-Parliament and UNITED NATIONS Department of Economic and Social Affairs. 2007. Akoma ntoso architecture for knowledge-oriented management of African normative texts using open standards and ontologies. URL `www.akomantoso.org`.
2. Agnoloni, T., E. Francesconi and P. Spinosa. 2007. xmLegesEditor: an OpenSource visual XML editor for supporting legal national standards." In *Proceedings of the V Legislative XML Workshop*, 239–251. Florence: European Press Academic Publishing.
3. Biagioli, C., A. Cappelli, E. Francesconi, and F. Turchi. 2007. Law making environment: Perspectives. In *Proceedings of the V Legislative XML Workshop*. Florence: European Press Academic Publishing.
4. Palmirani Monica, and Raffaella Brighi. 2003. An xml editor for legal information management. In *Proceedings of DEXA 2003, the 2nd International Conference on Electronic Government - EGOV 2003*, 421–429. Berlin: Springer.
5. Palmirani Monica, Raffaella Brighi, and M. Massini. 2005. Automated extraction of normative references in legal texts. In *Proceedings of the 9th International Conference on Artificial Intelligence and Law*, 105–106. New York, NY: ACM.

Chapter 5
Naming Legislative Resources

Enrico Francesconi

5.1 Introduction

In the last few years a number of initiatives have arisen in the field of legal document management.

Since 2001 the Italian Government, through the CNIPA (National Authority for Information Technology in the Public Administration), the Ministry of Justice and ITTIG-CNR (the Institute of Legal Information Theory and Techniques of the Italian National Research Council) promoted the NormeInRete project. It was aimed at introducing standards for sources of law description and identification using XML and URN techniques.

Other national initiatives in Europe introduced standards for the description of legal sources [6]: for example the MetaLex project, promoted by the University of Amsterdam and adopted by the Dutch Tax and Customs Administration, the Belgian Public Centers for Welfare and others; LexDania project in Denmark supported by the Danish Ministry of Justice; CHLexML in Switzerland developed by COPIUR, the Coordination Office for the Electronic Publication of Legal Data Federal Office of Justice; eLaw in Austria coordinated by the Austrian Parliament.

Such initiatives, based in synergies between government, national research institutes, and universities, have defined national XML standards for legal document management, as well as schemes for legal document identification.

Outside Europe, other initiatives have faced similar problems. For example, the Brazilian Senate carried out a feasibility study to provide unique and transparent identifiers to sources of law on the basis of the IFLA-FRBR model. Similarly, the Akoma Ntoso (Architecture for Knowledge-Oriented Management of African Normative Texts using Open Standards and Ontologies) project provides a set of guidelines for e-Parliament services in a Pan-African context by proposing an XML document schema providing sophisticated description possibilities for several Parliamentary document types (including bills, acts and parliamentary records,

E. Francesconi (✉)
ITTIG-CNR, Institute for Legal Information Theory and Techniques,
National Research Council of Italy, 50127 Florence, Italy
e-mail: francesconi@ittig.cnr.it

G. Sartor et al. (eds.), *Legislative XML for the Semantic Web*, Law, Governance and Technology Series 4, DOI 10.1007/978-94-007-1887-6_5,
© Springer Science+Business Media B.V. 2011

etc.). Finally, the Tasmanian Government provided advanced legislative information services through the EnAct project. It gave searchable consolidated Tasmanian legislation by automating much of the legislative drafting and consolidation process, as well as using SGML document representation. Numerous less-visible efforts in the United States and elsewhere have struggled with similar issues.

Most of these initiatives adopted a URI[1] schema for legal document identification. For example in Italy the NormeInRete project defined a URN standard to identify legislation and administrative acts, as well as the Danish LexDania and the Brazilian Lexml projects. All these standards have a common internal structure, regarding both the hierarchy and the elements content. Other projects, like Akoma-Ntoso, defined an identifier based on the http protocol, sharing common features with the URN based identifiers.

In today's information society the processes of political, social and economic integration of European Union member states as well as the increasing integration of the world-wide legal and economic processes are causing a growing interest in exchanging legal information knowledge at national and trans-national levels. The growing desire for improved quality and accessibility of legal information amplifies the need for interoperability among legal information systems across national boundaries. A common open standard used to identify sources of law at international level is an essential prerequisite for interoperability.

The need for a unequivocal identifier of sources of law in different EU Member States, based on open standards and able to provide advanced modalities of document hyper-linking, has been expressed in several conferences by representatives of the Publication Office of the European Union, with the aim of promoting interoperability among national and European institution information systems. Similar concerns have been raised by international groups concerned with free access to legal information, and the Permanent Bureau of the Hague Conference on Private International Law is considering a resolution that would encourage member states to "adopt neutral methods of citation of their legal materials, including methods that are medium-neutral, provider- neutral and internationally consistent". In a similar direction the CEN MetaLex initiative is moving, at European level, towards the definition of a standard interchange format for sources of law, including recommendations for defining naming conventions to them.

5.2 The FRBR Model

The most important and most recent initiatives aiming to provide unique identifiers to legislative resources are conceived in accordance with the Functional Requirements for Bibliographic Records (FRBR model) [13].[2] Such initiatives,

---

[1] Uniform Resource Identifier

[2] This section has been written in collaboration with Fabio Vitali

independently developed, share common features, identified within the CEN MetaLex initiative.

As in the FRBR model, the various CEN MetaLex compliant naming conventions identify a source of law as a bibliographic entity that can be described according to four level of abstraction:

- A bibliographic work is a bibliographic object, realized by one or more expressions, and created by one or more persons in a single creative process ending in a publication event. A work has an author or authors, and is the result of a publication event. We recognize the work through individual expressions of the work, but the work itself exists only in the commonality of context between and among the various expressions of the work: it is an intentional object.
- A bibliographic expression is a realization of one bibliographic work in the form of signs, words, sentences, paragraphs, etc. by the author of that work. Physical form aspects, as typeface or page-layout, are generally speaking not relevant for the expression level. Any change in content gives rise to a new expression. If an expression is revised or modified in content, the resulting expression is considered to be a new expression, no matter how minor the modification may be. Expression is an intentional object.
- A bibliographic manifestation embodies one expression of one bibliographic work. The boundaries between one manifestation and another are drawn on the basis of both content and physical form, e.g. the adoption of a specific data format, or its rendering as ink over sheets of paper. When the production process involves changes in physical form the resulting product is considered a new manifestation. Thus, a specific XML representation, a PDF file (as generated by printing into PDF a specific Word file with a specific PDF distiller), a printed booklet, all represent different manifestations of the same expression of a work. Manifestation is an intentional object. A MetaLex XML document is a bibliographic manifestation.
- A bibliographic item exemplifies one manifestation of one expression of one work: a specific copy of a book on a specific shelf in a library, a specific file stored on a specific computer in a specific location, etc. Items stored on a computer can be easily copied to another location, resulting in another item, but the same manifestation. This makes adding metadata about the item to the item in principle impossible. On the Internet generally speaking only the uniform resource locator (URL) is an item-specific datum. An item is a physical object (even when they are only just bytes on a physical disk).

An XML document is a standard manifestation of one or more bibliographic expressions of a source of law. Editing the XML markup and metadata of the XML document changes the manifestation of an expression. Changing the marked up text changes the expression embodied by the manifestation. Copying an exemplar of the MetaLex XML document creates a new item (Fig. 5.1).

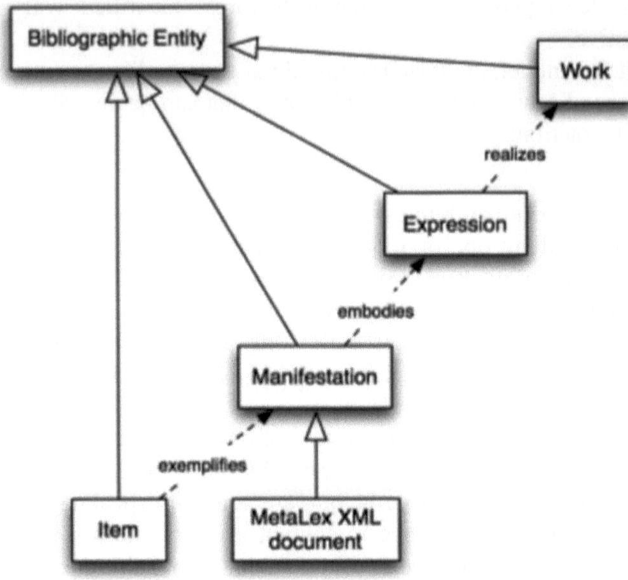

Fig. 5.1 The FRBR model describing sources of law according to different levels of abstraction

5.3 CEN MetaLex Naming Convention Principle and Features

Every CEN MetaLex compliant naming convention has to construct names that must be [2][3]

1. Persistent: names at all levels must maintain the same form over time regardless of the political, archival and technical events happened since their first generation;
2. Global: all relevant documents by all relevant bodies must be represented;
3. Memorizable: names should be easy to write down, easy to remember, easy to correct if they were written down wrongly;
4. Meaningful: names should mean something; It should be possible to make assumption about the kind, freshness and relevance of a citation by looking only at the document's name;
5. Guessable across levels: references to different levels of the same document must be similar; e.g., given a reference to an expression a user should be able to deduce the name of the work;
6. Guessable across document classes: references to different instances of the same document type must be similar; and
7. Guessable across document components: references to different components of the same document at the same level must be similar.

[3] This section has been written in collaboration with Fabio Vitali

A CEN MetaLex naming convention may use a number of document features for the purpose of creating the name of the bibliographic entity (at any level appropriate). Each of these features may contribute to a fragment of the overall name, whose presence is instrumental to uniquely identifying the relevant bibliographic entity. Depending on the naming convention, document type and syntax used, only some of these features may be known or relevant for identification purposes. There are at least four different ways in which (a subset of) these feature values can be specified:

1. As fragments of an URI (based on either the urn or the http protocol)
2. As property-value pairs within the document's metadata
3. As RDF/A statements within the document when expressed in XML or HTML
4. As RDF statements associated to or contained in the document

CEN MetaLex compliant naming conventions share common features (metadata set) able to identify sources of law at Work, Expression and Manifestation levels. Such common features at each level of abstraction, are here below summed up, where (*) represents a feature usually necessary for identification, while the others are additional features which can be useful for identification in specific cases.

Work-level Features

1. The country emanating the document; (*)
2. The document type; (*)
3. Any specification of document subtype, if appropriate;
4. The emanating actor, who may be implicitly deducible by the document type;(*)
5. The promulgating actor, who may be implicitly deducible either by the document type or by the emanating actor;
6. Any relevant creation date of the work; (*)
7. Any relevant number or disambiguating feature of the work (possibly including titles). (*)

Expression-level Features

1. The language(s) associated (could be multiple) (*)
2. The validity date(s) associated to actual content (could be multiple) (*)
3. Any content authoring information to determine the authoritativeness of the text content.
4. Any content-specification date (as opposed to validity dates)

Manifestation-level Features

1. The electronic data format chosen (*)
2. The markup authoring information to determine the authoritativeness of the markup and metadata (*)
3. Any relevant markup-specific date
4. Any additional markup-related annotation (e.g., the existence of multiple versions, of annotations, etc.)

In the following (Sections 5.4 and 5.5) two CEN MetaLex compliant standards for sources of law identification are described.

5.4 URN:LEX Standard

Uniform Resource Names (URNs) are conceived by the Internet community for providing unambiguous and lasting identifiers of network resources, independently from their physical locations, availability and actual publication.[4] In particular they play a key role in the legal domain where references to other legislative measures are very frequent and extremely important: the possibility of being able to immediately providing effective references and accessing legal documents is a desirable feature able to promote transparency and "legal certainty of law".

Moreover the growing necessity of improved quality and accessibility of legal information amplifies the need for interoperability among legal information systems in national and international setting. A persistent, shared, open standard identifier for legal documents at international level is an essential prerequisite for establish such interoperability.

Besides legal content providers, Internet content creators including publishers operating well outside the traditional arenas of legal publishing (news, technical documentation providers, etc.) can benefit by this standard because it facilitates the linking of legal documents and reduces the cost of maintaining documents that contain such references. This will result in a benefit for users as well, since they will enjoy a more richness and reliability of cross-referencing facilities, not only limited within the same information system as it is usually today.

In the last few years a number of initiatives both in and outside Europe have arisen in the field of legal document standards to improve legal document accessibility on the Internet [6]. In this section a standard for the identification of sources of law is described, recently submitted to the IETF as Internet Draft[5] [15]: it is based on a URN technique capable of scaling beyond national boundaries as well as on the definition of a namespace convention (LEX) and a structure that will create and manage identifiers for sources of law at international level.

The identifiers will be globally unique, transparent, persistent, location-independent, and language-neutral. These qualities will facilitate legal document management, moreover they will provide a mechanism of stable cross-collections and cross-country references. In this direction also the Permanent Bureau of the Hague Conference on Private International Law has recently expressed its opinion, encouraging EU Member States to adopt neutral methods of citation of their legal materials, including methods that are medium-neutral, provider-neutral and internationally consistent.

---

[4] This section has been written in collaboration with Pierluigi Spinosa

[5] `http://datatracker.ietf.org/doc/draft-spinosa-urn-lex/`

5.4.1 Structure of a URN:LEX Identifier

As usual, the problem is to provide the right amount guidance at the core of the standard while providing sufficient flexibility to cover a wide variety of needs. The proposed URN:LEX identifier standard does this by splitting the identifier into a hierarchy of components. Its main structure is [1]:

```
"urn:lex:"<NSS>
```

where "urn:lex" is the Namespace, which represents the domain in which the name has validity, as well as NSS is the Namespace Specific String composed as follows:

```
<NSS>::=<jurisdiction>":"<local-name>
```

where: `<jurisdiction>` is the part providing the identification of the jurisdiction, generally corresponding to the country, where the source of law is issued. issuing the source of law. It is also possible to represent international organizations (either states or public administrations or private entities)

`<local-name>` is the uniform name of the source of law in the country or jurisdiction where it is issued; its internal structure is common to the already adopted schemas. It is able to represent all the aspects of an intellectual production, as it is a legal document, from its initial idea, through its evolution during the time, to its realisation by different means (paper, digital, etc.).

The `<jurisdiction>` element is composed of two specific fields:

```
<jurisdiction>::=<jurisdiction-code>
                        [";"<jurisdiction-unit>]*
```

where:

`<jurisdiction-code>` is the identification code of the jurisdiction where the source of law is issued. In case of countries this code follows the standard [8] Alpha-2 (it=Italy, fr=France, dk=Denmark, etc.). In case of multi-national (e.g., European Union) or international (e.g., United Nations) organizations the Top Level Domain Name (e.g., "eu") or the Domain Name (e.g., un.org, wto.int) is used instead of ISO 3166 code; in case such multi-national or international organization does not have a registered domain, in order to avoid ambiguities or collisions with actual domains, a domain name (according to the English acronym of the organization name) under the virtual domain "lex" is used. For example, the jurisdiction code of the European Economic Community is "eec.lex";

`<jurisdiction-unit>` are the possible administrative hierarchical sub-structures defined by each country, or organisation, according to its own structure. This additional information can be used where two or more levels of legislative or judicial production exist (e.g., federal, state and municipality level) and the same bodies may be present in each jurisdiction. Then acts of the same type issued by similar authorities in different areas differ for the jurisdiction-unit specification.

5.4.2 Reference Model for the URN:LEX `<local-name>` Structure

As discussed the `<local-name>` will encode all the aspects of an intellectual production, as it is a legal document, from its initial idea, through its evolution during the time, to its realisation by different means (paper, digital, etc.). For these purposes it is based on the FRBR.[6] model developed by IFLA.[7] Following the FRBR model, in a source of law, as in any intellectual production, 4 fundamental entities (or aspects) can be specified.

The first 2 entities reflect its contents:

- Work: identifies a distinct intellectual creation; in our case, it identifies a source of law both in its being (as it has been issued) and in its becoming (as it is modified over time);
- Expression: identifies a specific intellectual realisation of a work; in our case it identifies every different (original or up-to-date) version of the act over time and/or language in which the text is expressed;

while the other 2 entities relate to its form:

- Manifestation: identifies a concrete realisation of an expression; in our case it identifies realizations in different media (printing, digital, etc.), encoding formats (XML, PDF, etc.), or other publishing characteristics;
- Item: identifies a specific copy of a manifestation; in our case it identifies individual physical copies as they are found in particular physical locations.

5.4.3 Structure of the URN:LEX `<local-name>`

The `<local-name>` component of the URN:LEX identifier contains all the necessary pieces of information enabling the unequivocal identification of a legal document, within a specific legal system. In the URN:LEX specification, a legal resource at "work" level is identified by four elements: the enacting authority, the type of measure, details (or terms) (like date of issue, number of the act, etc.) and possibly, any annex.

It is often necessary to differentiate various expressions, that is:

- the original version and all the amended versions of the same document;
- the versions of the text expressed in the different official languages of the state or organization.

[6] Functional Requirements for Bibliographic Record
[7] International Federation of Library Associations and Institutions

Finally the uniform name allows a distinction among diverse manifestations, which may be produced in multiple locations using different means and formats. In any case, the basic identifier of the source of law (work) remains the same, but information is added regarding the specific version under consideration (expression); similarly a suffix is added to the expression for representing the characteristics of the publication (manifestation). All this set of information is expressed in the jurisdiction official language; in case of more official languages, more names (aliases) are created for each language.

Therefore, the more general structure of the national name appears as follows:

```
<local-name>::=<work>["@"<expression>]?["$"<manifestation>]?
```

However, consistent with legislative practice, the uniform name of the original provision becomes the identifier of an entire class of documents which includes: the original document, the annexes, and all its versions, languages and formats subsequently generated.

5.4.4 Structure of the URN:LEX Identifier at Work Level

The structure of the document identifier at work level is made of the four fundamental elements mentioned above, chosen from those used in citations, clearly distinguished one from the other in accordance with an order identifying increasingly narrow domains and competences. The use of citation elements at work level allows to construct the URN of the cited act manually or by software tools implementing automatic hyperlinking of legal sources on the basis of the textual citations of the acts. The general structure of the identifier at work level is:

```
<work>::=<authority>":"<measure>":"<details>[":"<annex>]*
```

where:
`<authority>` is the issuing or proposing authority of the measure (e.g., State, Ministry, Municipality, Court, etc.);
`<measure>` is the type of the measure both public nature (e.g., constitution, act, treaty, regulation, decree, decision, etc.) as well as private one (e.g., license, agreement, etc);
`<details>` are the terms associated to the measure, typically a date and a number;
`<annex>` is the identifier of the annex, if any (e.g., Annex 1).

In case of annexes, both the main document and its annexes have their own uniform name so that they can individually be referenced; the identifier of the annex adds a suffix to that of the main document. In similar way the identifier of an annex of an annex adds a suffix to that of the annex which it is attached to. The main elements of the national name are generally divided into several elementary components, and, for each, specific rules of representation are established (criteria, modalities, syntax and order).[8] Examples of <work> identifiers are:

```
urn:lex:it:stato:legge:2006-05-14;22
urn:lex:uk:ministry.justice:decree:1999-10-07;45
urn:lex:ch;glarus:regiere:erlass:2007-10-15;963
urn:lex:es:tribunal.supremo:decision:2001-09-28;68
urn:lex:fr:assemblee.nationale:proposition.loi:13.
     legislature;1762
urn:lex:br:estado:constituicao:1988-10-05;lex-1
urn:lex:fsf.org:free.software.foundation:general.public.
     license:2007-06-29;lex-1
urn:lex:nl:hoge.raad:besluit:2008-04-01;bc8581
```

International treaties involve more jurisdictions (the signing ones) so they are represented through more identifiers, each of them related to an involved jurisdiction. For example, a bilateral France and Germany treaty is identified through two URNs belonging to either "fr" or "de" jurisdiction (e.g., `urn:lex:fr:etat:traite:...` and `urn:lex:de:staat:vertrag:...`) since it pertains to both the French and the German jurisdiction.

In the states or organisations that have more than one official language, a document has more identifiers, each of them expressed in a different official language, basically a set of equivalent aliases. This system permits manual or automated construction of the uniform name of the referred source of law in the same language used in the document itself (e.g., `urn:lex:eu:council:directive:2004-12-07;31`, `urn:lex:eu:consiglio:direttiva:2004-12-07;31`, etc.). Moreover, a document can be assigned more than one uniform namc in order to facilitate its linking to other documents. This option can be used for documents that, although unique, are commonly referenced from different perspectives: for example, a document promulgation or its specific content (e.g., a Regulation about privacy, promulgated through a Decree of the President of the Republic: it can be cited as Regulation about privacy, or as the Decree itself).

5.4.5 Structure of the URN:LEX Identifier at Expression Level

There may be several expressions of a legal text, connected to specific versions or languages. Each version is characterized by the period of time during which that text is to be considered as the valid text (in force or effective). The lifetime of a version ends with the issuing of the subsequent version. New versions of a text may be brought into existence by:

---

[8] For the details regarding each element, see Attachment B of the IETF Internet Draft `http://datatracker.ietf.org/doc/draft-spinosa-urn-lex/`

- changes as regards text or time (amendments) due to the issuing of other legal acts and to the subsequent production of updated or consolidated texts;
- correction of publication errors (rectification or errata corrige);
- entry into or departure from a particular time span, depending on the specific date in which different partitions of a text come into force.

Each of such version may be expressed in more than one language, with each language-version having its own specific identifier. The identifier of a source of law expression adds such information to the work identifier, using the following main structure:

```
<expression>::="@"<version>[":"<language>]?
```

where:
`<version>` is the identifier of the version of the (original or amended) source of law. In general it is expressed by the promulgation date of the amending act; anyway other specific information can be used for particular cases. If necessary, the original version is specified by the string "original";
`<language>` is the identification code of the language in which the document is expressed, according to ISO 639-1 [9] (it=Italian, fr=French, de=German, etc.); in case the code of a language is not included in this standard, the ISO 639-2 (3 letters) is used. This information is not necessary when the text is expressed in the unique official language of the country or jurisdiction.

Examples of document identifiers for expressions are:

```
urn:lex:ch:etat:lois:2006-05-14;22@originel:fr
```
(original version in French)

```
urn:lex:ch:staat:gesetz:2006-05-14;22@original:de
```
(original version in German)

```
urn:lex:ch:etat:lois:2006-05-14;22@2008-03-12:fr
```
(amended version in French)

```
urn:lex:ch:staat:gesetz:2006-05-14;22@2008-03-12:de
```
(amended version in German)

```
urn:lex:be:conseil.etat:decision:2008-07-09;185.273@originel:fr
```
(original version in French of a Belgian decision)

5.4.6 Structure of the URN:LEX Identifier at Manifestation Level

To identify a specific manifestation, the uniform name of the expression is followed by a suitable suffix describing the:

- digital format (e.g., XML, HTML, PDF, etc.) expressed according to the MIME Content-Type standard [7], where the "/" character is to be substituted by the "-" sign;
- publisher or editorial staff who produced it;
- possible components of the expressions contained in the manifestation. Such components are expressed by "body" (the default value), representing the whole or the main part of the document, or by the caption of the component itself (e.g. "Table 1", "Figure 2", etc.);
- other features of the document (e.g., anonymized decision text).

The <manifestation> suffix will thus read:

```
<manifestation>::=<format>[";"<specification>"]*
                  ":"<editor>[";"<specification>]*
                 [":"<component>[";"<specification>]*]?
                 [":"<feature>[";"<specification>]*]?
```

To indicate possible features or peculiarities, each main element of the manifestation may be followed by a further specification. For example, the original version the Italian act 3 April 2000, n. 56 might have the following manifestations with their relative uniform names:

PDF format (vers. 1.7) of the whole act edited by the Parliament:

```
urn:lex:it:stato:legge:2000-04-03;56$application-pdf;1.7:
  parliament
```

Furthermore, it is useful to assign a uniform name to a component of a manifestation in case non-textual objects are involved. These may be multimedia objects that are non-textual in their own right (e.g. geographic maps, photographs, etc.), mixed with textual parts. This way a "lex" name allows:

- exploitation of all the advantages of an unequivocal identifier that is independent of physical location;
- a means to provide choice among different existing manifestations (e.g. XML or PDF formats, resolution degree of an image etc.) of the same expression.

5.4.7 URN:LEX References

References to sources of law often refer to specific partitions of the act (article, paragraph, etc.) and not to the entire document. Therefore, for allowing applications to manage this information (e.g., pointing a specific partition of a document), it is necessary that a partition identifier within the act is present (i.e. an unequivocal label or ID). For enabling the construction of a partition identifier between different collections of documents, specific construction rules for IDs or labels should be defined and shared, within each country or jurisdiction, for any document type (e.g., for legislation, the paragraph 2 of the article 3 might have as label or ID the value "art3-par2", similarly for case-law, paragraph 22 of the judgment in Case 46/76 Bauhuis v Netherlands, might have as label or ID the value "par22").

Furthermore, it is useful to foresee the compatibility with applications able to manage this information (e.g., returning the proper element); these procedures are particularly useful in case of long acts, such as codes, constitutions, regulations, etc.

For this purpose it is necessary that the partition identifier is transmitted to the servers (resolution and application) and therefore it cannot be separated by the typical "#" character of URI fragment, which is not transmitted to the server.

According to these requirements, the syntax of a reference is:

```
<URN-reference>::=<URN-document>["~"<partition-id>]?
```

(e.g., to refer to the paragraph 3 of the article 15 of the French Act of 15 may 2004, n. 106, the reference is written
`urn:lex:fr:etat:loi:2004-05-15;106~art15-par3`).

Using a different separator ("~") from the document name, the partition ID is not withheld by the browser but it is transmitted to the resolution process. This enables the resolver to retrieve (for example, out of a database), if it is possible, only the referred partition, otherwise to return the whole act. Anyway, to make pointing to the indicated partition effective, the resolver should transform the partition ID of each returned URL in a URI fragment; this is obtained appending to URL the "#" character followed by the partition ID (in the example above, the returned URL will be `<URL-document>#art15-par3`).

It is also possible to use Web technology syntax (including "#"); in this case only the URN part of the reference is transmitted to the resolver, therefore the whole document will be always retrieved.

5.4.8 URN:LEX Identifier Resolution Service

The task of the resolution service is to associate a URN:LEX identifier with a specific document address. In contrast to systems that can be constructed around rigorous and enforceable engineering premises, such as DNS, the "lex" resolver will be expected to cope with a wide variety of "dirty" inputs, particularly those created by the automated extraction of references from incomplete or inaccurate texts.

A resolution system will have a distributed architecture based on two fundamental components: a chain of information in DNS (Domain Name System) and a series of resolution services from URNs to URLs, each competent within a specific domain of the namespace. Through the NAPTR records of the DNS (described in [10]), the client identifies the characteristics (protocol, port, site) of the service capable of associating the relative URLs with the URN in question, thereby allowing access to the document. A resolution service can delegate the resolution and management of hierarchically-dependent portions of the name. Delegation of this responsibility will not be unreasonably withheld provided that the processes for their resolution and management are robust and are followed.

The resolution service is based on two main elements: a knowledge base (consisting in a catalogue or a set of transformation rules) and a software to query the knowledge base itself.

5.4.8.1 Catalogues of Resolution

The architecture of the catalogue of resolution has to take into account that incompleteness and inaccuracy are rather frequent in legal citations, and incomplete or inaccurate uniform names of the referred document are thus likely to be built from textual references (this is even more frequent if they are created automatically through a specific parser).

Contrary with systems that can be constructed around rigorous and enforceable engineering premises, such as DNS, the LEX resolver will be expected to cope with a wide variety of "dirty" inputs, particularly those created by the automated extraction of references from incomplete or inaccurate texts. The result is a particular emphasis on a flexible and robust resolver design. For these reasons, the implementation of a catalogue, based on a relational-database, is suggested, as it will lead to a more higher flexibility in the resolution process able to deal with partial matches. In addition the catalogue must manage aliases, various versions and languages of the same source of law as well as related manifestations. It is suggested that each enacting authority implements its own catalogue, assigning a corresponding unambiguous uniform name to each resource.

5.4.8.2 Suggested Resolver Behaviour

First of all the resolution process should implement a normalization of the uniform name to be resolved. This may involve transforming some components to the canonical form (e.g., filling out the acronyms, expanding the abbreviations, unifying the institution names, standardizing the type of measures, etc.). For this function the registers of names and authorities organization, including validity time span, as well as the registers of the types of measure are useful.

The resolver should then query the catalogue searching for the URN which corresponds exactly to the given one (normalized if necessary). Since the names coming from the references may be inaccurate or incomplete, an iterative, heuristic approach (based on partial matches) is suggested. It is worth to note that incomplete references (not including all the elements to create the canonical uniform name) are normal and natural; for a human reader, the reference would be "completed" by contextual understanding given by the including document.

Lacking more specific indications, the resolver should select the best (most recent) version of the requested source of law, and provide all the manifestations with their related items.

A more specific indication in the uniform name to be resolved will, of course, result in a more selective retrieval, based on any suggested expression and/or manifestations components (e.g. date, language, format, etc.).

5.5 Http-Based Identifier Syntax

Another naming convention for sources of law, compliant with CEN MetaLex recommendations and used within the Akoma-Ntoso project, is based on the http protocol and syntax.[9] According to this syntax, at all levels, the resource URIs belong to the http:// scheme and are normally resolved using mechanisms widely available in browsers and web servers.

5.5.1 Absolute vs. Relative Http Forms

All http:// URIs are divided into absolute and relative forms. An absolute form of these URIs starts with the string "http://", which is then followed by an officially registered domain name, and the local part that starts off the first individual "/" character. A relative form of the same URI, on the other hand, has no indication of the scheme, no indication of the domain name, and may have further missing parts at the beginning of the whole string (no missing parts on the end, though). Browsers are able to build the absolute URI corresponding to the relative URI by adding at the beginning of the provided URI the missing parts that are taken from the URI of a base resource.

In XML manifestations, http:// URIs shall always be expressed in relative forms. This makes all URIs independent of the actual resolution mechanism, and allows for very flexible storage, access and reference mechanisms. This means that all resolution mechanisms used to access a document off another document will rely on the same resolution mechanism as the original one, regardless of the resolution mechanism employed to generate the documents themselves.

5.5.2 Global vs. Local Http Forms

A global http:// URI is a relative URI where all parts are explicit. Thus a global URI always starts with a slash, to indicate that only protocol and domain are omitted, but all other parts are explicitly specified. A local URI, on the other hand, may have one or more parts missing (necessarily from left to right), and the corresponding global (and, subsequently, absolute) URI is determined by adding the corresponding parts taken from the starting document, as usual with relative URI with missing parts.

In XML manifestations using http:// URIs, all work, expression and manifestation level references to whole documents must be global, and all references to

[9] This section has been written in collaboration with Fabio Vitali

individual components within the same level (or lower levels) must be local and are stored simply as the name of the corresponding component.

Thus, for instance, "/kn/act/2007-01-01/1/schedule1" is the relative, global work-level URI for schedule 1 of act 1/2007 of Kenya, but a work-level reference to schedule 1 placed within the main document of the act will only contain the local URI "schedule1" or "./schedule1". This guarantees that these references keep on working even after new expressions are created of the same work, both if the part containing the reference is changed or if it remains untouched. XML elements may refer to other documents according to different levels of the FRBR hierarchy. In particular they might point to work-level and occasionally expression-level URIs only, while object, img and attachment always point to manifestation-level URIs. As the global/local distinction is involved, reference elements always use global URIs for documents different than the host, while object, img and attachment always refer to components of the host document, and thus always use local references. A reference to a different act is always global, as specified in `<ref href="/kn/act/2006-08-10/123#sec12"> section 12 of act 13/2006 </ref>` while a reference to a specific attachment of the same act is always local, as specified in `<ref href = "./schedule01#par12"> paragraph 12 of schedule 1 of this act</ref>`

Analogously multimedia fragments (e.g., images) within the main document are specified using a local URI: `<img src="media/logo.tiff"/>`

The only exception to this rule is for external attachments, i.e., components that are external to the XML package.

5.5.3 Packages

In general, all manifestation components are stored within a package, and thus have a URI that is very similar to that of the manifestation itself. Sometimes, though, it could be appropriate to store the individual component elsewhere, as an independent document. Such situation may arise, for instance, when a document specifies another full document as one of its attachments, e.g. a ratification decree placing an international treaty as an attachment, etc. Since it is more appropriate to consider the important document the international treaty, it will constitute a work on its own and have its own URI of a completely different form than the one that the attachment would have.

In these cases, it is more appropriate that all references to the external attachment are global at the work level as well as at the expression and manifestation level.

5.5.4 Http-Based Identifier at Work Level

The http:// URI for the WORK is the baseline for building the URI for the Expression, which is the baseline for the URI of the MANIFESTATION. The http:// URI for the WORK consists of the following pieces:

- The base URL of a naming authority with URI-resolving capabilities (not relevant for the Naming Convention)
- A detail fragment organizing in a hierarchical fashion the additional data:
  - Country (a two-letter code according to ISO 3166-1 alpha-2)
  - Type of document
  - Date (expressed in YYYY-MM-DD format or just YYYY if the year is enough for identification purposes)
  - Number (when appropriate, otherwise the string nn)

All components are separated by forward slashes ("/") so as to exploit relative URIs in references, while all URIs in this specification are prefixed with the arbitrary domain name `[http://www.authority.org]` that stands for any of an arbitrarily large number of equivalent naming authorities.

- `[http://www.authority.org]/dz/debaterecord/2004-12-21`
  Algerian parliamentary debate record, 21st December 2004.
- `[http://www.authority.org]/sl/act/2004-02-13/2`
  Sierra Leone enacted legislation. Act number 2 of 2004.
- `[http://www.authority.org]/ng/bill/2003-05-14/19`
  Namibia Bill number 19 of 2003
- `[http://www.authority.org]/mg/act/2003-03-12/3`
  Madagascar. Act 3 from 2003

The naming convention provides naming support for individual components of a legal or legislative resource at the WORK level, too. Although conceptually components belong to expressions only, it often happens that the legislator makes work-level references to components, which thus need to have work-level URIs as well. It may also happen that the component (e.g., an attachment) may change name, or position, or even hierarchical placement, time after time.

For instance, we could have that an original act refers to table A of schedule 1, and after a little time schedule 1 is completely abrogated, and thus table A becomes (implicitly) an attachment of the main document. As such, it is important that all references to table A of schedule 1 are considered as references to table A of the main document after that event. This brings about the necessity to have URIs for Work Components. These are to be used when referring in a work-level fashion to components that have official names and positions, but may change in name and position with time. One problem is that a work-level component URI has no expression-level part, and yet the component part is AFTER the expression level part. Therefore, it is necessary to make sure that a work-level URI fragment is never mistaken for an expression-level or a component-level URI fragment.

But since:

1. The number part of the work-level URI (/nn/) is required even in unnumbered documents ("/nn/" for not numbered).
2. The expression fragment, if present, always has at least the language and the "@" character, and the @ character can only be used for expression fragments,

the absence of a part containing the "@" character indicates a work-level component reference after the 4th component (the number).

- `[http://www.authority.org]/kn/act/2007-01-01/1/schedule1`

  Kenya, schedule 1 of act 1 from 2007 (WorkComponent)

5.5.5 Http-Based Identifier at Expression Level

Characterizing the Expression is the specific identification of a content with respect to another content. This includes specifications of the version and the language of the expression. Therefore, different versions of the same work, or the same version of the same work expressed in different languages correspond to different Expressions and will have different URIs. Expressions are organized in components (the Expression Components), and therefore we need to identify separately the Expression as a whole from the individual URIs for each Expression Component. All of them are all immediately derived from the baseline, which is the URI for the Work.

The http:// URI for the Expression as a whole consists of the following pieces:

1. The URI of the corresponding Work
2. The character "/"
3. The human language code in which the expression is drafted (a three-letter code according to ISO 639-2 alpha-3)
4. The "@" character (required)
5. An optional version identifier:

   a. If an approved act, the version date of the expression in syntax YYYY-MM-DD.
   b. If a bill, the presentation date is appropriate, or the stage in the approval process that the current draft is the result of.

The absence of the version identifiers signals two different situations depending on the type of document:

- If the document is not versioned (e.g., the debate record of an assembly) then version identifier need not and cannot be present.
- If the document is versioned (e.g., an act in force), then the lack of version identifiers refers to the version in force at the moment of the resolution of the URI (i.e., the "current" version of the act, where "current" refers to the moment in time in which the URI is dereferenced, rather than the moment in time in which the document containing the URI was created: today for the reader, as opposed to today for the author of the references).

A particular expression is the first version of a Work. This Expression should not be confused with the Work itself (which considers the first Expression in no special way to all other possible Expressions), and it is a very specific, although peculiar,

Expression. The original version of an expression is referred to with an URI with a dangling "@" character (which implies that the actual version date is the first appropriate date for that work).

- `[http://www.authority.org]/dz/debaterecord/2004-12-21/fra` Algerian parliamentary debate record, 21st December 2004, French version
- `[http://www.authority.org]/sl/act/2004-02-13/2/eng`
  Sierra Leone enacted legislation. Act number 2 of 2004. English version, current version (as accessed today [according to the reader])
- `[http://www.authority.org]/sl/act/2004-02-13/2/eng@`
  Sierra Leone enacted Legislation. Act number 2 of 2004. English version, original version
- `[http://www.authority.org]/sl/act/2004-02-13/2/eng@2004-07-21`
  Sierra Leone enacted Legislation. Act number 2 of 2004. English version, as amended on July 2004
- `[http://www.authority.org]/ng/bill/2003-05-14/19/eng@first`
  Namibia Bill number 19 of 2003, first stage, English version
- `[http://www.authority.org]/mg/act/2003-03-12/3/mul`
  Madagascar. Act 3 from 2003 in French and Malagasy.

Some expressions have many components, some are only composed of a main document. In order to explicitly refer to individual components, it is therefore necessary to introduce a naming convention that identifies individual components, and still allows an easy connection between the component and the expression it belongs to. There are therefore two subcases:

- The expression is only composed of one component: in this case, the URI for the expression as a whole and for its main component are identical plus the name "main".
- The expression is composed of many components: the URI for each Expression Component consists in this case of the following pieces:

  1. The URI of the corresponding Expression as a whole
  2. The character "/"
  3. Either

     a. A unique name for the attachment
     b. The name "main" which is reserved for the main document. It we have different main they are numbered sequentially: main1, main2, etc.

- `[http://www.authority.org]/dz/minutes/2004-12-21/fra/main`
  Algerian parliamentary debate record, 21st December 2004, French version, main document
- `[http://www.authority.org]/sl/act/2004-02-13/2/eng/main`

Main body of the Sierra Leone enacted Legislation. Act number 2 of 2004. English version, current version (as accessed today)

- `[http://www.authority.org]/sl/act/2004-02-13/2/eng@2004-07-21/main/schedule1`
  Attachment "schedule01" of Sierra Leone enacted Legislation. Act number 2 of 2004. English version, as amended on July 2004
- `[http://www.authority.org]/ng/bill/2003-05-14/19/eng@first/main/schedule3`
  Third attachment of Namibia Bill number 19 of 2003, first stage, English version.

5.5.5.1 Hierarchies of Components

A frequent situation occurs when an attachment has itself further attachments. This creates a complex hierarchical situation in which the component should be considered, in a way, as an expression by itself, whose components need to be listed and properly differentiated. The process can be further iterated whenever not only an attachment has further attachments, but its attachments also have further attachments and so on. The situation must also foresee the situation in which attachments at different levels of the hierarchy end up having the same name (e.g., table A in schedule 1 and table A in schedule 2). In such situations, each ExpressionComponent must be considered as an expression by itself. Recursively, the URI of attachments are as follows:

1. if the attachment does not have further attachments, its URI is provided as detailed in the previous section, without further addenda.
2. If the attachment has further attachments, the URI as detailed in the previous section refers to the whole attachment, including its own attachments.
3. To refer to the main document of an attachment that has further attachments, a further "main" part should be added.
4. To refer to any further attachment of an attachment, a further "/" followed by a unique name for the attachment must be added to the attachment itself.

- `[http://www.authority.org]/sl/act/2004-02-13/2/eng@2004-07-21/main/schedule1`
  Whole attachment "schedule01" of the Sierra Leone enacted Legislation. Act number 2 of 2004. English version, English version, as amended on July 2004.
- `[http://www.authority.org]/sl/act/2004-02-13/2/eng@2004-07-21/main/schedule1/main`
  Main document of the attachment "schedule01" of Sierra Leone enacted Legislation. Act number 2 of 2004. English version, as amended on July 2004
- `[http://www.authority.org]/sl/act/2004-02-13/2/eng@2004-07-21/main/schedule1/tableA`
  Attachment "Table A" of the attachment "schedule01" of Sierra Leone enacted Legislation. Act number 2 of 2004. English version, as amended on July 2004
- `[http://www.authority.org]/sl/act/2004-02-13/2/eng@2004-07-21/main/schedule1/attachment1/main`

Main document of the attachment "attachment01" of the attachment "schedule01" of Sierra Leone enacted Legislation. Act number 2 of 2004. English version, amended on July 2004.

5.5.5.2 Virtual Expressions

In some situations the actual enter-in-force date of the expression is not known in advance, and it is necessary to create references or mentions of documents whose URI is now known completely (possibly, because their exact delivery date is not known yet). These are called virtual expressions (i.e., references to expressions that probably do not exist yet or ever, but can be unambiguously deduced once all relevant information are made available). There are at least three cases where such situation may take place:

1. the information is not known by the author of the expression (e.g., the legislator), in which case the act of actually retrieving the correct information is in itself an act of interpretation;
2. the information is not known by the editor of the expression (e.g., the publisher of the XML version of the document), in which case the information can theoretically be available, but is too much of a burden for the publisher to retrieve it.
3. the information is not know by the query system.

In all these cases, the syntax for the URI of the virtual expression uses a similar syntax to the specification of the actual expression, but the character ":" is used instead of the "@" after the specification of the work URI. For instance, if we need to reference the expression of an act in force on date "1/1/2007", we will probably need to refer to some expression whose enter in force date was in a previous date to 1/1/2007.

- `[http://www.authority.org]/sl/act/2004-02-13/2/eng:2004-07-21`
  Sierra Leone enacted Legislation. Act number 2 of 2004. English version, as amended on the closest date before July 21, 2004

5.5.6 Http-Based Identifier at Manifestation Level

Characterizing the Manifestation is the specific process that generated an electronic document in some specific format(s). This includes specifications of the data format(s) used. Therefore, different manifestations of the same expression generated using different data formats correspond to different manifestations and will have different URIs. Manifestations are organized in components (the ManifestationComponents), and therefore we must identify separately the Manifestation as a whole and the individual URIs for each Manifestation Component. All of them are all immediately derived from the baseline, which is the URI for the Expression.

The URI for the Manifestation as a whole consists of the following pieces:

- The URI of the corresponding Expression as a whole
- The character "."
- A unique three letter acronym of the data format in which the manifestation is drafted. The acronym can be "pdf" for PDF, "doc" for MS Word, or "xml" for the XML manifestation. The acronym "akn" is reserved for the package of all documents including XML version of the main document(s)
  - `[http://www.authority.org]/dz/debaterecord/2004-12-21/fra/main.doc`
    Word version of the Algerian parliamentary debate record, 21st December 2004, French version
  - `[http://www.authority.org]/sl/act/2004-02-13/2/eng/main.pdf`
    PDF version of the Sierra Leone enacted Legislation. Act number 2 of 2004. English version, current version (as accessed today)
  - `[http://www.authority.org]/sl/act/2004-02-13/2/eng@2004-07-21/main.akn`
    Package of all documents including XML versions of the Sierra Leone enacted Legislation. Act number 2 of 2004. English version, as amended in July 2004

Each Manifestation Component is an independent electronic structure (e.g., a file) in a single data format. Every type of manifestation has of course a different data structure and file structure. Therefore the actual format of the URIs of the components of the manifestation depend on the data format and cannot be formalized in general. In this section we therefore provide a grammar but not an exhaustive list of formats, that depends on the data format chosen for the manifestation. The URI for each Manifestation Component consists of the following pieces:

1. The URI of the corresponding Expression as a whole
2. The character "/"
3. Some unique identification of the ManifestationComponent with respect either to the manifestation as a whole or to the ExpressionComponent the component is the manifestation of.
4. The character "."
5. A unique extension of the data format in which the manifestation is drafted. The acronym can be "pdf" for PDF, "doc" for MS Word, "xml" for XML documents, "tif" for image formats, etc.

5.5.6.1 Packages Manifestation

A package manifestation is a very specific manifestation using a number of data formats (mainly XML but could include other multimedia formats as needed) with a very specific organization of parts and components. Since it makes explicit choices in terms of data formats and reciprocal references, it is important to provide clear and non-ambiguous rules as to the internal naming mechanism and its overall structure. A package manifestation is a package composed of one or more files organized in a flat fashion. The transportable format is a ZIP file whose extension is ".akn". Other formats are possible and acceptable as long as they adhere to these rules. The following are alternative options for a package:

- If the document is just composed of text and does not refer to any multimedia fragment of any form, then the ZIP package contains a single document called "main.xml".
- If the document is composed of many ManifestationComponents but does not refer to any multimedia fragment of any form, then the zip package is composed of many XML files, one for each ExpressionComponent. Each Manifestation-Component is then called as its corresponding ExpressionComponent, plus the ".xml" extension. The name "main" is reserved for the main component. Numbers are never used except when they are already part of the ExpressionComponent's name.
- If the document contains multimedia fragments of any kind, then each individual fragment does not have a corresponding ExpressionComponent, but is just a ManifestationComponent referred to in the img or object element. All multimedia components must be stored within an inner structure (e.g., a folder) called "media". Multimedia components can be called freely, but must use the appropriate extension to refer to their content type. Thus a logo can be called "logo.tif" or any other name, as long as the extension is correctly specifying the content type.

Reciprocal references to ManifestationComponents are necessary within a specific manifestation. For instance, the manifestation of the main document refers to the manifestations of its attachments via the attachment elements, and the schedule showing an image refers to the file of the image via the img element. In these cases, all references MUST be relative to the package (i.e., the manifestation as a whole):

1. attachment1.xml
   Manifestation of the first attachment of the current document
2. schedule3.xml
   Manifestation of the third attachment of the current document
3. media/logo.tif
   Manifestation of an image within the current document

References to ManifestationComponents are rarely, if ever, needed outside of the manifestation themselves. But if needed, they will refer to the file as follows:

1. The URI of the corresponding Expression as a whole
2. The character "/"
3. The relative reference to the required ManifestationComponent as specified above.

No assumption is made about the physical storage mechanism employed to maintain actual manifestations. As such, there is NO rule for URIs of the items, which are free to assume any form whatsoever and correspond to whatever storage mechanism has been employed locally. On the other hand, the actual URL for the item must be provided to a resolution mechanism in order for the hypertext feature of the legal and legislative publication systems to work correctly and automatically.

5.5.7 Http-Based Identifier Resolution Service

This naming architecture is built so as not to rely on the existence of a single storage architecture, since the URIs stored within documents are differentiated from the ones physically representing the resource being sought.

The mapping from architecture-independent URIs into accessible architecture-dependent URLs (representing the best Item for the document being sought) are realized through specific applications called URI resolvers.

The http:// naming architecture is built so as not to rely on the existence of any individual URI resolver, but assumes that all URIs are always correctly resolved to the best available Item regardless of the resolving mechanisms. In fact, each naming authority is given the global task of resolving any possible URIs, regardless of whether it belongs or not to the country or countries managed by the naming authority. This implies that the authority-specific details of URIs are purposefully omitted in this specification, and need to be considered only when first accessing a document.

For this reason, all URIs in this specification are prefixed with the arbitrary domain name [`http://www.authority.org`] that stands for any of an arbitrarily large number of equivalent naming authorities.

5.6 Current Implementations and Future Perspectives

In the legislative domain both urn-based and http-based standard for legal document identification have been proposed for standardization and implemented.

The URN:LEX schema for sources of law, compliant to the CEN MetaLex requirements, has been submitted to IETF for registration.[10] The syntax of the identifier and its usage in a multilanguage context has been shown, as well as the principles of a resolution service able to guarantee persistence of the links based on URN, independently from any change in document physical locations. National URN schemas, sharing the same principles of the URN:LEX schema, have been defined within the NormeInRete and Normattiva projects in Italy, the LexDania project in Denmark, as well as within the Senado Federal do Brazil.

Several examples of how the URN:LEX legal identifier standard can be applied to US legal documents, have been published on LexCraft,[11] the wiki for sharing best practices in legal information systems development, hosted by the legal information Institute (LII) at Cornell Law School, by LII Director Tom Bruce and John

---

[10] `http://datatracker.ietf.org/doc/draft-spinosa-urn-lex`

[11] `http://topics.law.cornell.edu/wiki/lexcraft/urn_lex_illustrative_examples`

Joergensen. In particular URN:LEX is one of the legal metadata standards proposed in the Law.gov legal open government data project.

The URN:LEX examples available on LexCraft are related to:

- U.S. federal statutes, regulations, and case law;
- U.S. state statutes and case law;
- U.S. municipal ordinances.

A first prototype of a URN:LEX resolver for France can be found at `http://urnlex.appspot.com`. Citability.org,[12] a U.S.-based project to create persistent URIs for government information, has expressed its interest to develop a URN:LEX parser and resolver. Moreover a URN:LEX standard within the Italian Senate of the Republic, as well as a tool to implement automatic legal references mark-up (automatic legal documents hyperlinking) as integrated within the Italian Senate Web site, have been implemented.

Currently a plug-in for Firefox has been developed by ITTIG-CNR to deal with the URN standard (URN schema handler): it allows a browser to natively exploit the URN schema, routing the resolution service through the DNS Internet infrastructure, with no need to transform a URN hyperlink attribute into an http query for the resolution system.

The main principles of the CEN MetaLex naming convention have been applied for defining an http-based identifier for sources of law within the Akoma-Ntoso project. Similarly an http-based persistent URIs identification schema for legal documents has been developed within the `legislation.gov.uk` project. The need to create a centralized database giving access to UK legislation allowed to exploit the advantages of an http-based schema, represented by a built-in, ready-made, widely deployed and cost-effective resolution mechanism for resolving the identifier to a document, and a document to a representation. Nonetheless the project responsibles have expressed their interest in supporting URN:LEX in addition to their own URI set.

A joint proposal aimed to harmonize the two schemas is actually desirable and it has been recently proposed to the European Parliament, to cope with legal documents identification within the EU Parliament workflow.

Recently a set of principles and technologies, known as "Linked Data", has been promoted as a basic infrastructure of the semantic web to enable data sharing and reuse on a massive scale.

Such principles, introduced by Tim Berners-Lee in his Web architecture note "Linked Data",[13] are

1. Use URIs as names for things.
2. Use HTTP URIs, so that people can look up those names.
3. When someone looks up a URI, provide useful information, using the standards (RDF, SPARQL).
4. Include links to other URIs, so that they can discover more things.

---

[12] `http://citability.org`

[13] `http://www.w3.org/DesignIssues/LinkedData.html`

The second principle is the one more affecting a discussion about the scheme to be used for legal resources identification; in particular to the aim of guaranteeing the access to the resources, http-based identifiers are suggested. This property is addressed as *dereferenceability*, meaning a resource retrieval mechanism using any of the Internet protocols (e.g. HTTP) so that HTTP clients, for instance, can look up the URI using the HTTP protocol and retrieve a description of the resource that is identified by the URI. Such property is available for http-based identifiers either with or without a resolver allowing a 1-to-1 association with the "best copy" of the resource, as discussed in Section 5.5.7. The same property holds for URN identifiers, as long as a resolver is properly set-up, allowing 1-to-n association with more copies of a resource, as discussed in Section 5.4.8.

References

1. Berners-Lee, T., R. Fielding, and L. Masinter. January 2005. Uniform Resource Identifiers (URI): Generic Syntax. STD 66, RFC 3986.
2. Boer, A., R. Hoekstra, E. de Maat, E. Hupkes, F. Vitali, M. Palmirani, and B. Rátai. (2009). CEN MetaLex Workshop Agreement.
3. Bradner, S. March 1997. Key words for use in RFCs to Indicate Requirement Levels. BCP 14, RFC 2119.
4. Daigle, D., L., van Gulik, D., Iannella, R., and P. Faltstrom. October 2002. Uniform Resource Names (URN) Namespace Definition Mechanisms. BCP 66, RFC 3406.
5. Daniel, R. June 1997. A trivial convention for using HTTP in URN. RFC 2169.
6. Francesconi, E. 2007. *Technologies for European Integration. Standards-based Interoperability of Legal Information Systems*. ISBN 978-88-8398-050-3. European Press Academic Publishing.
7. Freed, N., and N. Borenstein. November 1996. Multipurpose Internet Mail Extensions (MIME) Part One: Format of Internet Message Bodies. RFC 2045.
8. ISO 3166. Country name codes. ISO 3166-1:1997.
9. ISO 639. 1998, 2002. Codes for the representation of names of languages - Part 1: alpha-2 code - Part 2: alpha-3 code.
10. Mealling, M. October 2002. Dynamic Delegation Discovery System (DDDS), Part Three: The Domain Name System (DNS) Database. RFC 3403.
11. Moats, R., and K.R. Sollins. May 1997. URN Syntax. RFC 2141.
12. Narten, T., and H. Alvestrand. October 1998. Guidelines for writing an IANA considerations section in RFCs. BCP 26, RFC 2434.
13. Saur, K.G. 1998. Functional requirements for bibliographic records. UBCIM Publications – IFLA Section on Cataloguing, 19.
14. Spinosa, P.L. May 2006. The assignment of uniform names to Italian legal documents.
15. Spinosa, P., E. Francesconi, and C. Lupo. May 2010. A Uniform Resource Name (URN) Namespace for Sources of Law (LEX). `http://datatracker.ietf.org/doc/draft-spinosa-urn-lex/`.

Chapter 6
Akoma-Ntoso for Legal Documents

Monica Palmirani and Fabio Vitali

6.1 Introduction

6.1.1 Historical Introduction of Akoma-Ntoso

In 2004 and 2005, the UNITED NATIONS Department for Economics and Social Affairs (UN/DESA) project, “Strengthening Parliaments’ Information Systems in Africa” [14], has aimed at empowering legislatures to better fulfil their democratic functions, using ICTs to increase the quality of parliamentary services, facilitate the work of parliamentarians and create new ways to promote the access of civil society to parliamentary processes. Now the project is continued with a more largest objective under the name “Africa i-Parliament Action Plan”.

A strategic role in this project is played by the Akoma-Ntoso[1] [13] (Architecture for Knowledge-Oriented Management of Any Normative Texts using Open Standards and Ontologies) framework, a set of standards and guidelines for e-Parliament services in a Pan-African context. The framework addresses information content and recommends technical policies and specifications for building and connecting Parliament information systems, including three main results: (i) Akoma-Ntoso XML schema, (ii) naming convention for the legal resource identification (URI[2]), (iii) and Legislative Drafting Guidelines[3] for leading the draftsmen to produce well-structure legislative documents and in the meantime suggesting best practices of quality assurance.

This chapter was carried out with the following authors’ contributions: M. Palmirani paragraphs 6.1, 6.2.1, 6.2.2, 6.2.3, 6.5.5, 6.5.6, 6.5.7, 6.5.8, 6.5, 6.9, 6.6; F. Vitali paragraphs 6.2.4, 6.3, 6.4, 6.5.1, 6.5.2, 6.5.3, 6.5.4.

[1] “Akoma Ntoso” in the language of the Akan people of West Africa is the symbol that represents understanding and agreement, “linked hearts”.

[2] Uniform Resource Indentifier. `http://tools.ietf.org/html/rfc3986`

[3] Bota, C., T. Dorsey, M. Palmirani, and G. Sartor. 2007. Legislative Drafting Guidelines for Africa, UNDESA Report. `http://ldg.apkn.org/`

M. Palmirani (✉)
Faculty of Law CIRSFID, University of Bologna, 40126 Bologna, Italy
e-mail: monica.palmirani@unibo.it

G. Sartor et al. (eds.), *Legislative XML for the Semantic Web*, Law, Governance and Technology Series 4, DOI 10.1007/978-94-007-1887-6_6,
© Springer Science+Business Media B.V. 2011

Akoma-Ntoso XML schema (now called simply Akoma-Ntoso), in particularly, is a technology-neutral XML machine-readable descriptions of parliamentary, legislative and judiciary documents such as legislation, debate record, minutes, etc. that enable addition of descriptive structure (markup) to the content of parliamentary and legislative documents. Akoma-Ntoso schema makes the structure and semantic components of digital legislative documents fully accessible to machine readable processing thereby supporting the creation of high value legislative information services. This will greatly support improvement of efficiency and accountability in the parliamentary, legislative and judiciary contexts.

This also makes it possible to build software applications which can manipulate documents not just as plain undifferentiated text but also in terms of the structure and semantic context of the document. Such contextual access to legislative information makes it easier to use ICTs to assist institutions and citizens to be more involved in the legislative process.

Africa has been the first continent to promote a common open standard for parliamentary, legislative and judiciary documents. It is became a good practice also for the other countries that aim to customise and to adequate Akoma-Ntoso to their legal systems and parliament purposes. Good customisation of Akoma-Ntoso are LexML Brazil[4] from the Senate of Brazil and XML4EP[5] customization made by the European Parliament. Finally due to the strong similarity of architecture between Akoma-Ntoso and MetaLex/CEN standard design, an initiative is being undertaken for supporting the integration of these two standards into a single "Legal XML Family of Standards". In the next paragraphs we describes the pillars of Akoma-Ntoso architecture schema that are also the same into MetaLex/CEN.

6.1.2 Principles of Akoma-Ntoso XML-schema Design

Akoma-Ntoso and MetaLex/CEN architecture are funded on several basic principles that build the pillars of the XML-schema design. These two standards define, with these characteristics, a new usage of the XML into the legal domain and they set up a new generation into the Legal XML state of the art (see the paragraph 1.3) for guaranteeing the validity of the legal document over the time. Therefore Akoma-Ntoso supports the following features:

LEGAL AND LEGISLATIVE ORIENTATION: standard provides a representation of the main structures of legal and legislative documents using a principled approach that provides the best combination of technological excellence and sophisticated juridical competency.

RELIANCE ON EXISTING STANDARDS: standard completely and correctly makes use of and is based on web standards: XML, URIs, XML schema, XML Namespace, RDF, OWL, etc.

---

[4] `http://projeto.lexml.gov.br/`

[5] World e-Parliament Report 2010, page 100, chapter 5.

DESCRIPTIVENESS: standard preserves the original descriptiveness of the document and avoids an excessive generalization of the elements.

PRESCRIPTIVENESS: standard implements rules and constraints directly drawn from the legal domain that can be used to increase the quality of the legal information available to applications and users (e.g., support for the local legal drafting rules).

SELF-CONTAINMENT: standard provides a place within the document for all information needed to access, use and understand the content and the metadata of the document itself. This means that external resources (such as ontological specifications and traditional databases) become useful shortcuts, and not fundamental mechanisms for traditional and innovative uses of the documents. This is fundamental for their long-term preservation, since this makes document collections independent of the architectural choices and technological evolutions that may be found in different installations or become available in time.

STRUCTURE MODELLING: standard fully describes the original structure of the document when expressed into XML. The correct attention is given to the textual content and to the metadata associated to it.

METADATA MODELLING: standard associates documents with a rich set of metadata elements, designed for providing not just the values, but the semantics associated to them, providing a principled framework for the reasoning and the comparison of abstract and concrete concepts about the documents and their content.

SEPARATION OF LEVELS: standard strongly separates all the layers of the semantic web: content, structure, metadata, ontology, rules.

NAMING POLICY: standard adopts at all levels a syntax based on URI that can be used to precisely refer to the concept being sought. This allows the correct and specific support for a large class of references, including static legal references, dynamic legal references, data-level object inclusion, ontological references, etc.

TEMPORAL MODEL: standard correctly represents the temporal model underlying the concept of dynamicity over the time of the legal documents. Based on the naming policy, it allows to represent versions, variants, documents containing a plurality of versions, as well as static and dynamic references.

WORKFLOW MODEL: standard includes a mechanism for expressing workflow events connected also with a strong ontology of the context.

NEUTRAL DOCUMENT FORMAT: standard provides a homogeneous infrastructure for representing the structure of heterogeneous legal resources.

Not all Legal XML standards include those pillars above presented. The following sections aims to provide a review of the most important XML standards in legal domain. We propose a classification into four chronological generations using the characteristics just mentioned.

6.1.3 Legal XML Standard Generations

The state of the art of the last 10 years produced plenty of Legal XML standards for describing the document as legal resource. Before to introduce the basic elements of Akoma-Ntoso we want to provide a categorisation of the existing standards on the base of their main characteristics, especially respect the multi-layer subdivision above presented. We can identify four categories:

- the *first generation* of Legal document XML standard,[6] was oriented mostly to describe the legal text and its structure with an approach near to the database entities or the typography-word processing paradigms;
- the *second generation* posed more attention to the document modelling and to the description of text, structure and metadata.[7] Nevertheless the descriptiveness of the elements was not preceded by an abstract analysis of the classes of data and the result is a very long list of tags, a complex inclusions of DTDs or XML schema, with a frequent overlapping between metadata and text definition and a weak instruments for linking the text to any other layers;
- the *third generation* is based on pattern. The pattern defines the properties of the class and its grammar, content model, behaviour and hierarchy respect the other classes, so any additional tag belongs to an existing abstract class and in this way it is preserved the consistency over the time. A strong attention to divide the text, structure, metadata and ontology is a primary principle in order to track in robust way any new layer put on the top of the pure text. Because the pattern defines general rules that no longer impose real constraints in the mark-up action, so the clarity of design scarifies the prescriptiveness. Akoma-Ntoso and MetaLex/CEN [3, 4] are examples of this approach;
- the *four generation* uses the pattern jointly with co-constraint grammar like, among the others, RELEX NG [10], Schematron [7], DSD [8], etc. for resolving above mentioned problem of lack of prescriptiveness.

Akoma-Ntoso belongs to the third generation and it is a good candidate for becoming a four generation Legal XML standard.

6.1.4 Separation of Levels in Deep

Each legal resource has a complex multilayered information architecture that includes several perspectives of analysis. The separation of levels principles is one of the stronger pillar of the new generation Legal XML standards [1, 11] (Fig. 6.1):

TEXT. The aspect of the document officially approved by a legally competent authority.

TEXT'S STRUCTURE. The aspect of the document that describes the way the text is organized.

METADATA. Any additional information that was not deliberated by the legally competent authority. metadata can describe the document itself (e.g., by way of keywords), its workflow (e.g., procedural steps in the bill), its lifecycle (the document's

---

[6] Like EnAct or FORMEX.

[7] As NormeInRete or Lexdania [9].

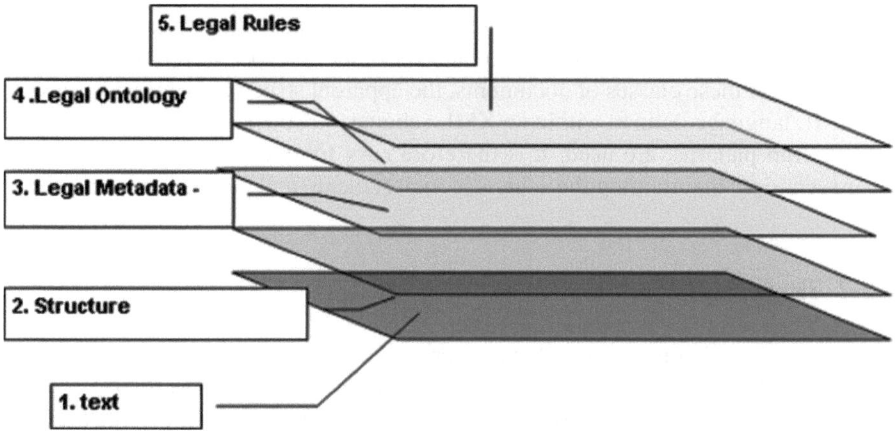

Fig. 6.1 Layers of representation in Legal Document Modelling

history), or its identification (e.g., by way of a URL, URI, or URN, or by specifying an annex).

ONTOLOGY. Any information specifying the legal or institutional setting in which the document plays a role—e.g., information identifying the document as a judgment or opinion about the legal system's concepts—or any concept which is invoked in the text and which needs modelling [5].

LEGAL RULES. The legal interpretation and modelling of the text's meaning. The transformation of the norms in logic rules for permitting legal reasoning [6, 12].

For example Akoma-Ntoso implements the first three levels of this cake and provides hooks and mechanisms for referring to external ontologies and to legal knowledge modeling. CEN MetaLex provides general mechanisms for coping with all the levels, and includes a document ontology able to manage the events, the rules, the authors, and other more fine grained legal knowledge models.

Fundamental part of this multilayer architecture is the IRI reference based naming convention that functions as the interface between levels.

The following sections aims to show how the above presented principles are used in the Akoma-Ntoso architecture and how the end-user can foster them during the markup.

6.2 Akoma-Ntoso Multilevel Architecture

Akoma-Ntoso is a Legal XML standard that belong to the third generation and it provides an explicit support of the first three levels of the semantic web layer cake: text and structure, metadata and ontology connection. In Akoma-Ntoso there are three main different document classes: (a) legislative documents, like bills and acts of Parliament; (b) debate documents, such as reports, debate records, an minutes; and (c) judgment documents, or judgments, meaning decisions rendered by a court of law (court rulings) or opinions issued by a judge; plus (d) a generic document format, called *doc*, for every other need and for other non specialized documents.

For each of these classes of documents, the apparent structure is defined as a special XML language defined within an XML schema. Abstract classes, implementing basic design patterns, are used. It is therefore easy to extend the XML schema to other scenarios, maintaining the schema concise, clean, and pattern oriented.

6.2.1 Text Level

At the *text level*, Akoma-Ntoso elements provide a way to capture textual elements such as blocks and headings, as well as semantic elements such as references and speakers inside of a debate. We can see in this following example (Fig. 6.2) the subdivision of the text in paragraphs (<p>), list and item. They are simple blocks without any particular meaning. We have just captured the text. Otherwise we see the markup of a normative reference (<ref>) that expresses a particular semantic: a citation.

An Act of Parliament to promote and develop in an orderly manner the carrying and content of communications under Act no. 9 of 2009

WHEREAS it is deemed necessary

- to facilitate development of a national infrastructure for an information-based society, and to enable access thereto;

- to provide a choice of services to the people of Kenya with a view to promoting plurality of news, views and information.

```
<p>An ACT of Parliament to
promote and develop in an orderly
manner the carriage and content
of communications according to
the
<ref id="ref1" href="un/act/2009-
12-12/9/main">Act. n. 9 at
2009.</ref>
</p>
<p>WHEREAS it is considered
necessary</p>
<list id="lst1">
  <item id="lst1-it1">
    <p>- to facilitate
development of a national
infrastructure for an information
based society, and to enable
access thereto;</p>
  </item>
  <item id=" lst1-it2">
    <p>- to provide a choice of
services with a view to promoting
plurality of news, views and
information.</p>
  </item>
</list>
```

Fig. 6.2 Example of text markup

6.2.2 Structure Level

At the *structural level*, elements capture and represent the text's organization, or its semantic structure. Preamble, article, and conclusions are just three examples of elements identifying the way a legislative act is organized, in the manner decided by the author in issuing the text. The following example (Fig. 6.3) shows the text structured in part, section (article) and subsection (comma). We can notice the heading (title of the article) markup used as particular structure annotation for indicating which role plays this specific text (Short title) in this particular position into the act. In other words "Short title" is no more longer a simple text, but it acquires a special meaning useful for information retrieval (e.g. give me all the sections with heading="Short title").

PART I. PRELIMINARY

Short title

1. This Act may be cited as the "First Example Act."

```
<body>
  <part id="prtI">
    <heading>PART I
PRELIMINARY</heading>
      <section id="sec1">
        <heading>Short
title</heading>
          <subsection id="sec1-
sub1">
            <content>
              <p>1. This <ref
id="ref12" href="/un/act/2010-01-
01/1/main">Act</ref> may be cited
as the First Example Act.</p>
            </content>
          </subsection>
      </section>
```

Fig. 6.3 Example of structure markup in Akoma-Ntoso

6.2.3 Metadata Level

At the *metadata level*, Akoma-Ntoso provides the necessary mechanisms for annotating the text with enriched data collected either in a separate block (metadata container) or in the text itself (inline elements). The metadata gathered in the metablock are connected directly to the text so as to make possible a multi-metadata annotation pertaining to the same document fragment. In this way the same text fragment can take multiple annotations, all of them fully and equally valid, coming from different editors expressing different points of view. The following example (Fig. 6.4) shows how the same text fragment (section 42, subsection 3) is subject to two different interpretations: editor1 annotates it as an authentic interpretive provision; editor2 takes the opposite view, saying it is an expectation. Both are a valid interpretations of the norm expressed in section 42, subsection 3.

```
<subsection id="sec42-sub3">
 <num>(3)</num>
 <content>
  <p>
   <mod id="mod1">In this section and
in <ref id="ref12" href="#sec44">
section 44</ref> "certificate of
ownership" means-</mod>
  </p>
  <list id="sec42-sub3-lst1">
   <item id="sec42-sub3-itma">
    <num>(a)</num>
      <p>a certificate of ownership
issued under any of the provisions of
this Act;</p>
   </item>
   <item id="sec42-sub3-itmb">
    <num>(b)</num>
      <p>a certificate of ownership
issued under any former law relating
to ACME; and</p>
   </item>
   <item id="sec42-sub3-itmc">
    <num>(c)</num>
      <p>a certificate of ownership
or equivalent documents issued by a
competent officer or other authority
of the country of origin.</p>
   </item>
  </list>
 </content>
</subsection>
```

```
<analysis source="#bungeni">
  <activeModifications>
    <meaningMod
type="authenticInterpretation"
id="am1" refersTo="editor1">
       <source href="#sec42-sub3"/>
       <destination href="#sec44"/>
    </meaningMod>
    <scopeMod
type="exceptionOfScope" id="am2"
refersTo=" editor2">
       <source href="#sec42-sub3"/>
       <destination href="#sec44"/>
    </scopeMod>
  </activeModifications>
</analysis>
```

Fig. 6.4 Example of metadata markup connected to the structured text

Most of these elements are shared by the different document types, and are left undifferentiated for all structures even if they locally acquire semantic meaning depending on the type of document where they are included. In the following example (Fig. 6.5), the tag *docProponent* is used in different ways in the document type *bill* and in the type *judgment*, but in either case it expresses the same general concept, for it represents the document's "proponent," or initiator (meaning the person or authority with whom the document originated), which in the former case is the Ministry of Local Government and in the latter the Supreme Court of Appeal.

In this way Akoma-Ntoso is kept compact, easy, clean, and light, even if it arguably becomes more complex to understand its application. All the elements belong to a shared conceptual architecture, while the semantics of each element take on a special *local* meaning.

<preface> <p class="heading">REPUBLIC OF AMCE</p> <p class="subheading"> <docTitle> GOVERNANCE FRAMEWORK BILL</docTitle> </p> <p class="subheading"> <docProponent>MINISTER FOR LOCAL GOVERNMENT of ACME </docProponent>) </p> </preface>	<header> <p> <b><docProponent refersTo="#SCOA"> SUPREME COURT OF APPEAL ACME</docProponent></b> </p> </header>

Fig. 6.5 Example of shared elements with different semantic meanings

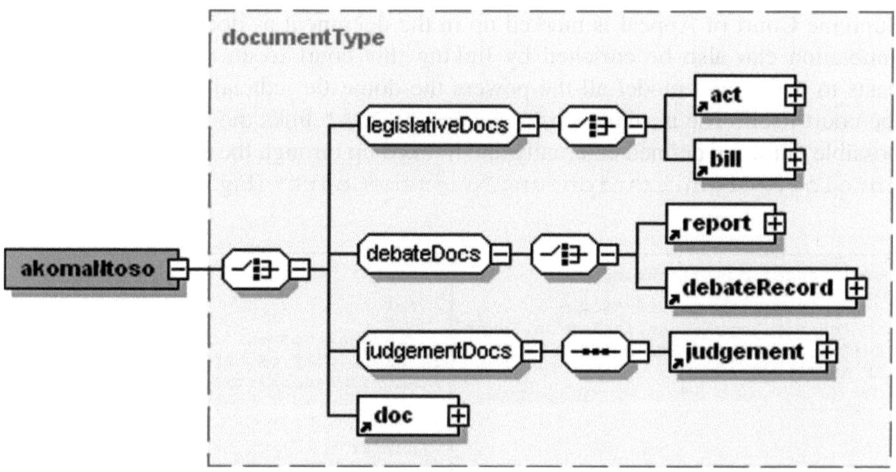

Fig. 6.6 Akoma-Ntoso document-type subdivision

New subschemas of the main XML schema are easy to implement using the design patterns principles, as the Amendment sub-schema designed by the EP demonstrates (Fig. 6.6).

6.2.4 Semantic Elements

Within structural and typographical elements, text fragments can be found that carry relevant meanings even though they have no particularly relevant structural role. These elements include semantic elements pertaining to the document's organization (elements such as quoted text, the specification of speakers, or name of a lawyer), or legal semantic elements such as normative references, events, the specification of recorded times, or a judge's dissenting opinion. It is important for semantic elements to be recorded, both because they add to the overall meaning of the documents being marked up and because they make it possible to disambiguate ambiguous information for subsequent semantic applications that might use these elements as a basis on which to produce reasoning and inferences. Thus, for example, semantic elements could be used to disambiguate a date such as "May 1 of the following year" or a reference to "the above-mentioned article," both strings requiring an understanding of the texts' semantic flow. The semantic elements in Akoma-Ntoso are in any event supported by factual evidence in the text so as to enable homogenous markup. Of course, how frequently and how deeply semantic elements are to be specified is a question left to legal analysis and to the discretion of the markup technician, but in principle markup can end up containing a considerable amount of specific and unambiguous information beyond that identifying the document's structural parts.

After semantic markup, the abstract concept can be linked to a particular hook positioned in the references block. The following example shows how the ACME Supreme Court of Appeal is marked up in the document as docProponent, but the annotation can also be enriched by linking this court to an ontology on which basis to define and model all the powers the domestic judicial system confers on the court itself. The attribute `refersTo="#SCOA"` links the local metadata to a possible ontology defined externally and hooked up through the attribute `href="/ontology/organization/un.SoupremeCourt"` (Fig. 6.7).

```
<references source="#bungeni">
   <TLCOrganization id="SCOA"
href="/ontology/organization/un.Soupr
emeCourt" showAs="THE SUPREME COURT
OF APPEAL OF ACME"/>
</references>
```

```
<header>
   <p>
   <b><docProponent refersTo="#SCOA">
SUPREME COURT OF APPEAL of
ACME</docProponent></b>
   </p>
</header>
```

Fig. 6.7 Example of connection between text and references (ontology level)

6.3 Generic Elements and Patterns

6.3.1 Generic Elements

Akoma-Ntoso provides more than 170 elements from which to choose in describing the fragment being considered. Generic elements are used in those cases (hopefully rare ones) in which no appropriate element can be found in the vocabulary, and some new element therefore needs to be invented, lest the fragment should be labeled by an inappropriate and vague term.

Generic Elements are thus meant to be used whenever a specific term is needed but none is available, and they represent an important source for extending the language itself. Generic elements are associated with specific structure models: they make the use of such structures consistent the rest of the schema, and they provide a mechanism with which to suggest a name (useful in displaying and characterizing the elements).

The generic elements are to be used in markup whenever a specific semantic or structural need arises for which no appropriate element is found in the element vocabulary. Akoma-Ntoso makes no claim to completeness in its vocabulary, and so there may well be a situation in which an explicitly named structure is present in the document and no corresponding element is found in the vocabulary.

It is for these situations that generic elements are appropriate. Generic Elements exist for all types of structures in the Akoma Ntoso vocabularies. This means that for every *named* element there exists an unnamed *generic* element having the same characteristics (an element that is *used* in the same way and has the same *content model*).

6.3.2 Patterns

As mentioned, named elements are organized into families, or *patterns*, that share a number of characteristics. Akoma-Ntoso defines the following patterns:

- *Containers*. Wrappers around other structural elements having no intervening text.
- *Hcontainers*, or hierarchical containers. These provide nested hierarchies as well as headings and numbers having no intervening text.
- *Blocks*. Structures containing text and smaller elements (the *inline* elements listed immediately below) organized vertically to aid reading and pagination. An example is text paragraphs.
- *Inline*. Elements within blocks describing features of smaller text fragments that do not break the document's vertical organization.
- *Milestones*. Empty elements used *within* the main flow of the text to define specific locations, such as the placement of an image or a page break.
- *Meta* or *metadata*. Empty elements used *outside* the main flow of the text to describe the document's overall features.
- *Mcontainers*, or metadata containers. These that organize metadata elements (and other *mcontainers*) but with no intervening content.

When a structure with no corresponding named element is found, the most appropriate strategy is to (a) find the element in the vocabulary that most closely resembles the structure's role, purpose, and use; and (b) find out what the structure's pattern is and use the generic element corresponding to that pattern. The generic element is then named using the name attribute: the chosen name should be that which the *specific* element would have if it existed.

One example are the elements container and hcontainer, the former representing a generic block set and the latter a hierarchical container set (Fig. 6.8).

APPENDIX 1 **OFFICIALS FROM THE DEPARTMENT OF DEFENCE**	<preface> <p class="heading"> <docType>APPENDIX 1</docType> <docTitle>OFFICIALS FROM THE DEPARTMENT OF DEFENCE </docTitle> </p> </preface> <mainContent> <container id="hco1" name="members" class="memberslist"> <ol id="hco1-oli1">
Mr. January (Secretary of Defence and Director General of the Department)	<li> Mr January (Secretary for Defence and Director General of the Department)</li>
Mr. February (Deputy Director General and Chief Director of Policy and Planning)	<li>Mr Feruray (Deputy Director General and Chief Director Policy and Planning)</li>
Lieutenant General March (SANDF Chief: Corporate Staff)	<li>Lieutenant General March </span>(SANDF Chief: Corporate Staff)</li> </ol> </container>

1. Introduction	<hcontainer id="iss1" name="issue"> <num>1. </num> <heading>Introduction</heading> <paragraph id="iss1-par1"> <content>
The Portfolio Committee on Defence considered the 2007/2008 Budget of the Department of Defence on 22–23 March 2007 as part of its oversight function over the Department of Defence. The report is based on both the budget hearings held on 22 March 2007 as well as the committee deliberations held on 23 March 2007.	<p>The Portfolio Committee on Defence considered the 2007/2008 Budget of the Department of Defence on 22 -23 March 2007, as part of its oversight function over the Department of Defence. The report is based on both the budget hearings held on 22 March 2007 as well as the committee deliberations on 23 March 2007. </p> </content> </paragraph> </hcontainer>

Fig. 6.8 Example of *container* and *hcontainer* markup

6.4 Metadata

6.4.1 Metadata Container in the Schema

Aside from marking up documents, Akoma-Ntoso also provides a large number of pre-established and common metadata categories. Among the common metadata categories we find identification metadata, publication details, classification data, lifecycle and workflow data, semantic analysis, references to other resources, and editorial footnotes (Fig. 6.9).

6.4.2 Metadata Blocks

Identification: This block identifies the document FRBR [2] metadata and assigns the URI to each level of the legal resource: work, expression, manifestation. Particular attention is focused on the components (annexes) as part of the entire legal document.

The following example (Fig. 6.10) shows the usage of the metadata blocks.

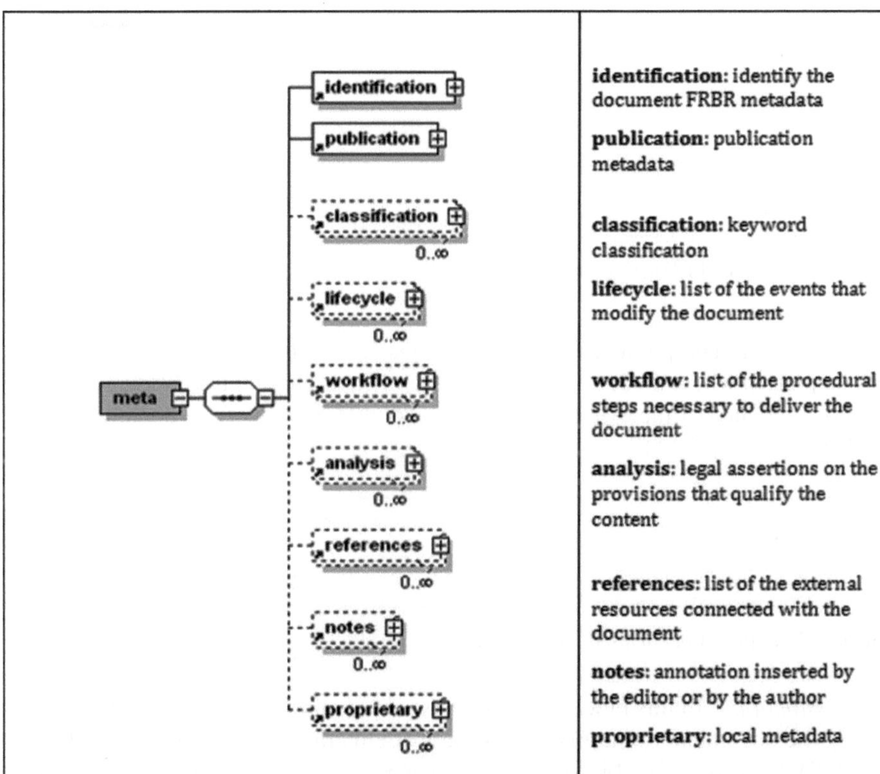

Fig. 6.9 Metadata roadmap

```
<meta>
  <identification source="#bungeni">
    <FRBRWork>
      <FRBRthis value="/un/judgement/2007-07-25/14-
2007/main"/>
      <FRBRuri value="/un/judgement/2007-07-25/14-
2007"/>
      <FRBRdate date="2007-07-25" name="Creation"/>
      <FRBRauthor href="#Scoa " as="#Author"/>
    </FRBRWork>
    <FRBRExpression>
      <FRBRthis value="/un/judgement/2007-07-25/14-
2007/eng@/main"/>
      <FRBRuri value="/un/judgement/2007-07-25/14-
2007/eng@"/>
      <FRBRdate date="2007-07-25" name="Delivery"/>
      <FRBRauthor href="#ACME" as="#Editor"/>
    </FRBRExpression>
    <FRBRManifestation>
      <FRBRthis value="/un/judgement/2007-07-25/14-
2007/eng@/main.xml"/>
      <FRBRuri value="/un/judgement/2007-07-25/14-
2007/eng@.akn"/>
      <FRBRdate date="2009-01-20"
name="XMLConversion"/>
      <FRBRauthor href="#ACME" as="#Editor"/>
    </FRBRManifestation>
  </identification>
```

Identification using the FRBR standard

Fig. 6.10 Example of *identification* metadata block

Publication: The publication metadata registers the information concerning the official journal where the legal document is published. These information guarantees a public evidence of the existence, validity and authenticity of the document in the legal system (Fig. 6.11).

```
  <publication date="2007-07-29" name="Law Report"
showAs="ACME Law Journal"/>
```

publication

Fig. 6.11 Example of *publication* metadata block

Classification: In this block documentalist could annotate the keywords for classifying the document. Sometime the assembly deliberates the keywords into the text (e.g. bill), therefore a double annotation is necessary: the first as part of the content (into the text) and the second into the metadata classification block as semantic data (Fig. 6.12).

```
<classification source="#bungeni">
   <keyword value="Human Right" showAs="human"
dictionary="UNVOC"/>
   <keyword value="Family Law" showAs="family"
dictionary="UNVOC"/>
</classification>
```

classification

Fig. 6.12 Example of *classification* metadata block

Lifecycle: The lifecycle block of metadata includes the list of each event that modifies the document over the time. These metadata is particularly relevant for tracking the modifications of the document. This mechanism permits to build software that support the consolidation process for producing in real-time the updated version of the document (e.g. bill, act) (Fig. 6.13).

```
<lifecycle source="#bungeni">
   <event date="2007-07-25" id="e1" source=""
type="generation"/>
</lifecycle>
```

lifecycle

Fig. 6.13 Example of *lifecycle* metadata block

Workflow: This block of metadata lists all the procedural events necessary to delivery the document in official format. This part makes a distinction from lifecycle events, because the internal office steps sometime don't affect the document with textual changes (e.g. deliberation in the assembly) and with legal effects. They are mostly the outcome of administrative procedure necessary for respecting of the national assembly regulation (Fig. 6.14).

```
<workflow source="#bungeni">
   <step date="2007-03-28" id="a1"/>
   <step date="2007-07-25" id="a2"/>
</workflow>
```

workflow

Fig. 6.14 Example of *workflow* metadata block

Analysis: This metadata block permits to annotate legal assertions on the provisions that qualify the content in semantic way (e.g. modifications, Shepard's citations classification into the judgment) (Fig. 6.15).

```
<analysis source="#bungeni">
  <judicial>
    <result type="deny"/>
    <supports id="jdc01">
      <source href="#ref01"/>
      <destination
href="/un/judgement/2000/123/eng@/main.xml"/>
    </supports>
  </judicial>
</analysis>
```

analysis

Fig. 6.15 Example of *analysis* metadata block

References: References block records all the relationships with external resources connected with the document including link to part of ontology (Fig. 6.16).

```
<references source="#bungeni">
  <TLCOrganization id="bungeni"
href="/ontology/organization/un/un.bungeni"
showAs="Bungeni"/>
  <TLCOrganization id="Scoa"
href="/ontology/organization/acme.SupremeCourt"
showAs="SUPREME COURT OF ACME "/>
  <TLCPerson id="ACME"
href="/ontology/persons/acme.SomeBody" showAs="Some
Body"/>
  <TLCRole id="Appellant"
href="/ontology/role/Appellant" showAs="Appellant"/>
  <TLCRole id="Respondant"
href="/ontology/role/Respondant"
showAs="Respondant"/>
  <TLCRole id="Advocate"
href="/ontology/role/Advocate" showAs="Advocate"/>
  <TLCRole id="Judge" href="/ontology/role/Judge"
showAs="Judge"/>
  <TLCRole id="Sollecitor"
href="/ontology/role/Sollecitor "
showAs="Sollecitor"/>
</references>
```

references

Fig. 6.16 Example of *references* metadata block

Notes: Note block aims to insert annotation by the editor or by the author. Special annotation are the consolidation notes that explain the effect of the modification (Fig. 6.17).

`<notes source="#bungeni">`	
`<note id="not1">`	
`<p> Some footnotes from author or editors.</p>`	notes
`</note>`	
`</notes>`	
`</meta>`	

Fig. 6.17 Example of *notes* metadata block

- *Proprietary*: this block permits to add new metadata block. If the proposed set of metadata elements is found to be inadequate, Akoma-Ntoso specifies a mechanism for adding new metadata elements depending on local rules and needs. This makes it possible to specify local sets of metadata elements for local applications and tools, without affecting the ability to share and reuse the documents themselves.

6.5 Legal Analysis of the Document

Before proceeding with XML markup of a document, the legal expert needs to undertake a legal analysis of it: this is the first and fundamental step in any markup. A legal analysis (usually done on paper) will identify the document's legal meaning and essential parts before proceeding to markup. It is an eight-step process as follows.

6.5.1 Identify the Type of Document

Correctly identifying the type of document in question is essential in making sure that any subsequent markup is effective. A document is identified as belonging to one type or another depending on whether its structure is hierarchical or not: in the former case, the document will be an act, a bill, or a judgment; in the latter, a report or debate record.

6.5.2 Distinguish Content from Metadata and the Presentation Layer

If the document has been issued by an official gazette, it will have plenty of information relative to its publication, such as footnotes, page numbers, a table of contents, and logos. So, once the document has been identified as belonging to one type or another, it needs to be cleaned up by removing from it the parts that do not need to be marked up and retaining only such parts as do have to be marked up (Fig. 6.18).

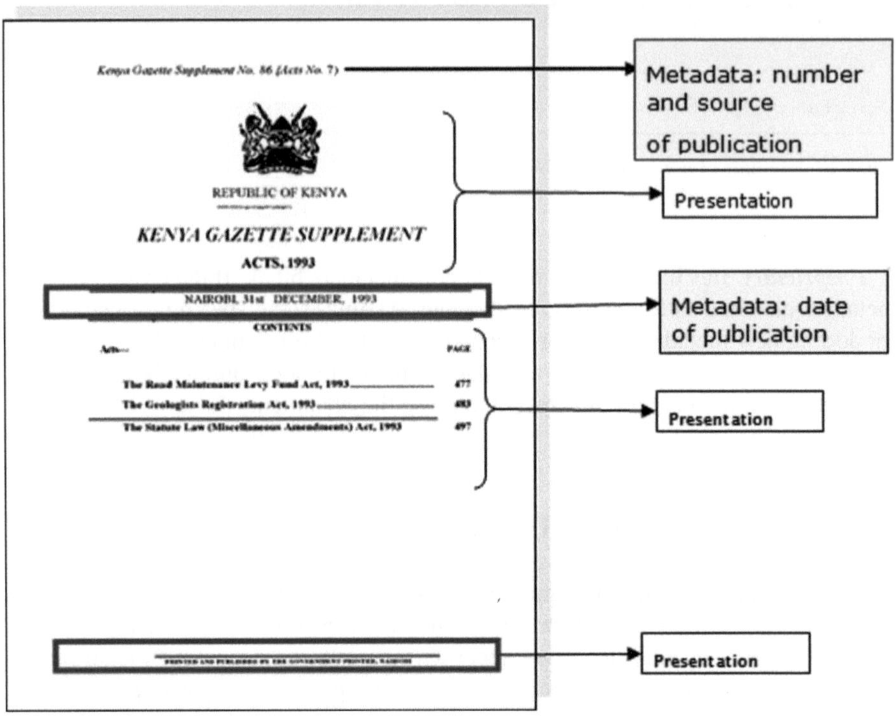

Fig. 6.18 Analysis of the content, metadata, and presentation blocks

6.5.3 Identify the Document's Main Legal Components

Each component in a document's Work level can be associated with a specific Expression and finally with a Manifestation. It is therefore important at this stage to go through the entire document and identify which of its components should be converted into an XML Manifestation and which ones are best preserved in other formats (such as PDF or TIFF). This analysis should be thorough and complete, covering the main document, its annexes, and its table of contents, and each of these components should be classified as belonging to a document type.

6.5.4 Define the Document's URI

Each of the document's three main layers—its Work, Expression, and Manifestation layer following FRBR standard (see also Chapter 7)—must be identified through a

URI (see Chapter 5). It is therefore important to define the type of document in question, its country of origin, its main language, and its date, and also its version if more than one exist. So, too, a legal document may different components, such as annexes, exhibits, tables of contents, and other official documents. It is therefore essential, when specifying URIs, to also analyze the way these components are structured, separating the logical organization imparted to the document by its author (such as a parliament or a judge) from the content's physical organization, usually based on technical criteria. In other words, the Work URI should reflect the original logical structure as set by the author, this to preserve over time the document's original form and the hierarchy of its annexes and other constituents. The document's physical organization may follow different criteria dependent on the purpose for which the document was issued and the technique used for its drafting. This means that we might find, for example, *three* components in a document's Work–and three corresponding URIs–but only *one* component in its Manifestation, with only a single URI, so as to make it easier to manage the document.

6.5.5 Isolate Each Main Legal Block in the Document

The main legal blocks are the front matter, the body, the conclusions, the tables of contents, and each of the main parts serving to interpret the document's structure in the correct legal way. The following example (Figs. 6.19 and 6.20) shows how the user have to divide conceptually the text in macro-block operating an interpretation on the text that could have relevant side effects on the future representation of the document into the web.

6.5.6 Identify Side Notes by the Author or Issuing Authority

Side notes, or marginal notes, no longer form the main part of a legal document, but they still need to be identified and isolated for an understanding of the way the document is organized. This is especially true of legislative documents in the common-law system, where marginal notes may serve the purpose of marking the structural parts of the document, which is often organized into chapters, as in the example below (Fig. 6.21).

6.5.7 Detect and Mark up the Text's Semantic Elements

There is an essential set of metadata that *any* legal document is bound to have depending on the kind it is. Thus, a *legislative* document will have in it metadata specifying, for example, its date of enactment, its issuing authority, its date of entry

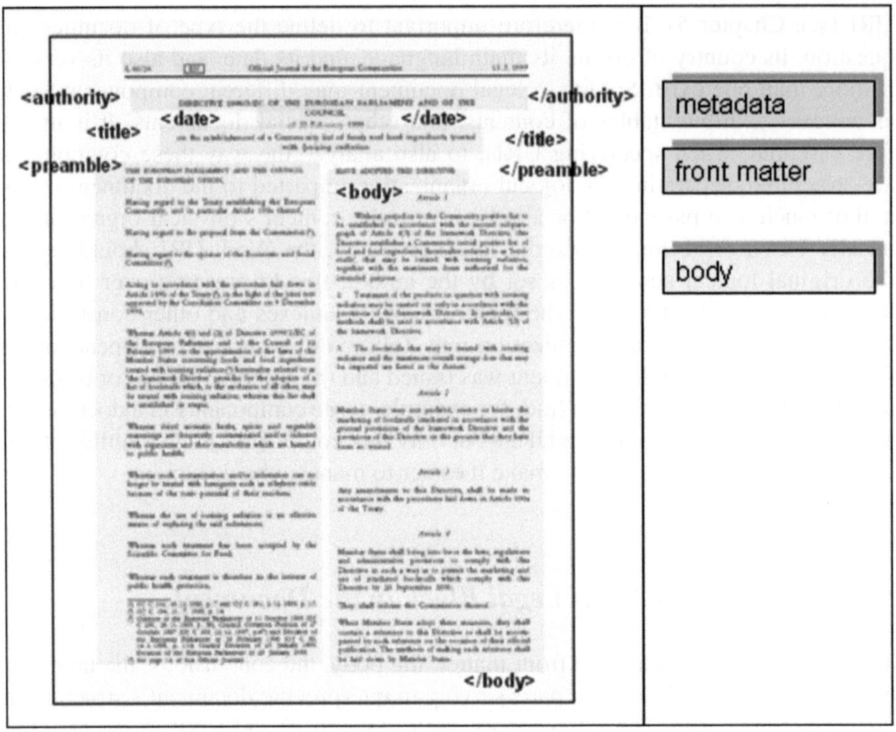

Fig. 6.19 Division of the text in macro-blocks

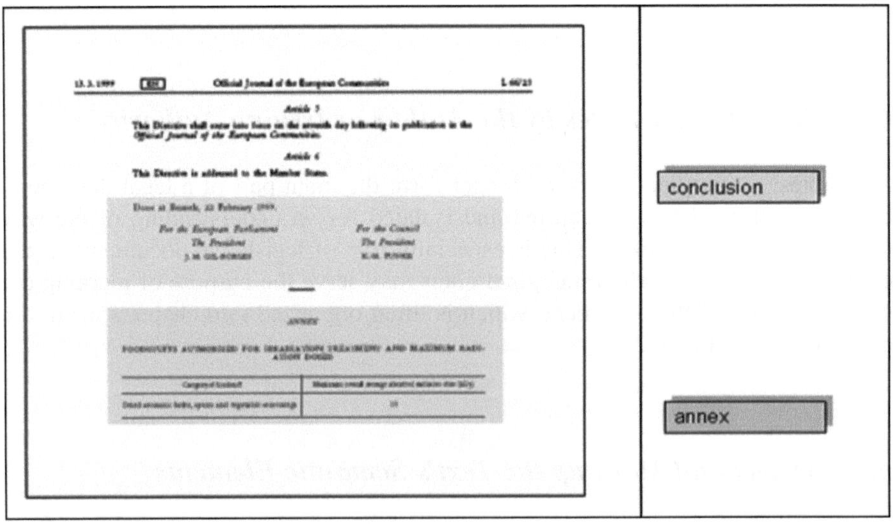

Fig. 6.20 Division of the text in macro-blocks

Chap. 21.	The Chief Justice may make rules governing the making of appeals and providing for the fees to be paid.	<subsection id="sec52-sub1"> <content> <p>The Chief Justice may make rules governing the making of appeals and providing for the fees to be paid.</p> </content> </subsection> -------- <outOfLines> <outOfLine id="sn01" type="sideNote" href="#sec52-sub1"> <p> Cap. 21. </p> </outOfLine>

Fig. 6.21 Example of side note in the *outOfLines* block

into force, its date of publication, and the outlet where the document is published (such as an official gazette); likewise, a debate record will have metadata specifying the date when the record itself was completed and when the debate took place, and a judgment (an opinion or court ruling) will specify the names of the attorneys involved in the suit out of which the ruling originated. Other semantic elements representing legal concepts in the text are *quotedText, quotedStructure, scene, judge*, etc. The corresponding parts should all be detected and analyzed by taking note of their *literal* meaning and assigning to them the correct *legal* meaning, this in preparation for the metadata markup.

There are two ways to proceed in marking up this information in the XML file, so the legal expert doing the markup should state from the outset which of these two methods he or she is using. Here they are:

1. The first is a two-step method using both *inline* elements and *meta* elements. Let us take, for example, the semantic inline element *quotedText*, which does two things: first, it isolates a text fragment that quotes another text; and, second, it forms part of a modification. For this latter reason the inline element *quotedText* may be used only in the *mod* block, because to mark up a text fragment by assigning to it the inline element *quotedText* is to do more than just single out a text string as quoted text (Fig. 6.22).

In Section 34 of the main Act, subsection (2), paragraph (a), is amended by deleting the words "balance sheet" and substituting the words "statement of assets and liabilities".	<p>In <mod id="mod10"> <ref id="ref9" href="/un/act/1997-08-22/3/main#sec34-sub2-itma">section 34 of the principal Act subsection (2) paragraph (a)</ref> is amended, by deleting, the words " <quotedText id="mod10-qtd1">balance sheet</quotedText>" and substituting therefor the words " <quotedText id="mod10-qtd2">statement of assets and liabilities </quotedText>" </mod>; </p>

Fig. 6.22 Identification of metadata inline elements in the text

The legal expert will then go back (at a later stage) and qualify the first and second *quotedText* element with special metadata inserted in the meta block, assigning to these semantic inline elements the role played in modification no. 10 (Fig. 6.23).

METADATA LEVEL	TEXT LEVEL
<analysis source="#bungeni"> <activeModifications> <textualMod type="substitution" id="am5"> <source href="#sec4-sub1-itma"/> <destination href="/un/act/1997-08-22/3/main#sec34-sub2-itma"/> <old href="#mod10-qtd1"/> <new href="#mod10-qtd2"/>	<quotedText id="mod10-qtd1">balance sheet </quotedText>" and substituting therefor the words " <quotedText id="mod10-qtd2">statement of assets and liabilities </quotedText>"

Fig. 6.23 Connection between text and metadata qualifications

2. The second method consists in using directly and exclusively the meta element in the meta block. This would be the method of choice for marking up the publication information printed in the header of an official gazette. The following example shows a European Directive published in the *Official Journal of the European Communities* (Fig. 6.24).

L 66/24 EN Official Journal of the European Communities 13. 3. 1999

DIRECTIVE 1999/3/EC OF THE EUROPEAN PARLIAMENT AND OF THE COUNCIL

of 22 February 1999

on the establishment of a Community list of foods and food ingredients treated with ionising radiation

Fig. 6.24 Publication metadata identification in the document

This information is identified by the legal expert and later recorded in the meta block (not in the text) (Fig. 6.25):

```
<publication name="OfficialJournal" date="1999-03-13"
number="L66/24" showAs=" Official Journal of the European
Communities" />
```

Fig. 6.25 Markup of the publication information within the meta block

6.5.8 Detect the Normative References

The normative references found in a legal document need special attention, for their URIs need to be correctly and completely identified. Indeed, if the reference is short, incomplete, or not explicit, end-users will have to resolve the ambiguity themselves by looking for the main elements of the URI, and that is an intellectual operation making it necessary to interpret the document's content in the correct legal way. In the example below, ACME (the Conservation and Management Act) is cited by way of an incomplete reference, so the legal expert needs to retrieve the missing information to complete the act's URI (Fig. 6.26).

```
<p>2. <ref id="ref1" href="/un/act/1980-01-01/1/main#sec2">Section 2
of the ACME (Conservation and Management) Act</ref>, in this Act
referred to as the principal Act, is amended -</p>
```

Fig. 6.26 Example of reference detection

6.5.9 Analyze the Normative Provisions

The normative provisions found in the text can be classified on the basis of the role they play in the document. The current version of Akoma-Ntoso makes it possible to qualify modificatory provisions as either active (outbound: activeModifications) or passive (inbound: passiveModifications), and we can also qualify judicial assertions (Fig. 6.27).

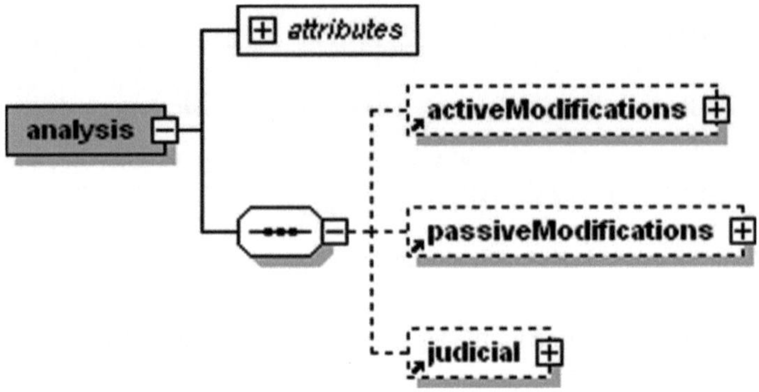

Fig. 6.27 Analysis metadata block in details

So we can add a modification qualification as well as we can qualify a judgment (a ruling) to represent a dissenting opinion or the majority opinion. A provision's qualification is represented in the meta block and connected with the corresponding text string using the id tag.

The example below shows how to classify the outcome of a case or trial in which the judge issues an opinion or judgment dismissing a claim or denying a request–this is done using the deny tag in conjunction with the result label, where "result" refers to the outcome of a trial–and it also shows how to qualify the judgment (the ruling) as supported by precedent, or how to indicate that precedent supports the judge's reasoning or argument (Fig. 6.28).

`<judicial>`
`<result type="deny"/>`
`<supports id="jdc01">`
`<source href="#par12"/>`
`<destination href="/gb/judgement/1829/QB273/eng@/main.xml"/>`
`</supports>`
`</judicial>`
	LEGEND
	Supports: There is a precedent supporting the judgment
	Source: The place in the document where the precedent is cited
	Destination: The judgment supported by the precedent so cited

Fig. 6.28 Example of judicial qualification

The example below shows a modificatory qualification composed of different pieces of semantic information: the action by which a norm is modified, the source of the modification so effected, the target norm (or destination) affected by the modification, textual parts of the modificatory action. In some cases we will also have the date on which the modification was made, any conditionals (i.e., the conditions subject to which the modification may take effect), the modification's duration (e.g., the time a suspension will last), along with other pieces of information (Fig. 6.29).

```
<analysis source="#bungeni">
  <activeModifications>
   <textualMod type="substitution" id="am5">
     <source href="#sec4-sub1-itma"/>
     <destination href="/un/act/1997-08-
22/3/main#sec34-sub2-itma"/>
     <old href="#mod10-qtd1"/>
     <new href="#mod10-qtd2"/>
  </textualMod>
  </activeModifications>
</analysis>
```

LEGEND

Action: The action of modifying a norm by substituting existing text with new text

Source: The norm from which the modification originates

Destination: The target norm receiving the modification

Old: The old text

New: The text as modified

Fig. 6.29 Example of *activeModifications*

6.6 Conclusions

We have explored in this chapter the Akoma-Ntoso standard and it is usage during concrete markup. We thus laid out the technological basis on which this language and standard are founded especially, explaining the technology's main features, the choices that account for its design, and the various types of legal documents that exist. And then we described step-by-step the method needed to generate a document fully conforming to the Akoma-Ntoso XML standard.

References

1. Barabucci, G., L. Cervone, A. Di Iorio, M. Palmirani, S. Peroni, and F. Vitali. 2010. Managing semantics in XML vocabularies: an experience in the legal and legislative domain. Presented at Balisage: The Markup Conference 2010, Montréal, Canada, August 3–6, vol. 5. In *Proceedings of Balisage: The Markup Conference 2010*. Balisage Series on Markup Technologies.
2. Bekiari, C., M. Doerr, and P. Le Boeuf. 2008. International Working Group on FRBR and CIDOC CRM Harmonization. FRBR object-oriented definition and mapping to FRBRER (v. 0.9 draft). `http://cidoc.ics.forth.gr/docs/frbr_oo/frbr_docs/FRBR_oo_V0.9.pdf`. Accessed 20 Aug 2009.
3. Boer, A., R. Winkels, and Vitali, F. 2008. MetaLex XML and the Legal Knowledge Interchange Format. In *Proceedings of Computable Models of the Law, Languages, Dialogues, Games, Ontologies*, 21–41. Springer.
4. Breuker, J., A. Boer, R. Hoekstra, and C. Van Den Berg. 2006. Developing content for LKIF: Ontologies and framework for legal reasoning. In *Legal knowledge and information systems, JURIX 2006*, 41–50. Amsterdam: ISO Press.
5. Breuker, J., P. Casanovas, M.C.A. Klein, and E. Francesconi. 2009. *Law, ontologies and the semantic web—channelling the legal information flood*. Amsterdam: IOS Press.
6. Gordon, Thomas, F. 2008. Constructing legal arguments with rules in the legal knowledge interchange format (LKIF). In *Computable models of the law, languages, dialogues, games, ontologies*, 162–184. Springer.
7. Jelliffe R. The Schematron Assertion Language 1.5. `http://www.ascc.net/xml/resource/schematron/Schematron2000`. Accessed 20 June 2009.

8. Klarlund, N., A. Moller, and M.I. Schwartzbach. 2000. DSD: A Schema Language for XML. In *Proceedings of the third workshop on Formal methods in software practice, Portland.*
9. Lupo, C., F. Vitali, E. Francesconi, M. Palmirani, R. Winkels, E. de Maat, A. Boer, and P. Mascellani. 2007. General xml format(s) for legal sources—Estrella European Project IST-2004-027655. Deliverable 3.1, Faculty of Law, University of Amsterdam, Amsterdam, The Netherlands.
10. Murata, M. 2009. RELAX (REgular LAnguage description for XML). `http://www.xml.gr.jp/relax`, 2000. Accessed 20 June 2009.
11. Palmirani, M., G. Contissa, and R. Rubino. 2009. Fill the gap in the legal knowledge modelling. *RuleML2009 proceeding*, 305–314.
12. Sartor, G. 2005. *Legal reasoning: A cognitive approach to the law*. Vol. 5. Treatise on Legal Philosophy and General Jurisprudence. Berlin: Springer.
13. Vitali, F. 2009. Akoma Ntoso release notes. `http://www.akomantoso.org`. Accessed 20 August 2009.
14. Vitali, F., and F. Zeni. 2007. Towards a country-independent data format: The Akoma-Ntoso experience. In *Proceedings of the V legislative XML workshop*, 67–86. Florence, Italy: European Press Academic Publishing.

Chapter 7
Legislative Change Management with Akoma-Ntoso

Monica Palmirani

7.1 Historical Introduction to the Problem

When a legal text is modified, the changes made to it wind up affecting the legal system as a whole. This interconnectedness of the law, coupled with its openness to change, gives rise to uncertainty, making it difficult to know what the law is in force, or what rules apply to the case at hand, and can disorient citizens and enterprises trying to figure out what rights and duties they have.

Several legal-information systems over the last 20 years have been developed to manage change in legal corpora—at first using technologies like databases, SGML, and HTML, and then XML and OWL—for the purpose of providing updated versions of the law in at any given time (through the so-called *point-in-time*[1] mechanism) [9].

The first system for producing point-in-time legislative database in SGML was EnAct [2], developed in 1995 by Timothy Arnold-Moore for the government of Tasmania. In 1992, at the Cornell Law School, the Legal Information Institute (LII), founded by Peter Martin and Tom Bruce [8], has made available online (in HTML format) the consolidated United States Code.[2] The Australasian Legal Information Institute (AustLII), cofounded by Graham Greenleaf in 1995, makes over 400 legal databases accessible on the Web today using HTML [13]. In 1999, EUR-Lex began to consolidate a database of European legislation using Formex, an SGML data standard now translated into XML (Formex v4).[3] On January 1, 2001, Norway activated a Web service by Lovdata to provide consolidated legislation.[4] In 2002, France

[1] Point-in-time is the function that makes it possible to manage all of a document's versions over time, rather than only compare the original document with its latest version.
[2] The URL is `http://www.law.cornell.edu/uscode/`
[3] The database is available at `http://formex.publications.europa.eu/index.html`.
[4] The database is available at `http://www.lovdata.no/info/lawdata.html`.

M. Palmirani (✉)
Faculty of Law CIRSFID, University of Bologna, 40126 Bologna, Italy
e-mail: monica.palmirani@unibo.it

G. Sartor et al. (eds.), *Legislative XML for the Semantic Web*, Law, Governance and Technology Series 4, DOI 10.1007/978-94-007-1887-6_7,

© Springer Science+Business Media B.V. 2011

turned the commercial service Jurifrance into a public Web portal called Legifrance that includes consolidated texts in a mixed format combining HTML, XML, and PDF.[5] In 2004, Austria launched the eLaw project [22], turning its previous database (RIS, set up in 1983) into a Web collection of authentic documents, thus completely dematerializing the country's Official Gazette.[6] In 2003 in Italy, Emilia-Romagna Region started consolidating the region's regulations using the NormeInRete XML schema.[7] The Italian High Court of Cassation started the same markup for the Italian Official Gazette's documents in 2005 and is now preparing to consolidate this set of documents (Fig. 7.1). On June 30, 2009, the Brazilian Senate launched the country's parliamentary consolidated database, called LexMLBrazil,[8] equipped with a point-in-time function based on a customisation of the XML Akoma Ntoso schema. The Chilean Library of Congress provides updated national legislation using the national XML schema for legal resources, and since 2009 it has been providing the LeyChile service,[9] which makes available all the legal documents in the national database in each of their versions going back to 1998. Finally, the Kenya Law Report[10] is

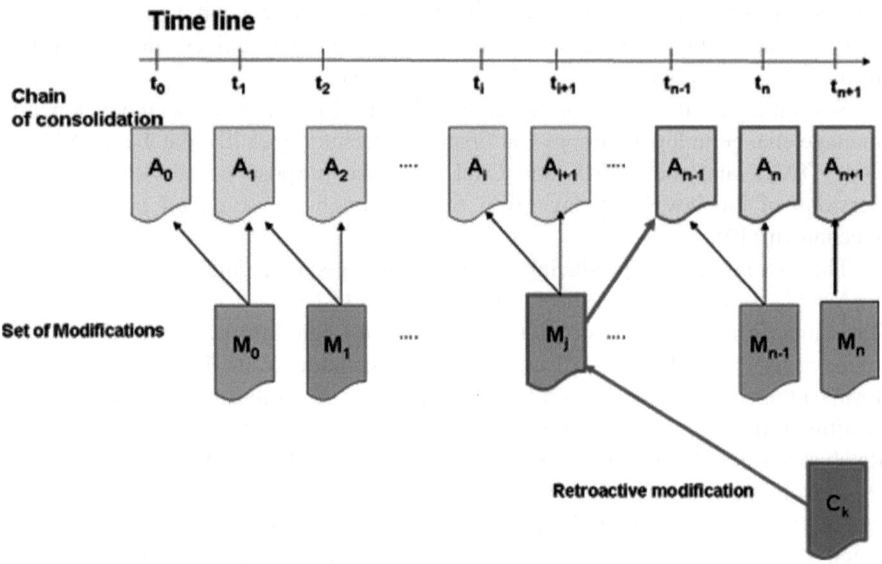

Fig. 7.1 *Point-in-Time* function of Norma-System (CIRSFID) applied to Italy's High Court of Cassation: all the versions are stored in the repository

[5] The database is available at `http://www.legifrance.gouv.fr/`.
[6] The database is available at `http://www.ris.bka.gv.at/`.
[7] The database is available at `http://demetra.regione.emilia-romagna.it/`.
[8] Online at `http://projeto.lexml.gov.br/documentacao/resumo-em-ingles`.
[9] Online at `http://www.leychile.cl/Consulta`.
[10] The database is available at `http://www.kenyalaw.org/update/index.php`.

now converting Kenya's database of laws into XML documents marked up using the Akoma Ntoso standard [24] (Fig. 7.1).

7.1.1 Methods for Managing Legislative Change

Three indispensable methods used throughout the world to reduce the costs associated with legislative management—as well as to make the legal system more functional and effective and easier to access—are consolidation, codification, and recasting. These methods can now avail themselves of XML technology, which is enabling functionalities that have never been possible before, such as integrating structural information with semantic metadata.

In what follows, we present three use-cases illustrating as many methods for managing a document's versioning over time.

7.1.1.1 Direct Method

This method proceeds from certain basic assumptions of legal theory. It particular, it assumes that the legal system changes by way of authoritative modifications introduced by official documents endorsed by an empowered institution. Proceeding from this assumption, the direct consolidation method takes the changes introduced through the official document (modificatory document) and applies them to the original document (basic working document) to achieve a consolidated version. A number of systems, organizations, and countries—including EnAct, AustLII, EUR-Lex, Emilia-Romagna Region, the Italian High Court of Cassation [16], Chile, Brazil) for producing the updated version of acts already promulgated and published in official journal. Chile, and Brazil—use this method successfully to produce updated versions of laws already promulgated and published in an official journal. It is a method typically used in the post-process legislative phase to produce a document's versions at specific points in its lifecycle (*point-in-time* versioning) after initial publication in an official gazette. This method is corroborated also by the theory of law: any modifications is a consequence of an evidence (e.g. empowered document, legal action, etc.) and any modification should be applied according with the principle of the temporal order (*lex posterior derogat priori*) (Fig. 7.2).

Fig. 7.2 The direct method of consolidation

7.1.1.2 Indirect Method

In this method (the inverse of the direct method), any and all changes are applied to the basic or original working document as they happen, and are then *inferred* by going back and removing the changes so introduced. Such reverse-engineering may occasionally yield outcomes out of keeping with what the legislators intended (e.g., just replacing the word "father" with "parent" is a single action that may result in many modifications throughout the document, with obvious material implications when the document is interpreted to determine its meaning and legal effect. This happens in the *vertical* or *implicit* modifications.) [14]. Other problems rise with particular cases: overlapping of modifications could be hidden each other, text style modifications (e.g. add an indent) are missed, relocation of the text are detected as new insertion. Some post reverse-engineering adjustments are therefore necessary for avoiding to obtain in automatic amendment texts not aligned with willingness of the author that usually wants to communicate concisely and effectively political messages. This method is useful in legislation drafting processes where a mixture of official and nonofficial changes are applied to a draft law (or bill). Two cases where this method has been used successfully are ITTIG's XMLeges editor [3, 23] of ITTIG and MetaVex editor [21] of the Leibniz Center for Law. In the XML4EP[11] and AM4EP the European Parliament has applied this method to the bill-amendment process by using a customisation of the Akoma Ntoso schema and a Web-application editor for capturing actions introduced directly by the Member of Parliament (or his/her staff) and transforming them into proposals to amend the bill text. This new functionality has also been integrated into the basic toolkit of the EnAct project [1] (Fig. 7.3).

7.1.1.3 Delta Method

This method is based on comparing two texts to automatically infer the changes between them. Problems may arise if text is replaced by *relocating* it within the document: as far as content is concerned, this means that instead of *new* norms being introduced in the document, we are looking at the *same* norms being moved to a dif-

Fig. 7.3 The indirect or reverse method

[11] For a description of the former project, see http://lexsummerschool.files.wordpress.com/2009/09/eu12-09-09.pdf; for a description of the latter, see http://www.ictparliament.org/wepc2009/presentations4november/wepc2009_sorensen.pdf.

Fig. 7.4 The delta method

ferent location within the document. In this case, the delta method doesn't infer that a document has changed by virtue of a relocation, but by virtue of a new inclusion and it provides a wrong outcome in the legislative process. It should be noted that if plain-text sources are used and the document is reformatted (e.g., by underlining, bolding, or italicising text), the delta algorithm will not help us detect these changes that sometime produce a different normative interpretation (e.g. add an indentation in a paragraph changes the logic consequentiality of the normative text). And, finally, the delta method can be made more effective by pre-XML markup of the documents being processed—which means we need a XML preliminary parser and must rely on its precision. This method is useful in the lawmaking process, especially when an document to needs circulate among different institutional bodies (e.g., the upper house, the lower house, and the executive), undergoing official revisions in the process. When one such institutional body takes up a new official version, it may need to compare it with its previous version in the workflow, when the document was in the hands of the body that passed it along in its current version [10] (Fig. 7.4).

These methods can gain from the XML standard, especially from a reliance on legal XML technical norms, and can also make it possible to reuse metadata and semantic annotations for different purposes not yet identified. In any event, there are two main tasks and corresponding end-products that legal XML needs to manage once it is remodelled on these methods: on the one hand it needs to manage changes (the modificatory document) and on the other hand it needs to enable versioning (the consolidation result). These two tasks are two sides of the same coin.

7.1.2 Legislative Change Management Principles

There are several characteristics a legal informatics system will need to embody if it is to apply these methods and be able to manage change and consolidation alike. We list ten such characteristics in what follows.

Event-Driven Approach. The full sequence of modificatory events is tracked in the modifying document and the modified document, this to enable direct consolidation and reverse inference. A temporal model capable of managing events and the priority of their application should be defined. This approach (event-driven) permits to develop the *point-in-time* functionality and so makes it possible to manage not just the first and last version of a document but also all interim versions. As the name suggests, point-in-time makes it possible to query the repository for any chosen point in time, and to take a snapshot of the legal system as it existed exactly at that time. Real point-in-time also ensures consistency while you browse and navigate from one normative reference to another. Thus, in a 2008 document, a cross-reference to Article 3 of Law No. 14/2004 will link to the updated 2008 version of that law (rather than to the law as it existed in 2004 or updated today). Point-in-time is especially difficult to implement for retroactive provisions or for an intervening *errata corrige* document version that takes effect under the *ex-tunc* principle.[12]

Self-containment. This means that the modificatory provisions can be annotated in the document where the changes are stated (*active* or *outbound* modification) or into the consolidated text (*passive* or *inbound* modification) or in both. This makes it possible to do direct consolidation or to infer the amendments by the reverse process previously explained as part of the indirect method.

Temporal Sequencing. This means that modifications can be applied to the new version in a correct *temporal sequence*, resolving as well the anomalies that come with retroactive modification, this in keeping the legal principles for resolving antinomies, especially the principles *Lex superior derogat inferiori*, *Lex specialis derogat generali*, and *Lex posterior derogat priori*.

Transparency and Traceability. Modifications need to be traceable, for in this way users can rely on neutral and objective elements (on hard facts) on which basis to determine on their own what happened during consolidation. Because the consolidation process is part-human, part-computerized, there is an intellectual component involved, and it therefore becomes essential that the new version be fully annotated with all of the modificatory actions that go into it. Using the direct consolidation it is possible to include also those human annotations coming from legal expertise.

Separation of Levels. An event (e.g. new amendment act) could produce several modificatory qualifications, and these qualifications are connected to the text where the modification is expressed or applied. A clear-cut separation is therefore necessary between content (e.g. text where the modification is expressed), on the one hand, and objective and subjective metadata (e.g. qualification of the modification and the connected event), on the other, for this will make it possible to annotate and qualify the same modificatory text multiple times if conflicting interpretations of it arise (e.g. suspension vs. exception) [4].

[12] Under the *Ex-tunc* principle, the normative effects owed to a modificatory event (repeal, substitution, annulment, etc.) enter into operation from the outset, going back to the time when the document was first created, despite the fact that the event (the document's modification) intervenes at a later time. Moreover, the normative effects deriving from the document's original version are erased as if that original version had never been.

Separation from Presentation. The graphical formatting and typographical styles used in the publication process should be kept separate from pure document content. This is the concept of "mother database" introduced by Jon Bing in 1970 [6], meaning that the document-management database should only contain neutral and valid legal resources. This separation is important for legal reasons connected with the long-term preservation in order to be able to recognize, in the future, the tags added for pure typographical reasons.

Granularity. The granularity of modifications should be not limited to the article or section level but it should make it possible to also go into each paragraph or paragraph fragment. This makes for greater accuracy and efficiency when managing change.

Validation Network. The consolidation process does not just involve two documents in isolation (a modifying document and a modified one): these documents exist in a network of normative references that need to be taken into account in applying each modification. Consolidation involves the entire legal system, and so whenever a modification is applied, the document must be checked for consistency with the other norms, for this makes it possible to detect anomalies, as when a norm is made retroactive, a modification is modified, a repeal is repealed, a modification is suspended, or the time when a modification is due to come into force is postponed. The complex relations among the parts and components of a legal system are contained in the "mother database", which captures the entire network through which such components are interlinked, and consolidation cannot properly proceed without checking for consistency with the network.

Completeness. This principle states that the consolidated version of a legal text must be produced taking into account all of the relevant legal sources. Even if one step is missed, the entire chain of consolidation stands affected and becomes subject to refutation.

Persistency. The chain of consolidation is the sequence of all the versions a document goes through over time (v1, v2, v3, v4, vn, vn+1). If a version in the middle of the chain receives a retroactive effect, the rest of the consolidation chain will no longer be persistent. Thus, for example, if version 3 (v3) was modified retroactively (e.g., Article 6 is repealed), all subsequent versions starting from time t3 could be invalid (e.g., v4 could embed some modifications into Article 6 even though the article did not exist in the preceding version v3). When dealing with retroactive changes, we need to duplicate the chain of versioning (forking the chain of consolidation into two chains), or we will have to go back and reconsider the entire consolidation process, looking at each of the assertions to check for persistency and consistency.

In the next section we analyse in depth the kind of user-scenario we have from the legal point of view, and we distinguish post-processing from pre-processing changes. This analysis will bring to light new requirements for the model on which basis to manage legislative change, and this is going to affect the way the XML schema is defined.

7.2 Change Management in the Legislative Scenario

7.2.1 Change Management of the Legislative Acts

A legislative act—understood as a public law or statute, one that has been enacted and published—can undergo change in any of three ways depending on the event that triggers the change: (i) a new law makes amendments and modifications to an existing law; (ii) the constitutional court issues decisions invalidating or modifying some laws (either in full or in part), often with retroactive effects; or (iii) supra-national law (e.g., a European Regulation) disapplies a national law, or the national law is diapplied by a regional law. These types of events account for a normative document's *lifecycle*, which we accordingly define as the set of events, belonging to any of the three aforementioned types, capable of changing the legal content or normative interpretation of the text contained in an act.

7.2.2 Change Management of the Legislative Process

Change also affects the *legislative drafting process*, which spans across the entire lawmaking process from the time a bill is introduced and debated in Parliament—involving as well a number of other participants, such as committees, government agencies, or associations—to the time it is made into law (enacted). During this phase we have to pay attention not only to normative changes (changes affecting the normative meaning of the law) but also to the administrative and institutional events (such as a vote taken in a parliamentary assembly) that determine the validity of the procedure. These administrative and institutional events change the document's status in some way, and together—as a series—they constitute the document's *workflow*. The workflow events, so defined, are annotated in the first useful document version for demonstrating the enforceability of the text and as certification of the lawmaking chain.

7.2.3 Change Management of the Legal System

A normative system, for its part, will be understood as a body of provisions that change over time, in a process where existing provisions are amended or ejected as new ones are introduced, or where a provision simply changes its normative content.[13] The provisions making up a normative system are therefore interconnected not only by their textual *structure* but also by their textual *meaning*: change one norm by amending its text and meaning, and you change the meaning of another norm. Thus, it will often happen that one provision should change another provision's text, purview, or term of enforceability through an amending clause embed-

[13] See [20] for a theory of diachronic normative system in the time useful for designing a information system.

ded in the provision itself (e.g., "in Article 125(1) and (2), the words 'until 31 December 2007' shall be replaced by 'until 31 December 2010'").[14] For this reason, we firmly believe that modificatory provisions should no longer be limited to textual amendments but should ontologically also extend to the modifications of a norm's time parameters (its time of entry into force or its period of efficacy), to its role (as when a national legal corpus comes to include an international treaty or implements a EU directive), to a legislative document's hierarchy within the normative system (delegation or delegification act), and surely to the scope of the norm's application.

Therefore, modificatory provisions also require special attention because they affect the entire normative system at different times: they can act instantaneously, retroactively, or in the future (e.g., "in Article 28, paragraph 2, Directive 79/1072/EEC shall be repealed effective 1 January 2010").[15] Therefore, it is important not only to detect a modificatory provision explicitly or implicitly stated in the text, but also to determine when such a provision should act on the normative system. It should be underscored, in this regard, that a lavish use normative modifications tends to undermine the certainty of the law, all the more so that the changes so introduced are sometimes fragmentary and incoherent, making it that much more difficult to arrive at a clear understanding of what the law is, or which of several versions of a provision counts as law.

7.3 Anatomy of a Modification

Having analyzed different consolidation methods, different use-cases (which typically involve managing change in the legislative process), and different aspects of modification, we can now turn to the essential elements of a modification and can offer a definition.

7.3.1 Taxonomy of a Modification

A normative modification is a change made to a legislative text—whether in part (as when one more clauses, articles, or other partitions are modified) or in full (as when an entire law is repealed)—or a change involving the relations that hold among the constituent provisions of a legal system (as when a decree-law is made into law). Each such change will correspond to an event represented as a point identifying the time (point in time) when the change takes place.

[14] Council Directive 2007/75/EC of 20 December 2007 amending Directive 2006/112/EC with regard to certain temporary provisions concerning rates of value added tax.

[15] Council Directive 2008/9/EC of 12 February 2008 laying down detailed rules for the refund of value added tax, provided for in Directive 2006/112/EC, to taxable persons not established in the Member State of refund but established in another Member State.

We can proceed on this basis to break down normative modifications into two main classes as follows.

7.3.1.1 Modifications Affecting Norms

This group of modifications changes the text's literal content (its language), its normative meaning, or the temporal dimension of the norms involved. In any of these cases, the modification changes the way the relevant norms need to be interpreted.

In this first group we can identify four sub-groups:

- TEXTUAL MODIFICATIONS. These are changes made to a norm's text or form (an integration, substitution, deletion, or relocation).
- MODIFICATIONS OF MEANING. These are modifications that change a norm's meaning without changing its text (a provision is authentically interpreted by another provision).
- MODIFICATIONS OF SCOPE. These are changes made to a norm's purview, i.e., the range of its subject matter or application. This kind of change may also come by way of a provision stating an exception to such a range.
- TEMPORAL MODIFICATIONS. These are changes made to a norm's temporal parameters. We have two different axes for managing temporal modifications: the time of its entry into force and the time when it takes effect or becomes operative (time or period of efficacy).

7.3.1.2 Modifications Affecting the Legal System

This group of modifications changes a document's status, or the role it plays in the legal system (as when an international treaty is adopted as part of a national legal system). These modifications usually do not change a norm's meaning, but they may change its application in the case-laws.

In this second group we can identify two sub-groups as follows.

- MODIFICATIONS OF A NORM'S STATUS. These are modifications that change the legal status a norm has within the legal system (an example, aside from that of an international treaty transposed into domestic law, is that of a decree-law made into law).
- MODIFICATIONS OF CONFERRED POWERS. These modifications change the powers a norm confers on people or institutions within the legal system (examples are a *legge delega*, by which the parliament entrusts the executive with issuing a legislative decree under which certain public laws may be passed, or a legislative decree empowering a ministry to deregulate a certain subject matter within its competence, or again a EU directive transposed into domestic law).

Figure 7.5 shows a complete taxonomy of modificatory provisions. This classification was arrived at by working together the modificatory forms described in legal theory and legal informatics, on the one hand, and the schemas functional to the consolidation of normative texts, on the other. As part of the NormeInRete project, CIRSFID modelled the first taxonomy of modifications [20] and in the Akoma

Super Class	Sub-Class	Type Level	Categories
Norm-specific modifications	**Modifications of content**	*textual modifications*	repeal substitution insertion replacement renumbering
		modifications of meaning	variation modification of the term authentic interpretation
		modifications of scope	exception/derogation extension
	Temporal modifications	*into force modifications*	entry into force end of enactment postponement of the entry into force prorogation of the entry into force re-enactment annulment
		efficacy modifications	entry into operation/efficacy end of the operation/efficacy disapplication retroactivity extraefficacy postponement of efficacy prorogation of efficacy
Legal-system modifications		*modifications of status*	conversion expiration reiteration remaking republication coordination/consolidation
		modifications of power	static reference implementation ratification application legislative delegation deregulation

Fig. 7.5 Taxonomy of modifications

Ntoso project this taxonomy was validated by reference to different legal traditions (both common law and civil law) [18].[16]

The taxonomy was also used for the *Legislative Drafting Guidelines for Africa*, a good-practices effort aimed at legal drafters. More to the point, the taxonomy was used to frame the guidelines in such a way that amendments would be drafted

---

[16] For an account of the validation conducted as part of the Akoma Ntoso project, see `http://www.akomantoso.org/docs/modificatory-provisions-for-legislative/credit-and-acknow`

taking into account not just the soundness of the amending text itself but also its final outcome.[17] When the objective is to have a consolidated text, the legal-theoretical forms need to be specified into further forms expressing the actions the passive or target norm is made to receive, but this specification must be effected in such a way that the resulting text does not lose its legal use or relevance.

The taxonomy has also been embedded into the LKIF-core ontology [18], designed to support the markup of modifications using the Metalex CEN standard [7] (see the Fig. 7.6). In this case, the taxonomy was represented in a different way, focusing on the semantic web metadata through RDF assertions. So all the modifications that entail annotation, and not literal textual amendment, were grouped as a single class called Semantic_Annotation.

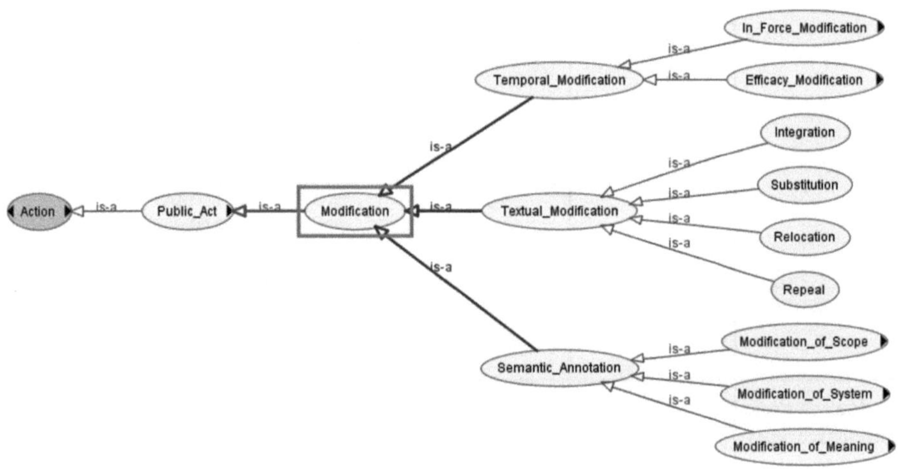

Fig. 7.6 Modification classes in the LKIF-core ontology

The taxonomy plays a fundamental role in making it possible to accurately identify (a) the action produced by a modificatory provision and (b) the consequences that such modificatory action entails for the target document (destination) as it changes over time. The attributes and the axioms connected each modification class help the system guide the end-user through the consolidation process. Several functions are possible using the taxonomy: (i) using NLP tools to extract from the text the modifications' qualification [11, 15, 23]; (ii) producing the consolidated text in semi-automatic way [16]; (iii) identifying the modificatory provisions by inference from the consolidated text; (iv) annotating the consolidated text with explanatory notes in an automatic way; (v) detecting and managing temporal anomalies, such as retroactiveness and suspension; (vii) helping semantic web information retrieval using the classification (tagging) of modificatory provisions [19]; (vii) supporting

[17] Thus Article 29.1 of the guidelines (on the Web at `http://ldg.apkn.org/`) says: "A provision can affect different aspects of other provisions: their content, their times of force or efficacy, their legal-value or status."

legal reasoning on the rule base (norms base), especially as concerns the norms' temporal dimensions [12, 17].

7.3.2 Modification Metadata in Akoma Ntoso

In Akoma Ntoso we have modelled the taxonomy in a simplified way, as illustrated in Fig. 7.7.

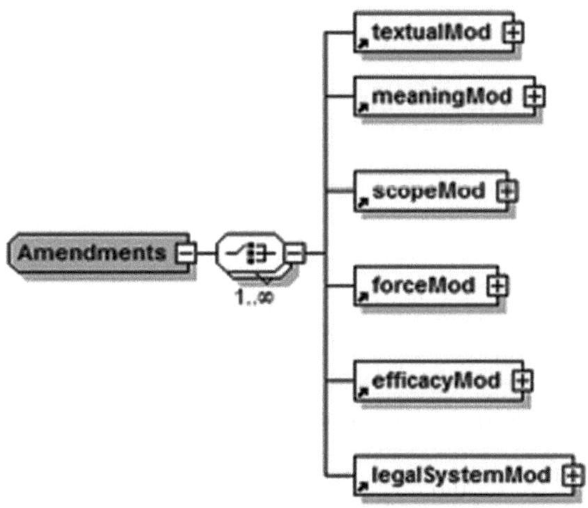

Fig. 7.7 Modification taxonomy in the Akoma Ntoso Schema

Akoma Ntoso can annotate the modificatory document with the appropriate metadata information using the block activeModification.

The element source indicates the position in the current document where the modifying provision is mentioned; destination identifies the act (law) being modified (the target of the modifying provision); new identifies the new text fragment introduced in the document; the type attribute specifies the type of modificatory action involved (Fig. 7.8).

```
<analysis source="#cirsfid">
   <activeModifications>
      <textualMod type="substitution" id="am1" complete="true">
         <source href="#ref2"/>
         <source href="#sec2-sub1-itma"/>
         <destination href="/ke/act/1997-08-22/3/main#sec2-sub1"/>
         <new href="#mod6-qtd1"/>
      </textualMod>
   </activeModifications>
</analysis>
```

Fig. 7.8 Metadata annotation in Akoma Ntoso: textual modification

The examples in Fig. 7.9 illustrates the markup of the pure text once we recognized the structural elements and annotated the existence of a modification (the mod tag), but all the information about relative to this change is assigned to the metadata block (Fig. 7.9).

```
<item id="sec2-sub1-itma">
   <num>(a)</num>
   <p>by deleting the definition of "financial year" and
      <mod id="mod6">
         <ref id="ref2" href="/ke/act/1997-08-22/3/main#sec2-
sub1">substituting</ref> therefor the following new definition -
            <quotedText id="mod6-qtd1">"financial year-"<eol/>
         (a) in relation to the Authority, has the meaning assigned to it in
               section 19;'<eol/>
         (b) in relation to a scheme, means such accounting period as may be
         prescribed in the scheme rules;
            </quotedText>
      </mod>
   </p>
</item>
```

Fig. 7.9 Markup of a modificatory provision in Akoma Ntoso

We should note that there is no duplication of text, and any semantic information is linked to the textual part using an href link. In this way, the text is independent of its semantic annotation, and in principle one can interpret the same fragment in two ways without thereby duplicating its content, as in the following example. In this new example we have the same text fragment (sec42-sub3) enriched by two different interpretations of the same modification: in one case one author sees this as an authentic interpretation, while another sees it as an exception. So we can track both authors' doctrinal visions (both interpretations) for future purposes (Fig. 7.10).

```
<analysis source="#bungeni">
   <activeModifications>
      <meaningMod type="authenticInterpretation" id="am1" refersTo="so">
            <source href="#sec42-sub3"/>
            <destination href="#sec44"/>
            <destination href="#n1"/>
      </meaningMod>
      <scopeMod type="exceptionOfScope" id="am2" refersTo="sb">
            <source href="#sec42-sub3"/>
            <destination href="#sec44"/>
      </scopeMod>
   </activeModifications>
```

Fig. 7.10 Metadata annotation in Akoma Ntoso: modification of a norm's meaning and scope

The text falls entirely within in the body of the document and so is not affected at all by this dispute: it is neutrally marked up only in the objective declarative part of the document (Fig. 7.11).

```
<subsection id="sec42-sub3">
   <num>(3)</num>
   <content>
      <p>
         <mod id="mod1">In this section and in <ref id="ref45"
href="#sec44">sections 44 and 45</ref> "certificate of ownership" means-</mod>
      </p>
      <list id="sec42-sub3-lst1">
         <item id="sec42-sub3-itma">
            <num>(a)</num>
            <p>a certificate of ownership issued under any of the provisions of
this Act;</p>
         </item>
         <item id="sec42-sub3-itmb">
            <num>(b)</num>
            <p>a certificate of ownership issued under any former law relating
to wildlife; and</p>
         </item>
         <item id="sec42-sub3-itmc">
            <num>(c)</num>
            <p>a certificate of ownership or equivalent documents issued by a
competent officer or other authority of the country of origin of the trophy
concerned.</p>
         </item>
      </list>
   </content>
</subsection>
```

Fig. 7.11 Markup of a modificatory provision in Akoma Ntoso

In conclusion, (a) the text is marked up with minimal information, as much as is necessary to identify its basic elements; (b) the metadata qualifies the modification (action, old text, new text, domain, temporal information, etc.); and finally (c) the lifecycle block and the references block record the modificatory events and the links to external documents, respectively. All layers are kept separate, so as not to duplicate content or information and to unambiguously distinguish content annotation from metadata enrichment.

7.3.3 A Modification's Semantic Elements and Attributes

Following is a list of semantic elements that can be used to model a modificatory provision while enabling all the foregoing functionalities.[18]

---

[18] We narrow our focus to modelling a modificatory provision, the part of the text that expresses a modification. A modificatory provision changes at least one other norm (its target norm), and in so doing it entails changes affecting the rules of law pertaining to the modification itself and to its

ActiveNorm (source). A provision expressing a modification.

PassiveNorm (target norm or destination). This is the provision targeted by the modification. The element PassiveNorm can be multiple when more than one provision is targeted, and it is often a problem to automatically identify all the subparts of a complex string of target provisions (e.g., "Articles 3, 4, 6, paragraph 2 and 8," where it is unclear whether the 8 identifies *paragraph* 8 or *article* 8). The element will be incomplete where the text does not include unambiguous or unique parameters for indentifying the provision referred to. Sometimes the passive norm is expressed through an exceptive sentence (e.g., "Repeal all chapters except the first one"), making it necessary to express this through a negative proposition: Repeal (not (Chapter I)).

Action. This is the modificatory action an active (or source) provision entails for the passive (or target) provision. Actions are sorted into classes within a taxonomy, and each action can have an application date different from the date of entry into force of the law (the active norm) where the provision is found. So it is possible to find that the modificatory action is retro-activated or postponed, and the provision's application date fixes the time of the action. In most of cases, this action starts on the date of entry into force of the document hosting the modificatory provision. Still, it is not so difficult to find different points in time when the action is to be activated. This date is a fundamental element for determining the correct and valid chronological sequence of legal events in the diachronic representation of the normative system.

Times (inforce, efficacy, application, duration). Time markers element can designate any of four intervals: we have (i) inforce,[19] indicating the period during which a norm or provision (and so also a modificatory provision) is in force; (ii) efficacy,[20] indicating the period during which a norm or provision is efficacious; (iii) application, indicating the period during which a norm or provision is applied by the judge to a concrete case-law; and (iv) duration,[21] indicating the period during which the action of modification continues to be. A modificatory provision is ultimately fixed by three dates: (a) the date of its entry into force, (b) the date on which it becomes efficacious, and (c) the date on which the modification is applied. All three pieces of information are necessary in tracing out the timeline of events accounting for the way any modificatory provision changes over time: all three therefore go into the process by change is managed in the versioning chain.

---

target norm. However, these ramifications—that is, the changes a modification entails for the rules of law—will not be treated in this chapter.

[19] Inforce: period when a norms is included in the Law System (in the civil law system usually after the vacation legis). A norm could be in the Law System but without effect: e.g. norm suspended.

[20] Efficacy: period when the norm expresses its effect and the judge may fully apply it in principle. A norm suspended could not be applied by the judge although in abstract.

[21] E.g. duration of the suspension.

Content (old text, new text, positions). Content is the part of the text that models the old text to be replaced or repealed in the modified provision. Any new text is inserted in the receiving norm, and the provision may indicate where the new text is to be inserted.

Domain. This part of the modificatory provision is sometimes used to indirectly describe a change in the target norm's range of application, or to point out an exception in this range, or to specify the way the range is to be interpreted.

Conditions. (event, space, facts). Sometimes a norm's efficacy is conditional on an event, or the condition may be framed by reference to a geographic space or a class of facts. When a modificatory provision is conditioned by an undefined event, this freezes the action until the conditional is resolved (e.g., "Estonia shall be granted a temporary derogation from the application of Article 21(1)(b) and (c) until 31 December 2012").[22] This part of the language is very difficult to detect, but the idea is to use a logic formalism to transform these cases into rules, so as to logically validate the time at which the conditions are satisfied. That will determine the time when the modificatory provision will take effect.

Reflexivity. When a source norm (ActiveNorm) and a target norm (PassiveNorm) collapse into each other in the document, we have a *reflexive* modificatory provision, one that acts recursively on the same text with an introversion modification. This kind of modification is usually aimed at postponing a norm's application (e.g., "7. The percentage referred to in paragraph 1(d) and paragraph 3 shall from 1 January 2011 be 25")[23] or at implementing an exception,

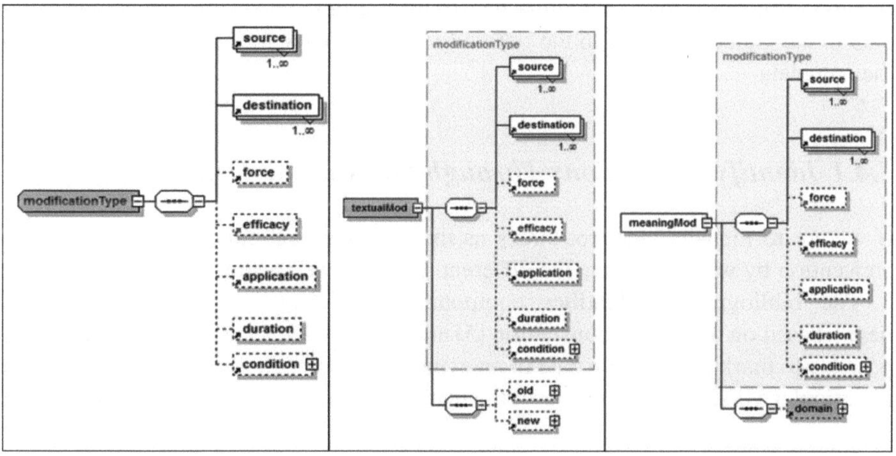

Fig. 7.12 Modification model in the Akoma Ntoso schema

[22] Directive 2008/3/EC.

[23] Council Directive 2003/48/EC.

condition, or geographic area restricting or expanding a norm's scope or geographic purview. This propriety of modificatory provisions is a challenge to detect, for the difficulty involved in distinguishing the *acting* text string from the string being acted upon (Fig. 7.12).

7.4 Anatomy of a Versioning Mechanism

The previously discussed functionalities and characteristics can all be managed using the Akoma Ntoso standard. The standard is neutral respect the different consolidation methods (direct, indirect, and delta), and it supports metadata annotation in several degrees of granularity without forcing the end-user to fully mark up a norm's complete setting. The main outcome of this markup activity is the consolidated document, enriched with all the events, notes, and information needed to render a transparent picture of the law's dynamicity over time.

The Akoma Ntoso mechanism for managing the consolidation of legal resources over time is based on three main apparatuses:

- a robust naming convention for managing versioning and variants identification respecting the FRBR model (identification block);
- a strong metadata mechanism for representing events, such as static data and dynamic intervals, especially as concerns the temporal parameters involved in the legal domain (lifecycle block); and
- a semantic model for annotating the modifications a text undergoes (analysis and note blocks).

In support of this scenario, Akoma Ntoso uses an instrument for connecting metadata to the concept classes in the ontology, and similarly for connecting the text to the metadata.

7.4.1 Identifying Versions Through the Naming Convention

If we are to manage legal resources as they change over time, we need a robust convention by which to name the different versions each resource has.

The bibliographic identifier component (the document's univocal identifier)—based on the FRBR convention [5] and the Metalex CEN ontology—makes it possible to mark the creation date of an expression,[24] which is the element by which a particular version of a legal resource can be identified. An expression's creation

[24] An *expression* is what realises an abstract idea called a *work*; a *manifestation* is a concrete representation of a particular expression; and an *item* is the specific medium on which the manifestation is delivered or made accessible. Thus, for example, the Italian data-protection law is an abstract *work*; the realisation of this abstract concept in the form of Law No. 169/2003 is an expression; the XML representation of document no. 196/2003 is a *manifestation* of that expression; and, finally, every individual copy or file of this XML representation on the Web is an item.

date (ExpressionCreationDate) is a fundamental metadata element for tracking the change over time and for providing an alignment with the FRBR model: it marks the date of a particular version of a legal document (a bill being debated in Parliament, an act or law, or what have you), and the choice of this date depends on the type of document in question, on the expression's creation process, and on background legal tradition. In the Akoma Ntoso schema, the resource names are identified through a hierarchy of elements: (a) the country where the document was drafted; (b) the issuing institution; the document's (c) type, (d) date, (e) number, (f) language, and (g) version date (@date); and finally the components of the document package (annexes, main document, etc.). The syntax for specifying this information is based on the permanent URI rules.[25]

Here are two examples (Fig. 7.13):

`http://www.parliament.sl/sl/parliament/act/2004-02-13/2/en@2004-07-21/main/schedule01`	Whole attachment "schedule01" of the Sierra Leone enacted Legislation. Act number 2 of 2004. English version, as amended on July 2004.
`http://www.parliament.sl/sl/parliament/act/2004-02-13/2/en@2004-07-21/main/schedule01/tableA`	Attachment "Table A" of the attachment "schedule01" of Sierra Leone enacted Legislation. Act number 2 of 2004. English version, as amended on 21 July 2004

Fig. 7.13 Fragment showing the naming convention in use in Akoma Ntoso

One problem is that of managing cases where multiple versions of a document are all valid at the same time (in these cases we say that the document has multiple *variants*). More to the point, when a document has multiple expressions created on the same date (e.g., different variant of the same bill, all created on the same date), the bibliographic identifier component will have to include *two* types of date: one for the document's initial expression (@ExpressioCreationDate) and one for its so-called fictional expressions (FictionalExpressioDate). The fictional expression date is the date when a new variant is introduced. Thus, for example, suppose the same version of a bill (version no. 5) is processed in parallel by three different commissions, each tasked with making proposals for amendment: whenever a new proposal is drafted and presented, it will have a FictionalExpressioDate specifying the date when it was presented (e.g., proposal no. 42 of version no. 5 of bill no. 239/2010).

Another example is where an act is annulled (as if it had never existed to begin with). Here we may have a situation where a court ruling issued *before* the annul-

[25] On the Web at `http://purl.oclc.org/docs/index.html`.

ment refers to the act as valid, whereas a case pending trial will have to be decided considering the act as null and void; which means that we have two different simultaneous and fully valid versions of the same act, namely, one version where the act is on the books and in force (adjudicated cases) and another one (having the same creation date) where it is instead null and void (for cases pending trial) (Fig. 7.14).

http://www.parliament.eu/eu/parliament/commissionIII/bill/2010-01-10/1026/en@2010-01-21;2010-07-30/main/schedule01¤	Variant·of·the·commission·III·in·date·of·2010-07-30·of·the·bill·has·approved·in·assembly·in·the·date·2010-01-21·(last·official·version)¤

Fig. 7.14 Fragment showing the of naming convention in use in Akoma Ntoso

In Akoma Ntoso this mechanism is managed in the meta block and in particular in the identification part. The example below shows the identification block for Bill No. 1026, official version 2010-01-21, amended by the third commission on July 30 of the same year (Fig. 7.15):

```
<FRBRExpression>
  <FRBRthis value="/eu/parliament/commissionIII/bill/2010-01-10/1026/en@2010-
01-21;2010-07-30/main"/>
  <FRBRuri value="/eu/parliament/commissionIII/bill/2010-01-10/1026/en@2010-01-
21;2010-07-30"/>
  <FRBRdate date="2010-08-28" name="Generation"/>
  <FRBRauthor href="#bungeni" as="#jurist"/>
  <components>
   <component id="emain" href="/ eu/parliament/commissionIII/bill/2010-01-
10/1026/en@2010-01-21;2010-07-30/main/schedule01" name="schedule"
showAs="schedule"/>
   </components>
</FRBRExpression>
```

Fig. 7.15 Fragment in Akoma Ntoso: Identifier block

7.4.2 Temporal Metadata

7.4.2.1 Metadata on the Static Date

In the legislative process we can distinguish static dates and dynamic dates. Static dates record legal events important for the life of a legislative document.

Five types of static legislative events can be distinguished as follows:

- *Legislative Creation*. This is the event in the legislative procedure through which a document is first created (it may be, for example, the first drafting of a bill).

- *Legislative Delivery*. This event marks the time when the first version of a document is officially approved by a institutional body (e.g., assembly, court, committee) empowered to do so.
- *Legislative Enter into Force*. This event marks the time of enactment, when the act fully enter into the Legal System.
- *Legislative Operation*. This refers to a legislative document's efficacy, specifying the date starting from which a judge, court, or other competent person or body may apply the document.
- Legislative Process Date.These are all the dates involved in a document's legislative workflow.

In Akoma Ntoso, the date can be marked using the neutral tag <date> , and for the different classes of static legislative events (which may be defined through an external ontology, such as Metalex CEN or LKIF-core), we can use the references block (Fig. 7.16):

```
<preface>
   <p>Kenya Gazette Supplement No. 63 (Acts No. 4)<eol/>REPUBLIC OF
KENYA<eol/>KENYA GAZETTE SUPPLEMENT<eol/>ACTS, 1997<eol/>NAIROBI, 29th August,
1997<eol/>
    <docTitle id="ActTitle">THE RETIREMENTS BENEFITS ACT, 1997</docTitle>
    <eol/>No. <docNumber>3</docNumber> of 1997<eol/>
    Date of Assent: <date date="1997-08-22" refersTo="#dateAssent">22nd August,
1997</date>
    <eol/>Date of Commencement:-<date date="1997-09-12"
refersTo="#dateCommencement">12nd September, 1997</date>
   </p>
</preface>
```

Fig. 7.16 Fragment in Akoma Ntoso: preface

In the references block illustrated in Fig. 7.17 we have included the definition of two types of events, namely, assent and commencement:

```
<TLCEvent id="dateAssent" href="/ontology/roles/dateAssent" showAs="Assent"/>
<TLCEvent id="dateCommencement" href="/ontology/roles/dateCommencement"
showAs="Commencement"/>
```

Fig. 7.17 Fragment in Akoma Ntoso: TopClassEvent

This mechanism provides a flexible instrument for extending the definition of static legislative events without overfilling the XML schema with tags, especially as there are issues among legal scholars as to how such events ought to be legally defined (which in turn raises issues as to what the proper tagging is for documents that reflect these events).

Still, the major static legislative events raise no such issues, and embedded into the XML schema are some basic tags with which to mark them up. Thus, for example,

- the publication date is embedded in the metadata block (Fig. 7.18):

```
<publication name="internal" date="2003-12-19" showAs=""/>
```

Fig. 7.18 Fragment in Akoma Ntoso: document's publication metadata

- the date of delivery is embedded in the preface block (Fig. 7.19):

```
<docDate date="2003-12-10">10th December, 2003</docDate>
```

Fig. 7.19 Fragment in Akoma Ntoso: document's date

- the first event in the document's lifecycle is embedded in the lifecycle metadata block, which specifies the document's date of entry into force using the attribute type="generation" (Fig. 7.20).

```
<lifecycle source="#bungeni">
   <event id="e1" date="2004-01-01" source="#rol" type="generation"/>
</lifecycle>
```

Fig. 7.20 Fragment in Akoma Ntoso: document's lifecycle

7.4.2.2 Metadata Relative to Dynamic Time

We have introduced into Akoma Ntoso some typical elements with which to manage the intervals framing a legislative text's dynamic time (especially with a view to managing as well the dynamic time of the rules and norms based on those textual provisions).

Three such elements are start, end, and duration (the last of these enriched with elements by which to describe different periods, such as months, hours, weeks, and years). The start and end elements combine with the inforce and efficacy intervals to give startEfficacy and endEfficacy, respectively. These attributes are valid for any textual fragment, to be sure, but they are an insufficient basis on which to represent all types of events and intervals.

Intervals are managed using attributes available in any tags. We are using start, end and startEfficacy, endEfficacy, so we can model only two kinds of events and intervals near the inline tags (we can only model a norm's entry into force and its period of efficacy). If a need arises for more kinds of intervals or more temporal parameters (such as application or duration), this model will be insufficient. The following fragment shows an updated version of a definition (the definition of *pooled fund*) that (a) enters into force at time e2 (usually date when the modificatory provision enters into force) and (b) enters into operation at time e3. We can annotate any part of the literal text, and in this way we can track its evolution over time. These attributes make it possible to immediately detect new, recently inserted fragments (Fig. 7.21).

```
<span start="e2" startEfficacy="e3">"pooled fund" means a fund established by a
limited liability company, other than an approved issuer, for purposes of
pooling scheme funds for collective investment;
   <noteRef href="#n2" num="2"/>
</span>
```

Fig. 7.21 Fragment in Akoma Ntoso: inline temporal annotation using attributes

Also, when it comes to modelling the duration of a modificatory action, there is no mechanism by which to mark up an interval having a starting event and a duration. In the example given in Fig. 7.22, we need to calculate the dates in a static way and fix them into the markup.

```
<p>The Financial year of the Authority shall be the period of twelve months
ending on the thirtieth June in each year.</p>
```

```
<p>The present text shall be apply after six months to the enter into operation
of this law</p>
```

Fig. 7.22 Fragment in Akoma Ntoso: paragraphs

It is otherwise important to mark up temporal information in the text *dynamically*, so as to make it easier to model cases involving modifications of modifications or simply to apply some reasoning mechanism (e.g., in working out the question, How long is norm X applicable?).

Imagine we have the sentence (row a) and the following modification paragraph (row b) (Fig. 7.23):

a)	`<p>The present text shall be apply after six months to the enter into operation of this law</p>`
b)	`</p>substitute "six" with "ten"</p>`

Fig. 7.23 Fragment in Akoma Ntoso: paragraphs

If the word "six" in sentence a is marked up with a temporal meaning, we can use that temporal information to automatically recalculate the period of the law's application when modification b takes place. From the above limitation we can conclude that we need a robust mechanism for marking up:

- he definition of an interval and its duration; and
- inline date and time parameters to be represented in text fragments through the markup mechanism.

The Akoma Ntoso schema will thus be enriched with the following elements in its next release. Each text fragment has an attribute, temporalGroup, that specifies all intervals between dates without limiting the types or the number of intervals (temporalGroup has the id=p1 and the span element, that identifies the part of the text to connect with the temporalGroup information, uses the attribute period for creating a idref) (Fig. 7.24):

```
<span period="#p1">"pooled fund" means a fund established by a limited
liability company, other than an approved issuer, for purposes of pooling
scheme funds for collective investment;
      <authorialNote id="ath1" marker="#art2-lst1-itma" refersTo="#sideNote">
            <p>Side note of publication just for example</p>
      </authorialNote>
</span>
```

Fig. 7.24 Fragment in Akoma Ntoso: temporal information

The events making up a document's lifecycle are recorded using the classes defined in the ontology (LegislativeEnterInForce) (Fig. 7.25):

```
      <lifecycle source="#bungeni">
            <event id="e1" date="1997-08-29" source="#ro1" type="generation"
refersTo="#LegislativeEnterInforce"/>
            <event id="e1" date="2003-12-19" source="#ro1" type="modification"
refersTo="#LegislativeModification"/>
      </lifecycle>
```

Fig. 7.25 Fragment in Akoma Ntoso: lifecycle events

The metadata block specifies the intervals containing the events making up the document's lifecycle. The fragment in Fig. 7.26 describes two intervals, the first definite (or bounded on both ends: from e1 to e2) and the second indefinite (bounded on one end only: from e1 toe1 + duration).

```
<temporalData>
      <temporalGroup id="p1">
            <timeInterval refersTo="#inforce" from="#e1" to="#e2"/>
            <timeInterval refersTo="#efficacy" from="#e1" duration="P6M15D25"/>
      </temporalGroup>
</temporalData>
```

Fig. 7.26 Fragment in Akoma Ntoso: intervals defined[26]

[26] http://www.w3schools.com/Schema/schemadtypesdate.asp

In the references metadata block we connect events with the corresponding ontology classes (the example uses the Metalex document ontology). We should to stress that we have *two* definitions of *inforce*: one is dynamic (this is the interval during which the text is valid), whereas the other (LegislativeEnterInForce), is static, identifying the date on which the document's original version first enters into force (this is the first time the document enters as part of the legal system) (Fig. 7.27).

```
<TLCEvent id="inforce" href="[Metalex:Inforce]" showAs="Inforce"/>
<TLCEvent id="efficacy" href="[Metalex:Efficacy]" showAs="Efficacy"/>
<TLCEvent id="LegistaltiveEnterInForce" href="[Metalex:EnterInForce]"
showAs="EnterInForce"/>
```

Fig. 7.27 Fragment in Akoma Ntoso: top-class event connected with Metalex ontology classes

7.4.3 Versioned Document Metadata in Akoma Ntoso

Some documents exist in single versions, while others (notably acts, meaning laws, statutes) exist in different forms that change over time depending on their position within their lifecycle. Some versions are authoritative—they have formally been issued by their official authors, and such issuance took place at a specific point in time—whereas others are the result of editorial work, with no special authority. Some have legal validity because approved by the competent body; others are simply informational documents. A case in point is when amendments are made to an existing act. For documents that evolve, Akoma Ntoso provides not only a robust conceptual schema (in the form of the FRBR model) but also a series of constructs specifically designed to manage document versions and the track changes within each document.

In particular, all documents marked up with the Akoma Ntoso XML vocabulary must declare whether they are *original versions* (i.e., exactly as issued by their official authors), modified *single versions* (i.e., versions whose content reflects the editorial process of making amendments to an existing text), or modified *multiple versions* (a name often shortened to *multiversion*), where the document can contain multiple instances of the same fragment, each instance having been modified in different versions of the document, but all of them correctly labelled, and with the labels all *simultaneously* correct. Each instance is associated with several dates (start date of applicability, end date of application, etc.) by which the content of each version contained in the multiversion document is unambiguously associated with a precise moment in time. Any and all text that has not changed in any of the specified versions therefore occurs only once, while all text that has changed occurs in as many forms as it has taken in all of the specified versions.

This enables the application to both (a) display the document's content and (b) immediately show how such content has evolved, while also providing tools by which to compare versions, concentrating on the differences and not on the parts that have remained unchanged. This multiversion method is particularly useful in the *drafting stage* of the lawmaking process (up until the time a bill is signed into law). By contrast, the single-versioning approach is best when it comes to producing document versions that have been approved by the issuing authority (and in some cases signed) and are not subject to an external extraction mechanism. This is especially true when the document involves retroactive modifications, which can complicate the relations among provisions and can therefore affect the rendering of the document. And in cases where provisions are suspended on multiple occasions over time, there is also the serious possibility of having not just one valid rendering but several, thus engendering uncertainty in the legal system—the kind of uncertainty that can only be removed by authoritative manual interpretation. This happens as well when the editors' comments and annotations modify not only the specific article or article being commented or annotated but also some other parts that have been manually edited to make the text consistent (by adjusting the syntax for correctness and the language generally).

The *versioned document* is managed using four tools included in the meta block. Below is a brief discussion of these tools (namely, lifecycle, references, analysis, and notes), which work in combination with the previously explained mechanism for identifying document versions.

- The document's lifecycle is the tool that tracks any and all events affecting the document over time (Fig. 7.28).

```
<lifecycle source="#bungeni">
   <event id="e1" date="1980-01-01" source="#ro1" type="generation"
refersTo="#LegislativeCreation"/>
   <event id="e2" date="1989-12-15" source="#rp1" type="amendment"
refersTo="#LegislativeModification"/>
   <event id="e3" date="2003-05-25" source="#rp2" type="amendment"
refersTo="#LegislativeModification">
   <event id="e4" date="2004-01-01" source="#rp2" type="amendment"
refersTo="#LegislativeModification"/>
</lifecycle>
```

Fig. 7.28 Example of a document's lifecycle

- The references tool is the area where we annotate the URIs of all the modifying documents. Thus, for example, event e2 is marked as having the value of the source attribute (the value rp1), which corresponds to the passiveRef, with URI/acme/act/1989-12-01/16/eng@/main. In this way the event is connected with the appropriate document, the one that generates the event. It is also possible for the same document to contain multiple events, such as event e4 (Fig. 7.29).
- The analysis tool (in the analysis block) records any modification affecting the current version. Passive (inbound) modifications annotate the source of the

```
<references source="#bungeni">
  <original id="ro1" href="/acme/act/1980-01-01/1/eng@/main" showAs="Act 1
of 1980"/>
  <passiveRef id="rp1" href="/acme/act/1989-12-01/16/eng@/main" showAs="Act
16 of 1989"/>
  <passiveRef id="rp1" href="/acme/act/2003-05-10/20/eng@/main" showAs="Act
20 of 2003"/>
    <activeRef id="rp2" href="/acme/act/2008-10-21/34/eng@/main" showAs="Act
34 of 2008"/>
</references>
```

Fig. 7.29 Example of passive references

```
<analysis source="#bungeni">
 <passiveModifications>
  <textualMod type="insertion" id="pm1">
    <source href="/acme/act/1989-12-06/16/eng@/main#mod6"/>
    <destination href="#sec3.a"/>
  </textualMod>
  <textualMod type="repeal" id="pm2">
    <source href="/acme/act/1989-12-06/16/eng@/main#mod15"/>
    <destination href="#sec52-sub3"/>
  </textualMod>
  <textualMod type="substitution" id="pm3">
    <source href="/acme/act/1989-12-06/16/eng@/main#mod10"/>
    <destination href="#sec50-sub2"/>
  </textualMod>
 </passiveModifications>
</analysis>
```

Fig. 7.30 Example of modification qualification

modification and its destination (or target), thus making it possible to track over time the changes embedded in the document and to improve transparency (Fig. 7.30).

- The notes tool (in the notes block) describes all of an editor's modifications. The tool allows for multiple annotation by different editors, as shown in the example in Fig. 7.31.

Inserted in the new text is the attribute start, specifying the date starting from which the text fragment (Section 3A in the example given in Fig. 7.32) enters into force (the date referring to the document in its new version). The inline element noteRef provides a hook for linking to the note written in the notes block.

```
<notes source="#ed1">
  <note id="n10">
    <p>10. Insertion of the following partition: Section
3.a.<eol/>Modification effective as from: 15/12/1989.<eol/>
    <a href="/un/act/1989-12-06/16/eng@/main#ref6"
title="modifiyng">Modificatory document</a>: act n. 16 06/12/1989.</p>
  </note>
</notes>
<notes source="#ed2">
  <note id="n101">
    <p>10. Section 3.a. is inserted by the modificatory <a
href="/un/act/1989-12-06/16/eng@/main#ref6" title="modifiyng"> Act n. 16
06/12/1989 </a>  with effective date from 15/12/1989.<eol/>
</p>
  </note>
</notes>
```

Fig. 7.31 Example of consolidated notes

```
<section id="sec3.a" period="#e2">
  <num>3A. <noteRef num="1" href="#n1"/></num>
  <heading>
    <b>Functions of the Service</b>
  </heading>
  <subsection id="sec3.a-sub1">
    <content>
      <p>
        <b>3A. The functions of the Service shall be to -</b>
      </p>
    </content>
  </subsection>
</section>
```

Fig. 7.32 Example of versioning markup within the text

7.5 Conclusions

In this chapter we introduced some methods for managing legislative change, discussing the characteristics and foundational elements necessary in implementing the point-in-time function in the legislative domain. We also presented the mechanisms embedded into the Akoma Ntoso to deal with the problem of managing legislative change/of implementing the point-in-time function and to ensure a wall of separation between content markup and the metadata needed to manage versioning. We have also introduced a temporal model for managing the modifications, a model based on at least three axes: a document's entry into force, its efficacy, and its application. Finally, we looked at the current limitations of the Akoma Ntoso syntax for representing the interval and the duration associated with a modificatory action lasting for an indefinite period. We therefore envisaged a solution that we hope to implement in the next release. The challenge going forward will be to make legal resources not just accessible on the Web but accessible in such a way as to ensure their authoritativeness, completeness, relevance, consistency, and persistence. Finally, the success with which the Akoma Ntoso standard has been applied in Brazil, the European Parliament, and Kenya is encouraging us to continue along this path, seeking to exploit the advantages of XML in the legal domain, all the while ensuring that each legislative corpus is validly produced and consolidated, this in the interests of transparency, democracy, and free accessibility to legal resources online.

References

1. Arnold-Moore, T., and C. Jane. 2000. Connected to the law: Tasmanian legislation using EnAct. *Journal of Information, Law and Technology* 2000(1).
2. Arnold-Moore, T. 1995. Automatically processing amendments to legislation. In *ICAIL 1995*, 297–306. College Park, Maryland, USA: ACM. ISBN 0-89791-758-8.
3. Bacci, L., P. Spinosa, C. Marchetti, and R. Battistoni. 2009. Automatic mark-up of legislative documents and its application to parallel text generation. In *Proceedings of LOAIT Workshop*, 45–54.
4. Barabucci, G., L. Cervone, A. Di Iorio, M. Palmirani, S. Peroni, and F. Vitali. 2010. Managing semantics in XML vocabularies: an experience in the legal and legislative domain. Presented at Balisage: The Markup Conference 2010, Montréal, Canada, August 3–6, vol. 5. In *Proceedings of Balisage: The Markup Conference 2010*. Balisage Series on Markup Technologies.
5. Bekiari, C., M. Doerr, and P. Le Boeuf. 2008. International Working Group on FRBR and CIDOC CRM Harmonization. FRBR object-oriented definition and mapping to FRBRER (v. 0.9 draft).
6. Bing, J. 2003. *The policies of legal information services: A perspective of three decades*. Yulex. ISBN 82-7226-077-8, 35–57.
7. Boer, A., R. Winkels, and Vitali, F. 2008. MetaLex XML and the Legal Knowledge Interchange Format. *In Proceedings of Computable Models of the Law, Languages, Dialogues, Games, Ontologies*, 21–41. Springer.
8. Bruce, T., and P.W. Martin. 1994. The legal information institute: What is it and why is it? *Cornell Law Forum*, 2–6.
9. Consolidation Interim report of the working group, European Forum of Official Gazettes, 5th meeting Madrid, 25th – 26th September, 2008.
10. Di Iorio, A., M. Schirinzi, F. Vitali, and C. Marchetti. 2009. A natural and multi-layered approach to detect changes in tree-based textual documents. In *ICEIS 2009*, 90–101. Lecture Notes in Business Information Processing 24 Springer 2009. Milan, Italy. ISBN 978-3-642-01346-1
11. Francesconi, E., S. Montemagni, W. Peters, and D. Tiscornia. 2010. *Semantic processing of legal texts: Where the language of law meets the law of language*. Springer.
12. Governatori, G., and A. Rotolo. 2010. Changing legal systems: Legal abrogations and annulments in defeasible logic. *Logic Journal of the IGPL* 18(1):157–194.

13. Greenleaf, G. 2004. Jon Bing and the history of computerised legal research – Some missing links.' In *Et tilbakeblikk p fremtiden ("Looking back at the future")*, eds. Olav Torvund and Lee Bygrave, 61–75. Oslo: Institutt for Rettsinformatikk.
14. Maat, E. de, and R. Winkels. 2009. A next step towards automated modelling of sources of law. In *Proceedings of ICAIL 2009*, 31–39.
15. Mazzei, A., D.P. Radicioni, and R. Brighi. 2009. NLP-based Extraction of Modificatory Provisions Semantics. In *Proceedings of the International Conference on ARTIFICIAL INTELLIGENCE and LAW, ICAIL09*, 50–57. Barcelona, Spain: ACM.
16. Palmirani, M., and F. Benigni. 2007. Norma-system: A legal information system for managing time. In *Proceedings of the V legislative XML workshop V legislative XML workshop, 14–16 Giugno*, Vol. 1, 205–224. Firenze: European Press Academic Publishing (ITALY).
17. Palmirani, M., G. Contissa, and R. Rubino. 2009. Fill the gap in the legal knowledge modelling. *RuleML* 2009:305–314.
18. Palmirani, M. 2007. *Classification of the modificatory provisions for the legislative consolidation: The case of Africa legislative traditions*, 48. Nairobi: UNDESA (KENYA).
19. Palmirani, M., and L. Cervone. 2009. Legal change management with a native XML repository. In *Proceeding of JURIX 2009, Frontiers in artificial intelligence and applications*, ed. G. Governatori, Vol. 205, 146–155. Amsterdam, The Netherlands: IOS Press.
20. Palmirani, M. 2005. Time model in normative information systems. In *The Proceeding of Workshop "The Role of the Legal Knowledge in the eGoverment"*, ICAIL 2005, Proceedings of the Conference, June 6–11. Bologna, Italy: ACM. ISBN 1-59593-081-7
21. van de Ven, S., Rinke Hoekstra, Radboud Winkels, Emile de Maat, and dm Kollar. 2008. MetaVex: Regulation drafting meets the semantic web. In *Computable models of the law. Languages, dialogues, games, ontologies*, eds. P. Casanovas, G. Sartor, N. Casellas, and R. Rubino, 42–55. Lecture Notes in Artificial Intelligence, Vol. 4884. Berlin: Springer.
22. Schefbeck, G. 2009. Free access to legal and legislative information: The Austrian approach. In *Law via the internet: Free access, quality of information, effectiveness of rights*, eds. M. Ragona and G. Peruginelli, 207–218. Florence: European Press Academy Publishing.
23. Spinosa, P., G. Giardiello, M. Cherubini, S. Marchi, G. Venturi, and S. Montemagni. 2009. NLP-based metadata extraction for legal text consolidation. *ICAIL 2009*, 40–49. Barcelona, Spain: ACM.
24. Vitali, F., and F. Zeni. 2007. Towards a country-independent data format: The Akoma Ntoso experience. In *Proceedings of the V Legislative XML Workshop*, 67–86. Florence: European Press Academic Publishing.

Chapter 8
A MetaLex and Metadata Primer: Concepts, Use, and Implementation

Alexander Boer and Tom van Engers

8.1 Introduction

The development of the Internet has created a new potential for government service delivery at lower cost and improved quality, and has lead to new governmental services using that technology. This development called electronic government or eGovernment. Electronic government invariably involves web technologies including XML for legal sources, as these sources are as essential to governments and their public administrations as the ball is to a ball game. Many governments disseminate legislation and official publications primarily using internet technology. However publication of legislation, and the development of tools for working with legislation is at the moment still a jurisdiction-specific enterprise, although it is usually standardized at the jurisdiction level.

Some years ago a group of users and academics, noticing the problems created by many different standards in an increasingly globalized world, decided to create a jurisdiction-independent XML standard, called *MetaLex*, that can be used for interchange, but also—maybe more importantly—as a platform for development of generic legal software.

For vendors of legal software this standard opens up new markets, and for the institutional consumers of legislation in XML it solves an acute problem: how to handle very different XML formats in the same IT infrastructure. Increasing legal convergence between governments in the European Union, and the growing importance of traffic of people, services, goods, and money over borders of jurisdictions has led to an increased need for managing legislation from different sources, even in public bodies and courts.

EU tax administrations for instance need access to all VAT regimes of other member countries to correctly apply EU law, and EU civil courts may nowadays for instance be confronted with the need to understand foreign law on labour contracts

A. Boer (✉)
Leibniz Center for Law, University of Amsterdam, 1000 BA Amsterdam, The Netherlands
e-mail: A.W.F.Boer@uva.nl

G. Sartor et al. (eds.), *Legislative XML for the Semantic Web*, Law, Governance and Technology Series 4, DOI 10.1007/978-94-007-1887-6_8,
© Springer Science+Business Media B.V. 2011

to decide on cases involving employees with a foreign labour contract choosing domicile in the country where the court has jurisdiction.

This chapter gives an overview of the MetaLex XML standard. MetaLex XML positions itself as an interchange format, a lowest common denominator for other standards, intended not to necessarily replace jurisdiction-specific standards in the publications process but to impose a standardized view on this data for the purposes of software development at the consumer side.

MetaLex is a generic and extensible interchange framework for the XML encoding of the structure of, and metadata about, documents that function as a source of law. It aims to be jurisdiction and language-neutral, and is based on modern XML publishing concepts like a strict separation between text, markup, and metadata, building on top of structure instead of syntax, accommodation of transformation pipelines and standard APIs, and integration of semantic web standards.

MetaLex defines mechanisms for schema extension, for adding and extracting metadata, for cross referencing, for constructing compound documents by reference, for legally sound version management, and for implementation of a naming convention. MetaLex ideally subsumes existing XML standards, requiring only minimal syntactic changes to existing XML document instances, making MetaLex compliance an unobtrusive addition to existing XML document processing and dereferencing frameworks.

In Section 8.3 we introduce several important MetaLex concepts. MetaLex is especially useful for legal purposes because it standardizes legal bibliographic identity. The determination of bibliographic identity of sources of law is essential for correct citation of sources of law, and for deciding on the applicability in time and space of legal rules presented in those sources of law.

For purposes of reference and self-identification, MetaLex requires adherence to an IRI[1] based, open, persistent, globally unique, memorizable, meaningful, and—in a sense—*guessable* naming convention for legislative resources based on provenance information.

This provenance information can be extracted in RDF form and used in semantic web technologies [3]. Provenance information is described in terms of events that happened to the documents, or that the document played a role in.

MetaLex and the MetaLex naming conventions strictly distinguish the source of law as a published work from its set of expressions over time, and the expression from its various manifestations, and the various locatable items that exemplify these manifestations, as recommended by the Functional Requirements for Bibliographic Records.

In Section 8.4 present the MetaLex approach to standardization of metadata about sources of law, and its integration into the semantic web. As a special case and example, we focus on the implementation of a naming convention in the MetaLex metadata framework in Section 8.4.4.

In Section 8.5 the key observations of the chapter are summarized.

---

[1] Internationalized resource identifier.

8.2 About the MetaLex Standard

MetaLex is a common document interchange format, document and metadata processing model, metadata set, and ontology for software development, standardized by a CEN/ISSS[2] committee specification in 2006 and 2010. The MetaLex standard is managed by the *CEN Workshop on an Open XML interchange Format for Legal and Legislative Resources (MetaLex).*

The latest version of the specification prepared by the technical committee of the workshop can always be found at `http://www.metalex.eu/WA/proposal`.

8.2.1 History of the Standard

The name MetaLex dates from 2002 (cf. [4]). The MetaLex standard has however been redesigned from scratch in the *CEN Workshop on an Open XML interchange Format for Legal and Legislative Resources (MetaLex)*, taking into account lessons learned from *Norme in Rete*—the Italian standard for legislation—and *Akoma-Ntoso*—the Pan-African standard for parliamentary information. It has been accepted as a prenorm by the CEN in 2006 [6] and has, with some modifications, been renewed in 2010.

A significant contribution to the activities of the CEN workshop has been made by the Estrella project [10, 11], with matching finances from the EC.

8.2.2 Scope of the Standard

The CEN workshop declares, by way of its title *an Open XML interchange Format for Legal and Legislative Resources*, an interest in legal and legislative resources, but the scope statement of the first workshop agreement limits the applicability of the proposed XML standard to sources of law and references to sources of law.

As understood by the workshop, the source of law is a writing that can be, is, was, or presumably will be used to back an argument concerning the existence of a legal rule in a certain legal system, or, alternatively, a writing used by a competent legislator to communicate the existence of a legal rule to a certain group of addressees. Because the CEN Workshop is concerned only with an XML standard, it chooses not to appeal to other common ingredients of definitions of law that have no relevant counterpart in the information dimension.

Source of law is a familiar concept in law schools, and may be used to refer to legislators (compare *fonti delle leggi, sources des lois*) or legislation, case law, and custom (compare *fonti del diritto, sources du droit, rechtsbron*). In the context of MetaLex it strictly refers to communication in writing that functions as a source

---

[2] `http://www.cen.eu`

of rights. There are two main categories of source of law in writing: legislative resources and case law.

The organizations involved in the process of legislating may produce writings that are clearly precursors or legally required ingredients of the end product. These writings are also included in the notion of a legislative resource, but in this case it is not easy to give straightforward rules for deciding whether they are, or are not to be considered legislative resources.

The notion of case law has not been defined by the workshop, and no specific extensions for case law have been made as yet. CEN MetaLex can however be applied to case law to the extent appropriate; any future specific extensions for case law will be based on the same design principles.

8.2.3 MetaLex Conformance Requirements

The MetaLex standard consists of a written specification, the CEN workshop agreement proper, an XML schema that describes the structural features of MetaLex documents, and an OWL schema that describes MetaLex metadata. MetaLex defines a mechanism for schema extension, for adding and extracting metadata, for cross referencing, for constructing compound documents, and for implementation of a naming convention.

MetaLex positions itself as a metastandard for other standards. The conformance question therefore normally speaking arises for classes of documents—described by a standard that claims to implement MetaLex—rather than for individual XML documents. Conformance of XML documents to the MetaLex standard means:

1. validation of XML documents against a schema that restricts the MetaLex XML schema;
2. the theoretical possibility of obtaining an XML document that uses solely MetaLex generic elements and validates against the MetaLex XML schema by way of simple substitution;
3. the availability of sufficient metadata;
4. conformance to a naming convention;
5. declaration of a GRDDL specification that extracts metadata and implements a naming convention; and
6. conformance to all other CEN MetaLex Workshop Agreement written guidelines.

An example of a comforming standard is Akoma-Ntoso. Some standards support specific aspects of the MetaLex framework, without claiming a conforming implementation.

8.2.4 The Use of MetaLex

The major use of MetaLex follows from its function as an interchange standard: it enables producers of one particular XML document expressed in a more specific but MetaLex conformant XML schema to interpret it as a MetaLex document or to export it in a generic MetaLex format. MetaLex conformance guarantees that many generic functions that one would want to apply to a document, including version management and interpreting references, can be realized.

Consumers may reinterpret the document in terms of another MetaLex-conforming schema. Reinterpreting a more specific and more detailed standard in terms of the more abstract MetaLex format may come at the price of losing some meaning, although MetaLex rarely causes the loss of information. Reinterpretation of a generic MetaLex document into a more specific and richer XML format may obviously require additional metadata that was not available in the original document.

MetaLex may also be used as a basis for a more detailed and specific schema, thus respecting its design principles and hence creating a MetaLex compliant XML schema. One may also build upon an existing, more specific, MetaLex compliant schema and then prune undesired elements and add desired ones. This gives the designers of such schema the possibilities to tap into the community of practitioners of that language and it may reduce development time compared to designing an XML schema from scratch. The European Parliament has chosen this strategy, basing their schema on Akoma-Ntoso, a fine example of a schema conforming to the MetaLex standard that was developed for African countries and is in use in various countries, also outside Africa.

Examples of functionalities supported by MetaLex can be found in various editors which have been developed to support legislation drafters. The xmLeges editor, developed at ITTIG/CNR, the Norma editor and its successor the Bungeni editor developed by the University of Bologna, and the MetaVex editor developed by the Leibniz Center for Law, support document search using identification data, like the date of publication and delivery, allow for resolution of references, and support consolidation. The editor currently under development at the European Parliament, the Authoring Tool for legislation drafting (AT4LEX), which is intended to support members of the European Parliament in the near future, will support similar functionalities.

Users of MetaLex may also choose to only support the MetaLex ontology and use a compatible metadata delivery framework, as demonstrated by the Single Legislation Service (SLS) of the UK.

8.3 Important Concepts in MetaLex

Concepts of central importance in the MetaLex standard are the naming mechanism, the bibliographic identity concept, and the action and event as central concepts in MetaLex metadata. Design principles of central importance are the nature of the MetaLex XML schema as a metaschema that defines generic content models instead of prescribing a document structure, and the integration of MetaLex metadata into the Resource Description Framework. The following subsections address these concepts.

8.3.1 MetaLex Content Models and XML Schemas

The MetaLex XML schema defines structures that allow existing XML documents (conforming to other XML schemas) to conform to the MetaLex basic content models content model. This is achieved by defining the elements of that XML document as implementations of MetaLex content models in a schema that extends the MetaLex XML schema. The structure of the existing XML document does not have to be modified to achieve this.

A schema extension specifies the names of elements used in XML documents and allows for additional attributes on these elements. It may also be used to further constrain the allowed content models if the schema extension is intended to be normative, for instance if the schema is used in an editor to validate the structure of the document before it is published.

The MetaLex XML syntax strictly distinguishes syntactic elements (structure) and the implied meaning of elements by distinguishing for each element its name and its content model. A content model (cf. [2, 13]) is an algebraic expression of the elements that may (or must) be found in the content of an element. Generic elements, on the other hand, are named after the content model: they are merely a label identifying the type of content model.

All content models are constrained to just twelve different abstract complex types, of which five fundamental (the patterns) and seven specialized for specific purposes. MetaLex also defines quoted content models, to be used when one source of law quotes the content, usually the prospective content for purposes of modification, of another source of law.

8.3.2 Naming Conventions and the Bibliographic Identity of Legal Documents

MetaLex aims to standardize legal bibliographic identity. The determination of bibliographic identity of sources of law is essential for purposes of reference, and for deciding on the applicability in time of legal rules presented in the sources of law. Identification is based on two important design principles: firstly, the naming convention mechanism, and secondly the use of an ontology of bibliographic entities.

Every conformant implementation uses some naming mechanism that conforms to a number of rules, and distinguishes documents qua work, expression, manifestation, and item.

MetaLex and the MetaLex naming convention mechanism distinguish the source of law as a published work from its set of expressions over time, and the expression from its various manifestations, and the various locatable items that exemplify these manifestations, as recommended by the IFLA Functional Requirements for Bibliographic Records (FRBR; cf. [12]).

A MetaLex XML document is a standard manifestation of a bibliographic expression of a source of law. Editing the MetaLex XML markup and metadata of the XML document changes the manifestation of an expression. Changing the marked up text changes the expression embodied by the manifestation. Copying an example of the MetaLex XML document creates a new item. The work, as the result of an original act of bibliographic creation, realized by one or more expressions, does not change. Each bibliographic item exemplifies exactly one manifestation that embodies exactly one expression that realizes exactly one work.

Work, expression, and manifestation are intentional objects. They exist only as the object of ones thoughts and communication acts, and not as a physical object. An item is on the other hand clearly a physical object, that can be located in space and time, even if it is not tangible.

Items stored on a computer can be easily copied to another location, resulting in another item, but still an instance of the same manifestation. This makes adding metadata about the item to the item in principle impossible. On the Internet generally speaking only the uniform resource locator (URL), used for identifying and dereferencing items, is an item-specific datum. The item level is therefore not very relevant to XML standards.

The MetaLex standard is primarily concerned with identification of legal bibliographic entities on the basis of literal content, i.e. on the expression level, and prescribes a single standard manifestation of an expression in XML. Different expressions can be versions or variants (for instance translations) of the same work.

MetaLex extends the FRBR with a jurisdiction-independent model of the lifecycle of sources of law, that models the source of law as a succession of consolidated versions, and optionally *ex tunc* consolidations.

The concept of ex tunc expressions captures the possibility of retroactive correction (errata corrige), or annulment of modifications to a legislative text by a constitutional court. In these cases the version timeline is changed retroactively. See for instance [8] for an explanation of the practical ramifications of annulment, and more generally an overview of the complexities involved in change of the law. Note that while MetaLex permits the identification of versions in different timelines, the involved reasoning requires defeasibility, and the use of a knowledge representation language that allows for that.

MetaLex requires adherence to an IRI-based, open, persistent, globally unique, memorizable, meaningful, and "guessable" *naming convention* for legislative resources based on provenance information. This provenance information can be extracted in RDF form and used in OWL2 [3]. Names of bibliographic entities must be associated to an identifying permanent IRI reference as defined by RFC 3987.

MetaLex *names* are used in self-identification of documents, citation of other documents, and inclusion of document components. Names must be persistent and cover all relevant legal and legislative bibliographic entities. Work, expression, manifestation, and items have distinct names and identifiable fragments of the document and components attached to the document also have names derived from the name of the document. The distinction between works, expressions, and manifestations is also made for names of components and fragments.

There are few technical limitations on names acceptable to the new MetaLex standard. MetaLex accepts PURLs, relative URI, URNs, OpenURLs, and any metadata-based naming method based on a set of key-value pairs associated to an IRI reference, for instance in RDF. MetaLex makes no assumptions about Internet-based document *dereferencing* frameworks for obtaining items, which may be based on PURL, OpenURL, URN resolver, metadata-based search, or simply non-existent.

The naming convention requirements are intended to cover representative existing IRI reference-based or metadata-based naming mechanisms for sources of law, for instance the Juriconnect identifiers of the Netherlands, NormeInRete (NIR) identifiers in Italy, the pan-African Akoma-Ntoso identifiers, the future European Case Law Identifiers (ECLI), and those in use in the Single legislation Service[3] of the UK.

The following are examples of IRI reference-based names of naming schemes considered in the context of the MetaLex standardization (Fig. 8.1):

1. NIR, Italian work: urn:lex:it:stato:legge:2006-05-14;22
2. Single Legislation Service, UK work: /id/ukpga/1985/67
3. Akoma-Ntoso, fictional Tuvalu work: /tv/act/2004-02-13

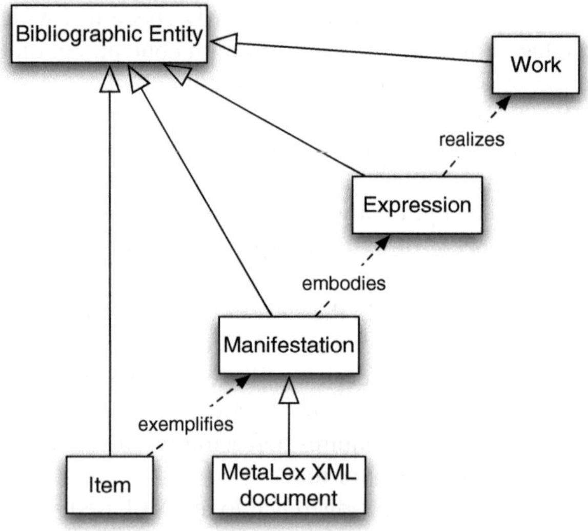

Fig. 8.1 Taxonomy of bibliographic entities in MetaLex, and their relata, based on FRBR

[3] See `http://www.juriconnect.nl`, `http://www.nir.it`, `http://www.akomantoso.org`. The UK SLS legislation portal is working on a web-based API, which supports i.a. RDF/OWL and MetaLex: `http://www.legislation.gov.uk`

Note that these examples all order descriptors from generic to specific, but different separators are used, and the last two are intended to be used as relative references, relative to an implicit base IRI. Other naming schemes, for instance in the Netherlands, are based on key-value pairs, either encoded in proprietary XML structures, in common metadata syntaxes like RDF, the HTML and XHTML *meta* tag, or in IRI references as *key=value* pairs separated by *&* (for instance as an OpenURL).

In Section 8.4.4 the implementation of naming conventions, and the enforcement of naming requirements in the metadata framework is discussed in more detail.

This paper leaves some content-specific naming requirements undiscussed, focusing instead on the mechanisms involved. There is for instance also a list of metadata that *should* be used as constituents of MetaLex names if possible (including such things as the country code, emanating actor, electronic data format, date of publication of the work, date of commencement of the modification producing an expression, etc). Adherence to the URN:LEX standard[4] is also worth recommending.

The use of MetaLex identification and referencing solves one aspect of the traceability problem often encountered in large organizations. In current organizational practice links are more often than not made to locatable items, often without formal agreements about the permanence of the used item identifiers. Correct references to the right bibliographic abstraction (generally work or expression depending on the purpose of the reference) is essential. MetaLex makes this concern explicit, and provides some tools to address it.

8.3.3 Semantic Web Integration

MetaLex metadata is usually *XML* metadata, i.e. metadata that describes the context of production of the bibliographic entity the metadata is about. It may be extended in conforming implementations with metadata about contexts of use for sources of law, or even knowledge representation of the meaning of text fragments contained in the expression.

Example integrations of MetaLex metadata into knowledge representation languages are for instance found in LKIF [2] and Agile [5]. In Section 8.4 the integration of MetaLex into the Semantic Web is discussed in detail.

The MetaLex metadata requirements were designed with integration into the semantic web in mind. MetaLex metadata can be easily mined as *open data* and can be transparently used as data for reasoning in RDF and OWL compatible knowledge representation languages, for instance to answer the question whether a source of law is applicable to a case.

MetaLex metadata is based on the abstract data model of the Resource Description Framework (RDF). The standard specifies what metadata must be present in a conforming XML manifestation, includes an ontology specified in an OWL schema

[4] See `http://tools.ietf.org/html/draft-spinosa-urn-lex-00`

with design patterns for XML metadata, and requires the presence of a translator that transforms the contained metadata to RDF syntax.

The MetaLex OWL schema should be used for RDF metadata if appropriate, regardless of whether this metadata is serialized in or stored outside a MetaLex XML document. The MetaLex OWL schema defines metadata for describing both hierarchical and relational ways of positioning and identifying bibliographic objects, at least at the work and expression level, at the relevant levels of granularity, including fragments and components attached to the document. As such it describes a basic reference implementation of a naming convention that should be used or extended wherever appropriate.

It is common in knowledge representation to make a direct mapping between knowledge representation structures and the structure of the text for purposes of maintaining isomorphism [1], or because the knowledge representation is based on a linguistic analysis of the text, as in the following simplistic and fictional example:

```
<rule>A <antecedent>motorcycle</antecedent> is a
<consequent>vehicle</consequent>.</rule>
```

The metadata mechanism of MetaLex, and the possibility of naming ones own inline elements, make it possible to emulate the same mechanism in MetaLex. The rule element can refer to an OWL axiom that states that motorcycle is a subclass of vehicle, while the antecedent element refers to the OWL concept motorcycle and the consequent refers to the OWL concept vehicle. The MetaLex standard itself does not commit to such a reading, however.

8.3.4 Event Descriptions for Situated Metadata about Legal Documents

An important design feature of MetaLex is that XML metadata is conceptually organized around actions performed on documents and events that happen to documents, or rather bibliographic entities as explained in Section 8.3.2, instead of around the documents themselves. In Section 8.4.3.2 we return to event descriptions.

In most metadata standards for documents a single attribute-value pair is used for such information items as the date of promulgation, with the source of law as implicit subject of the statement, instead of reifying the publication/promulgation event and treating the date as an attribute of the event like MetaLex recommends.

There are two independent lines of argument for organizing metadata about sources of law around events and acts [2]. The first argument is one of knowledge representation tactics, and the second argument is based on legal theory and practice.

A particular metadata description is usually about (a snapshot of) some entity (taken) in a particular state—a perceived stability of the entity over a particular time interval that does not take account of changes that are outside the domain of interest. The granularity of that snapshot varies across metadata vocabularies, depending on the targeted community.

This is apparent in the FRBR conceptualization of bibliographic objects (cf. [12]) used in MetaLex: it groups hierarchically the products of different types of events in the categories work, expression, manifestation, and item. When you make a copy, the item identity changes, but descriptive metadata stays the same. When you add or change metadata statements attached the document, which apply to manifestation, expression, or work, the manifestation changes, but the expression stays the same, when you edit the text, the expression changes, but the work usually stays the same, etc.

To a community that works with certain legislation daily, the insertion of a new provision is for instance an important event to be noted, and even to prepare for; For the casual reader it happens to be just one of the many constituting parts of that document at the moment of consulting, and what it was before or will be is usually of little interest.

There are several good reasons, from the point of view of knowledge representation, to explicitly reify the events.

One is supplied by Lagoze (see [9]): for establishing semantic interoperability between different metadata vocabularies and for developing mechanisms to translate between them it is only natural to exploit the fact that some types of entities—people, organizations, places, dates, and events—are so frequently encountered that they do not fall clearly into the domain of any particular metadata vocabulary but apply across all of them.

It is very clearly the event, and the act, that play the mediating role between these entities and the resource the metadata description is about. The natural coherence between for instance between author, publication date, and publication channel information (e.g. state gazette bibliographic information) is found in their participation in the publication (promulgation) act.

Some other reasons were noted by i.a. the author of this paper elsewhere [7]. Relevant events often modify input resources into output resources, at the expression or manifestation level, and the respective metadata descriptions for those input and output resources are often the data about the event, i.e. they are shared by the input and output resource: only the perspective is different.

In formal legislation, there is for instance a natural coherence between the old consolidation, the new consolidation, the modifying legislation, the modifying authority, and the modification date. The modification event, if identified explicitly, links together three different but related resources, and interesting metadata about them.

Different perspectives on this exact same event, because it was not reified and identified, may yield incompatible metadata descriptions, result in unnecessary duplication of metadata. This creates several separate occasions in which to make mistakes, unnecessary maintenance, and, lastly, the loss of relevant references between documents. Explicitly identifying events increases the reliability of the metadating process.

Keeping track of changes is especially relevant in the field of law because we have to presume that the law does not become better over time. For most written resources, whether fiction or non-fiction, the last version dominates all others because it is the best: only rarely are we interested in anything other than the current state of the work. We trust that if there is a notable difference at all between todays edition of a book and the first one, todays version will be better. Nobody would ever bother to pick up a 17th century physics textbook to check whether the law of gravity already existed in order to decide on the question of whether 17th century witches could really fly. In law we are often asked to do exactly that: the law that applies to an event, is the law in force during that event, barring the complications of retroactive or delayed activity.

A tax administration will for instance routinely work at any point in time with at least three different versions: the running tax year, the previous tax year, which is processed now, and the next tax year, which is being prepared.

In [7] the point is also made that the expectation of certain events also functions as a conceptual coat rack for missing information—for instance a future date of modification x not yet decided—which is essential in the preparation for future legislation. Important was in this case that the IRI used in RDF metadata is not a unique name: multiple identifiers can refer to the same event (but not vice versa), and what are initially believed to be separate events can—by just stating their equality—be unified without changing the metadata.

There is also a legal theoretic argument to be made for the importance of event and act descriptions, and that one is found in the institutional interpretation of the role of legislation (or contracts, or driver's licenses, tax statement forms): One undertakes a legal act on the institutional level by producing a written statement in accordance with a certain procedure. In this reading the document is the mere physical residue of the intentional act that is really important: it functions as physical evidence that a constitutive act that modified institutional reality happened, and it declares the intent of the act.

Evidence is not only found in the central position of legal action and declaration of intent (or will) in legal doctrine, but also in concepts like the *Act of Parliament* when one is referring in actuality to the physical result of that act of Parliament.

The majority of XML schemas don't reify events. There appears to be a dislike of them on esthetic grounds: they are perceived as in some way less real or objective than dates, persons, and places, and there are no established standards for identifying them, comparable to those for times, places, and persons. In law it is however generally quite clear whether legislative acts (signature, promulgation, enactment, modification, repeal, etc.) happened, and their determination obviously cannot be less objective than for instance the determination of the dates at which they happened.

8.4 MetaLex and the Semantic Web

Having explained the general principles, we now address the Resource Description Framework and the Web Ontology Language OWL, for those readers not familiar with them, and then proceed to explain the relation between these standards and MetaLex, and the content of the MetaLex OWL ontology.

8.4.1 The Resource Description Framework

metadata in CEN MetaLex must be based on the abstract data model of the Resource Description Framework (RDF). The concrete syntax of its implementation inside an XML document manifestation is however not restricted.

An RDF description of a resource consists of a set of statements so-called triples of the form (subject, predicate, object), where subject and predicate are individuals identified by an IRI reference, and the object is either an individual identified by an IRI reference or a literal value. The subject is the resource described by the statement, the predicate is the property used to relate subject to an object, and the object is the value of the property as it holds for the subject.

The following are for instance valid abstract RDF statements:

(/persons/1, /properties/name, "Alexander Boer") A properties/name of the individual identified by persons/1 is (literal value) Alexander Boer

(/persons/1, /properties/friend, persons/2) A properties/friend of the individual identified by persons/1 is /persons/2

The following is not a valid abstract RDF statement, because a literal may not function as subject node: ("Alexander Boer", /properties/name, /persons/1)

Note that the examples use relative IRI references. In semantic interpretation these must be resolved to full IRI: it must therefore be possible to establish a useful and stable XML base for an RDF document. It is also syntactically permitted to use CURIEs instead of IRIs. A CURIE (short for Compact URI) is an abbreviated URI expressed in safe CURIE syntax, for instance e.g. metalex:component for `http://www.metalex.eu/metalex/1.0#component`.

Semantically, sets of RDF statements are interpreted as labeled, directed graphs. Predicates are labels on the edges, and subjects and objects are nodes. IRI referenced individuals shared by RDF statements are merged into one node in the interpretation graph. Note that in principle, more than one IRI reference may be used to refer to one and the same individual. Different nodes in the graph do not necessarily refer to different individuals. Literal values are not merged: they have only one incoming edge. They are therefore always leaf nodes of the graph.

There is an alternative interpretation of RDF statements which reifies the statements themselves statement = (subject, predicate, object), as IRI-referenced individuals declared in the namespace given by the XML base of RDF data structure. This feature is useful for creating metadata about metadata statements. This is yet another reason for making the XML base of an RDF data structure explicit. For the syntax and semantics of RDF statements, this document defers to the respective RDF specifications.[5]

[5] `http://www.w3.org/TR/rdf-syntax-grammar/` and `http://www.w3.org/TR/rdf-mt/`

8.4.1.1 Classes and Properties in OWL Schemas

The OWL schema is a method for specification of the operational semantics of classes and properties used in RDF statements using description logic axioms. For the syntax and semantics of OWL, this document defers to the respective OWL specifications.[6] The use of properties has already been demonstrated in the previous section. Membership of a class is stated as, for instance (/persons/1, rdf:type, /classes/person).

An OWL schema can itself be expressed in RDF, and uses the IRI references of the subject classes and properties, and can therefore be merged into graphs that use those classes and properties for description. Schema files are usually imported into RDF graphs. If a method of embedding RDF statements into the XML manifestation is sufficiently general, it is possible to directly embed the operational semantics of classes and properties into the XML manifestation. This is sometimes useful.

MetaLex implementations define their own schema, extending MetaLex. Note that the existing MetaLex schema does not yet follow the newest version of the standard. The MetaLex ontology is identified as `http://www.metalex.eu/metalex/1.0`), and behaves as a hash namespace.

8.4.2 Implementation of MetaLex Metadata

MetaLex XML adopts the RDF Annotations (RDFa) recommendation as a default implementation for the inline specification of metadata attributes. Metadata, including the metadata prescribed by a naming convention, should be specified as RDFa statements inside the MetaLex XML document, and if metadata is not available as RDFa, it must be systematically translatable from the proprietary implementation to RDF. The translation from a proprietary metadata format to RDF must be publicly available following the Gleaning Resource Descriptions from Dialects of Languages (GRDDL) specification.

MetaLex specifies no explicit mechanism for linking a MetaLex XML document to RDF metadata stored outside this document, other than through shared IRI references. The difference between storage of RDF inside and outside a standard MetaLex XML manifestation may be used for the identification of the metadata author. Metadata inside the document is associated to the editor of the manifestation, who can be assumed to be the author of the metadata.

8.4.2.1 Delivery Mechanisms for Metadata

The mechanism by which applications retrieve RDF metadata, given an item IRI reference, is beyond the scope of MetaLex. The MetaLex standards only prescribes that it must be possible to extract RDF metadata from the MetaLex XML document using a GRDDL translator.

---

[6] `http://www.w3.org/TR/owl2-overview/`

For traditional hierarchic IRIs that take the form of URLs, the dereferencing of item IRIs may follow the guidelines set out by the HTTP/1.1 protocol in RFC 2616, and the additional guidelines of the *Best Practice Recipes for Publishing RDF Vocabularies*.[7] For IRIs that take the form of URNs, an alternative resolution mechanism is appropriate.

8.4.3 Use of the MetaLex Ontology

In the process of deciding on the abstract data model for expressing metadata the MetaLex ontology plays a central role. Classes and properties from the MetaLex OWL schema should be used where reasonable, and newly created properties and classes should be defined in a new schema that extends the MetaLex OWL schema.

The process of implementing the MetaLex metadata requirements starts by deciding what relevant metadata may be available about:

1. The document as a whole, as a work, as an expression, and as a manifestation;
2. IRI identified parts of the document, on the work, expression, and manifestation level;
3. IRI identified components of the document, as a work, as an expression, and as a manifestation; and
4. Cited IRI identified documents, and IRI identified parts or components of documents in the document, on the work, expression, and manifestation level.

It is natural to think of metadata in terms of literal values, like names and dates. Keep in mind that literal values are not merged in the semantic interpretation of RDF, while it is eminently desirable to identify and merge nodes representing for instance points in time and persons. It is therefore better to identify an author as /persons/1, named "Alexander Boer", than directly as "Alexander Boer", and better to identify a date as /dates/1, represented in ISO 8601 as "2010-01-01". One of the advantages of distinguishing the identity of a date from its value, is that it becomes possible to say for instance that things happened on the same date (or one date is after the other one) without committing oneself to providing a value for those dates. This is often useful in the legislative drafting and implementation process.

For amongst many others the same reason, that is to have appropriate IRI-references for decisions to merge subgraphs (also from different sources), the MetaLex ontology insists on a strict distinction between work, expression, manifestation, and item, and on the use of event and action descriptions. In the next two subsections we identify certain required and commonly occurring structures.

The merging of nodes depends on explicit sets of properties that function as names. This of course a fortiori applies to the naming convention metadata, but the metadata will also contain such sets for dates, specific actions or events, or

[7] `http://www.w3.org/TR/swbp-vocab-pub/`

specific persons. The semantic enforcement of naming conventions is addressed in Section 8.4.4.

8.4.3.1 Bibliographic Identity, Components, and Identifiable Fragments and Positions

A MetaLex XML manifestation identifies itself with an IRI reference, conforming to a naming convention. The IRI reference naming the manifestation, here */w/e/m*, contains the information necessary to construct the IRI of the embodied expression */w/e*, and the realized work */w*.

The abstract data model should contain, for each named bibliographic object, including the ones cited and included as components, a structure that functions as a backbone for the metadata about the bibliographic manifestation consisting of a reference to the embodied expression and a reference to the realized work from the expression (see 1,2).

1. (/w/e/m, metalex:embodies, /w/e)
2. (/w/e, metalex:realizes, /w)
3. (/w/e/m, metalex:exemplifiedBy, /w/e/m/i)
4. (/w/e/m, metalex:fragment, /w/e/m#id) */w/e/m has a fragment /w/e/m#id*
5. (/w/e/m#id, metalex:component, /w/e/m/comp) *milestone element /w/e/m#id includes a component /w/e/m/comp by referring to it*
6. (/w/e/m#id, metalex:cites, /w#id) */w/e/m#id holds a citation of fragment #id of work /w (in this case a self-reference)*

All relevant metadata structures have one of these three IRI as subject. The only (optional) item-level metadata property is the *metalex:exemplifiedBy* property, which takes the manifestation level IRI as object, and the item level IRI chosen for delivery as subject (3).

A schema should make explicit to which level a metadata statement pertains. Making no such distinction between levels creates ambiguity. The required type of subject and object of each metadata property should be set in the OWL schema. IRI conforming to a naming convention will also convey information about the structure of a bibliographic object. From the IRI reference of the component, the IRI reference of the containing document can be constructed (5). From a hash namespace fragment identifier, the containing document can be inferred (4). These hierarchical relations must also be made explicit.

As a general rule, the complete hierarchical structure that exists between relevant explicitly named bibliographic entities should be made explicit. Fragments should be explicitly included if they hold a component, or hold a citation of another bibliographic object. Citations should also be made explicit (6).

8.4.3.2 Event Descriptions

XML information about the context of production and use of bibliographic objects, also the provenance information that contributes to the naming convention, should be organized around actions performed on documents, or events if no action exists. In MetaLex, a bibliographic object is produced by an event or action, here */a* (1).

1. (/w/e/, metalex:resultOf, /a) or (/a, metalex:result, /w/e/)
2. (/w/e/, metalex:instrumentOf, /a) or (/a, metalex:instrument, /w/e/)
3. (/w/e/, metalex:matterOf, /a) or (/a, metalex:matter, /w/e/)
4. (/dates/1, metalex:dateOf, /a) or (/a, metalex:date, /dates/1)
5. (/persons/1, metalex:agentOf, /a) or (/a, metalex:agent, /persons/1)

A bibliographic object may be used in an action (for instance modifying or power-conferring legislation, see 2), and an event or action may happen to a bibliographic object (for instance enactment or repeal, or it was input for a modification, see 3). Actions and events happen at dates (4), and actions are performed by persons in the agent role (5).

Persons may also for instance play the role of recipient. The thematic roles presented are of course generic. The idea is that specific subproperties are created, and new domain specific events are defined as subtypes of the given ones.

In the MetaLex ontology we for instance find stub classes for the creation, translation and modification of expressions, enactment, repeal, commencement, etc. These can be used as a starting point for extension.

8.4.4 Implementation of Naming Conventions in Metadata

To comply with MetaLex transformation requirements, the naming convention must be implemented into the GRDDL translator used for extracting metadata. The IRI reference conforming to the naming convention must refer to the unique individual described by the set of provenance metadata extracted from it. This would equally apply to other adopted naming conventions for dates, languages, persons, organizations, etc.

The IRI is a globally unique identifier. Identifiers are typically based on an injective function; They identify only one entity, but they are not necessarily the only identifier of that entity. A name typically not only identifies just one entity, but it is also, within the namespace described by a naming convention, the only identifier of the entity. This is the unique name assumption, which holds that there is a bijective function from names to entities named.

The new version of OWL, OWL2, provides an instrument for the enforcement of this very useful semantic assumption in specific cases, which depends on the notion of an inverse functional data property. Inverse functionality says that any individual s which participates in a triple (s, p, o), where o is some literal value, is the same individual. This allows us to say that an ISO 8601 date value refers to one unique day, that an ISO 639-2 alpha-3 language code refers to one unique language, etc. Automated enforcement of these constraints guarantees correct node merging behavior in the abstract data model in its RDF interpretation.

This means that */dates/1* and */dates/2* in the following statements necessarily refer to the same node if ex:dateValue is inverse functional (and the semantic processor aware of ISO 8601 dates processing).

1. (/dates/1, ex:dateValue, "1981-04-05")
2. (/dates/2, ex:dateValue, "19810405")

The identification of works, expressions, and manifestations however depends on more than a single data property. The complexities of enforcement in this case are discussed in [3]. Let $/v_1/v_2/\ldots/v_n$ be a transparent IRI reference to the entity described by a list of property-value pairs, formulated in a description logic that can be expressed in OWL as $\exists P_1.\{v_1\} \sqcap \exists P_2.\{v_2\} \sqcap \ldots \sqcap \exists P_n.\{v_n\}$. Generally, a naming axiom has the following form in description logic syntax [3]:

$$\{v_1/v_2/\ldots/v_n\} \equiv \exists P_1.\{v_1\} \sqcap \exists P_2.\{v_2\} \sqcap \ldots \sqcap \exists P_n.\{v_n\}$$

Nominal *generic concept inclusion* axioms like this are generally rather complex for automated reasoning in OWL [3]. Firstly, the computational cost of inserting new individuals into the knowledge base is usually high because this rather uncommon insertion case is often not very well optimized. Secondly, subclass axioms with a complex concept expression on the left hand side introduce a high degree of non-determinism in tableaux expansion.

The fact that there is in principle a sound procedure for determining whether bibliographic entities are definitely the same, definitely different, or possibly the same, is very valuable for validation purposes. There are useful semantic workarounds that allow one to work efficiently with the metadata [3].

8.5 Conclusions

MetaLex is a generic and extensible interchange framework for XML encoded documents that function as a manifestation of a source of law, with embedded metadata, managed by the CEN Workshop on an Open XML interchange Format for Legal and Legislative Resources (MetaLex).

The key features of the MetaLex XML standard are its unobtrusiveness in implementation in existing XML formats, and the way in which it standardizes the availability of metadata about sources of law that (1) uniquely name it, and (2) provide a description of the context of production of the source of law.

Unobtrusiveness is a result of the use of a metaschema with design patterns to be extended rather than a concrete schema to be implemented, and of the decision to only require the existence of an extraction mechanism that produces RDF metadata. The same mechanism can be used for making other metadata, not required by MetaLex, available.

The generic naming mechanism is a unique selling point of MetaLex. A name typically not only identifies just one entity, but it is also, within the namespace described by a naming convention, the only identifier of the entity. This is known as the unique name assumption, which is useful for node merging in the semantic interpretation of RDF graphs. Names are moreover to some extent guessable if one knows the naming convention.

Because of its unobtrusiveness, and its generic semantic web approach to metadata, MetaLex conformance has great benefits while the implementing organization incurs only modest costs.

References

1. Bench-Capon, T., and T.F. Gordon. 2009. Isomorphism and argumentation. In *ICAIL '09: Proceedings of the 12th International Conference on Artificial Intelligence and Law*, 11–20, ACM, New York, NY.
2. Boer, A. 2007. Using event descriptions for metadata about legal documents. In *Electronic proceedings of the workshop on standards for legislative XML, in conjunction with Jurix 2007*, eds. R. Winkels and E. Francesconi. Leiden, The Netherlands.
3. Boer, A. 2009. Metalex naming conventions and the semantic web. In *Legal knowledge and information systems*, ed. G. Governatori, 31–36, Amsterdam: IOS Press.
4. Boer, A., R. Hoekstra, R. Winkels, T. van Engers, and F. Willaert. 2002. Proposal for a Dutch legal XML standard. In *Electronic Government (EGOV 2002)*, eds. R. Traunmüller and K. Lenk. Springer Lecture Notes in Computer Science, 142–149. Aix en Provence, France: DEXA.
5. Boer, A., T. van Engers, and R. Winkels. 2010. Traceability and change in legal requirements engineering. In *AI approaches to the complexity of legal systems: complex systems, the semantic web, ontologies, argumentation, and dialogue: international workshops AICOL-I/IVR-XXIV, Beijing, China, September 19, 2009 and AICOL-II/JURIX 2009*, eds. P. Casanovas, U. Pagallo, G. Ajani, and G. Sartor, 74–92. Springer Lecture Notes in Computer Science, Vol. 6237. Rotterdam, The Netherlands.
6. Boer, A., F. Vitali, and E. de Maat. 2006. CEN Workshop Agreement on MetaLex XML, an open XML Interchange Format for Legal and Legislative Resources (CWA 15710). Technical report, European Committee for Standardization (CEN), 2006.
7. Boer, A., R. Winkels, T. van Engers, and E. de Maat. 2004. A content management system based on an event-based model of version management information in legislation. In *Legal knowledge and information systems. Jurix 2004: The seventeenth annual conference*, ed. T. Gordon. Frontiers in Artificial Intelligence and Applications, 19–28, Amsterdam: IOS Press.
8. Governatori, G., and A. Rotolo. 2010. Changing legal systems: Legal abrogations and annulments in defeasible logic. *Logic Journal of the IGPL* 18(1):157–194.
9. Lagoze, C. 2000. Business unusual: How event-awareness may breathe life into the catalog. In *Proceedings of the bicentennial conference on bibliographic control for the new millennium, November 15–17, 2000*, ed. A.M. Sandberg-Fox. Washington, DC: Library of Congress Cataloging Directorate.
10. Lupo, C., F. Vitali, E. Francesconi, M. Palmirani, R. Winkels, E. de Maat, A. Boer, and P. Mascellani. 2007. General XML format(s) for legal sources. Deliverable 3.1, Estrella.
11. Palmirani, M., G. Sartor, R. Rubino, A. Boer, E. de Maat, F. Vitali, and E. Francesconi. 2007. Guidelines for applying the new format. Deliverable 3.2, Estrella.
12. IFLA Study Group on the Functional Requirements for Bibliographic Records, & International Federation of Library Associations and Institutions. 1998. *Functional requirements for bibliographic records: Final report*. München, Germany: K.G. Saur.
13. Vitali, F., A.D. Iorio, and D. Gubellini. 2005. Design patterns for document substructures. In *Extreme markup 2005 conference. Montreal, 1–5 August 2005*. Montréal, QC, Canada.

Chapter 9
Semantic Resources for Managing Legislative Information

Maria Angela Biasiotti

9.1 Background

XML tagging offers the possibility of embedding semantic information in legislative documents, namely, information about the normative content of the legal text [1, 4, 7, 24, 41, 44, 49].

The embedded semantic information can have different levels of depth and can have different articulated structure [3, 7].

At a first level, it only consists of keywords that are added to the text to facilitate the retrieval of it or of its parts [6, 30, 38].

At a second level, it consists of conceptual structures meant to specify the objects of the text and of its parts [7, 12, 21].

At a third level, it may also indicate the entities involved in the regulation and the role they play in it as agents, obligations, etc. [8, 46].

Finally, it may include the formal specification of the rules expressed by the text [3, 7, 8, 46].

Here, we focus only on the first two layers, which are addressed in most of the applications that have been developed so far. In particular, we highlight ways to provide standardised and interoperable semantic tagging and I argue, for that purpose, that it is necessary to rely on existing terminological and semantic resources.

9.1.1 Overview of Language and Knowledge Resources: Thesauri, Lightweight and Foundational Ontologies

The management of legislation can greatly profit from the support of linguistic resources providing sets of language data and descriptions in machine readable form, such as written or spoken corpora and lexical resources (annotated or not), multi-modal resources, grammars, terminology or domain-specific databases

---

M.A. Biasiotti (✉)
ITTIG-CNR, Institute for Legal Information Theory and Techniques, National Research Council of Italy, 50127 Florence, Italy
e-mail: biasiotti@ittig.cnr.it

G. Sartor et al. (eds.), *Legislative XML for the Semantic Web*, Law, Governance and Technology Series 4, DOI 10.1007/978-94-007-1887-6_9,
© Springer Science+Business Media B.V. 2011

and dictionaries, ontologies, multimedia databases, etc. So the majority of public actors who produce legislative texts, choose to offer the user (citizens) facilities to access legal information, annotating the digital documentation by utilizing semantic resources. Generally speaking, within the definition "semantic resource", three kind of strategic tools can be identified among those existing: thesauri, semantic nets (or taxonomies) and ontologies.

More specifically and in brief ontologies are controlled vocabulary expressed in an ontology representation language (OWL), whereas taxonomies or semantic nets are collections of controlled vocabulary terms organized into a hierarchical structure and thesauri are networked collections of controlled vocabulary terms. Each term in a taxonomy is in one or more parent-child relationship to other terms, while in a thesaurus associative relationships are used in addition to parent-child relationships. Generally speaking, we should bear in mind that [5, 9–11, 13, 26, 28], at European level, apart from the EUROVOC semantic standard, there are no common and shared semantic standards. There only are some good practices at national level in almost each Member State, facilitating citizens to have access to legislative information.

At a basic level of the Language Resources Pyramid we find the thesaurus which is the most widespread and utilized language tool. It can be defined as a *classification tool* to assist libraries, archives or other centres of documentation to manage their records and other information. This tool is designed to facilitate users in identifying preferred terms for classifying and titling records and to provide a range of paths to reach these terms. The thesaurus also facilitates strategies for retrieving documents reducing the probability of an unsuccessful search, or one resulting in a confusing or irrelevant outcome. This functionality is achieved by establishing paths between terms in accordance with ISO level (International Standards Organization) standards. The definition of "thesaurus" supplied by ISO guidelines is as follows: a thesaurus is *the vocabulary of a controlled indexing language, formally organized so that the a-priori relationships between concepts (for example as "broader" and "narrower")* are made explicit.[1] Furthermore, if the thesaurus is multilingual ISO provides the following definition: *a thesaurus containing terms selected from more than one natural language. It displays not only the interrelationships between terms, but also equivalent terms in each of the languages covered* (Fig. 9.1).[2]

Going up in the pyramid of the semantic resource, we find more advanced tools such as "lightweight ontologies" or semantic nets (such as *WordNet*, *FrameNet* and the *CYC*, described in the next paragraph) and highly formalised ontologies, also called foundational ontologies (such as SUMO[3] and DOLCE[4]).

---

[1] ISO: 5964:1985 guidelines for the establishment and development of multilingual thesaurus

[2] ISO: 5964:1985 guidelines for the establishment and development of multilingual thesaurus

[3] The Suggested Upper Merged Ontology (SUMO) and its domain ontologies form the largest formal public ontology in existence today. The Standard Upper Ontology (SUO) is an effort by IEEE members to create a high-level ontology, for use by expert systems and intelligent agents within a variety of domains. The goal is to create a framework by which disparate systems may utilize a common knowledge base from which more domain-specific ontologies may be derived

[4] DOLCE (Descriptive Ontology for Linguistic and Cognitive Engineering) is a foundational ontology (FO) developed originally in the EU WonderWeb project. FOs are domain-independent

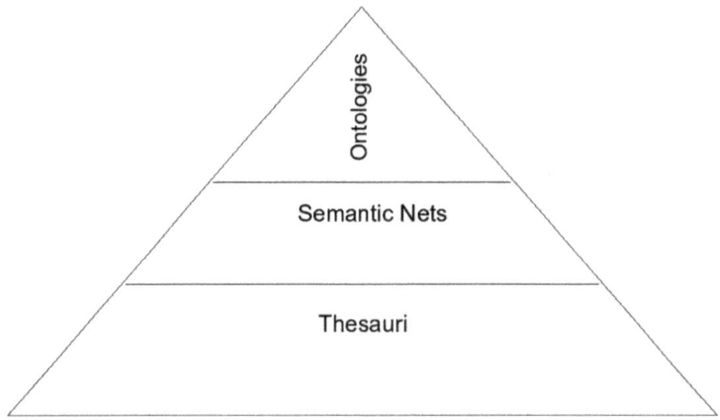

Fig. 9.1 Use of the language resources pyramid

Ontology is a central concept in emerging ICT development and the ontology-based approach seems to be one of the most promising solutions to the "semantic problem" in the web.

The term "ontology" is a concept coming from philosophy, but in the IT context, in particular, in the AI, it represents a field studying how to represent reality correctly in order to allow the deeper sharing of information and knowledge. The term has acquired several specifications in the information technology context, such as *lightweight* and *formal, axiomatic ontologies*.

Lightweight ontologies or semantic nets appear as simple taxonomic structures of primitive or composite terms together with associated definitions. Lightweight ontologies are often a kind of computational lexicon, and are used to represent semantic relationships among terms in order to facilitate content-based access to the (Web) data produced by a given community. In this case, the intended meaning of primitive terms is more or less known in advance by the members of such a community.

Lightweight ontologies, such as lexicons, show only a limited kind of formal modelling, as they are generic and based on a weak abstraction model; the elements (classes, properties, and individuals) of the ontology depend primarily on the acceptance of existing lexical entries. In a lexical ontology, such as WordNet,[5] many of the hyper/hyponymy links are not logically consistent, as it was designed as a lexical resource.[6] In lexical ontologies constraints over relations and consistency

axiomatic theories, containing a rich axiomatization of their vocabulary, and are used to make the rationales and alternatives underlying different ontological choices as explicit as possible.

[5] Fellbaum, C. ed. 1998. *WordNet: An electronic lexical database*. London, England: The MIT Press, Cambridge.

[6] See (Gangemi, A., N. Guarino, and A. Oltramari. 2001. Conceptual analysis of lexical taxonomies: The case of WordNet Top-Level. In *Formal Ontology in Information Systems. Proceedings of FOIS2001*. C. Welty and S. Barry eds., 285–296. ACM Press.), for an interesting analysis of the logical consistency of the top level hierarchies of WordNet.

are ruled by the grammatical distinctions of language (language-based approach) [25, 34, 35, 37, 42, 54].

However, the need for precise agreement regarding the meaning of terms *becomes crucial as soon as a community of users evolves, or multicultural and multilingual communities need to exchange data and services* [36].

To capture (or at least approximate) such subtle distinctions we need an explicit representation of the so-called *ontological commitment* about the meaning of terms, in order to remove terminological and conceptual ambiguities. This is the role of *foundational ontologies.*[7]

Foundational ontologies are axiomatic theories about domain-independent *top level* categories, such as *object, attribute, event, parenthood, dependence and space-time connection.* They amount to repositories of highly general information modelling concepts that can be reused in the design of application ontologies for all kinds of domains.[8] By providing boxes of standardised knowledge representation, foundational ontologies also enhance semantic interoperability between communicating actors.

According to artificial intelligence wisdom, ontology is nothing other than *the formal statement of a shared conceptualisation* [27] and *foundational ontologies* are the top-level reference ontologies, to drive the construction of *domain ontologies*[9]; although their starting point is the set of common-sense intuitions that make up the human conceptualisation of reality, they ultimately aim at describing the categorical structure of the world as a whole. Generally in information science, an upper ontology (top-level ontology or foundation ontology) is an attempt to create an ontology which describes very general concepts that are the same across all domains. The aim is to have a large number of domain ontologies accessible under this upper ontology. It is usually a hierarchy of entities and associated rules (both theorems and regulations) that attempts to describe those general entities that do not belong to a specific problem domain.

The role and nature of foundational ontologies (and axiomatic ontologies in general) is complementary to that of lightweight ontologies: the latter can be built semi-automatically, e.g., by exploiting machine learning techniques; the former requires

---

[7] Gangemi, A., C. Catenacci, and M. Battaglia. 2004. The inflammation ontology design pattern: An exercise in building a core biomedical ontology with descriptions and situations. In *Biomedical Ontologies*. D. Pisanelli ed. Amsterdam: IOS Press.

[8] Gangemi, A., N. Guarino, C. Masolo, A. Oltramari, and L. Schneider. 2002. Sweetening ontologies with DOLCE. In *Proceedings of EKAW 2002*, Siguenza, Spain.

[9] Gruber, T. R. 1993a. Toward principles for the design of ontologies used for knowledge sharing. In *Formal ontology in conceptual analysis and knowledge representation*. N. Guarino, and R. Poli eds. Deventer, The Netherlands: Kluwer. See also, Gangemi, A., D.M. Pisanelli, and G. Steve. 1999. An overview of the ONIONS project: Applying ontologies to the integration of medical terminologies. *Data and Knowledge Engineering* 31:183–220.

more human labour, which can benefit from the results and methodologies of disciplines such as philosophy, linguistics, and cognitive science.[10]

Generally in the concrete application of ontologies, the different views provided as well as the representation of the reality given by them can be combined and integrated by means of the *core ontology* or to a *domain ontology*. A core legal ontology is a *complete and extensible ontology that expresses the basic concepts of a domain and that can provide the basis for specialization in domain-specific concepts and vocabulary-core ontologies* [43]. Whereas according to Guarino's definition *Domain ontologies and task ontologies describe, respectively, the vocabulary related to a generic domain or a generic task or activity, by specializing the terms introduced in the top-level ontology* [29].

Key basic concepts identified in core and domain ontologies form the basic conceptual vocabulary of the domain, and cover the ontological requirements of the majority of tasks at a general level. To give an example, the ontology of a specific regulatory field (consumer protection, IPR Management, private law [19]) is indirectly linked to the foundational ontology by a Legal Core Ontology which describes the basic entities (legal roles, legal situations, duties, sanction, organisations, etc.) of the legal reality.[11]

By way of conclusion on semantic resources, the following should be noted. The above mentioned resources share the fact that they are all made up of terms, descriptors or concepts thought to be significant for describing a certain domain. From the opposite point of view, they are characterized by different *concept density*, different *constraint density* and finally by different degrees of *language dependence* and *domain orientation*.

Regarding *concept density*, meaning specifically the number of concepts or terms for a given coverage, this is quite low in foundational ontologies and in upper level ontologies whilst very high in lexical resources. In terms of *constraint density*, that is, the number or relations/constraints for a given coverage, this is low in taxonomies and leightweight ontologies and increasing in foundational ontologies. As to *dependence from language*, this is very high in thesauri and taxonomies whilst it decreases in lightweight and foundational ontologies. Finally, *domain orientation* is also different for each resource: relationships of a thesaurus are fixed and inexpressive of domain relationships and meaning is limited to BT, NT, RT, UF and is therefore not specific to the domain, whilst those of a lightweight ontology or foundational ontology do reflect those of a specific domain.

---

[10] Masolo, C., S. Borgo, A. Gangemi, N. Guarino, and A. Oltramari. 2003. The wonderWeb library of foundational ontologies, IST 2001-33052 wonder web. `http://wonderweb.semanticweb.org/deliverables/documents/D18.pdf`.

[11] e.g. Hoekstra, R., J. Breuker, M. Di Bello, and A. Boer. June 2007. The LKIF core ontology of basic legal concepts. In *Proceedings of the workshop on legal ontologies and artificial intelligence techniques (LOAIT 2007)*, eds. Pompeu Casanovas, Maria Angela Biasiotti, Enrico Francesconi, and Maria Teresa Sagri, `http://www.estrellaproject.org/lkif-core`.

9.2 Lexical Resources

In this section some of the most relevant lexical resources will be analyzed in general and specifically for the legal domain [15, 17, 20, 46, 53].

9.2.1 General

9.2.1.1 WordNet

WordNet[12] is a lexical database containing information about English nouns, verbs, adjectives and adverbs and it is organized around the notion of *synsets*. A synset is a set of words with the same part-of-speech that can be interchanged in a certain context.[13]

WordNet can be used for supporting semantic inferences, for finding alternative expressions or wordings, for expanding words to sets of semantically related or close words (in, for example, information retrieval), for automatic text analysis and artificial intelligence applications.

Every synset contains a group of synonymous words that go together to form a specific meaning; different senses of a word are in different synsets. The meaning of synsets is further clarified with short defining glosses. Synsets are connected to other synsets via a number of semantic relations. These relations include: *hyp(er)onymy, troponymy, holo(mero)nymy, entailment* and *the cause relation.*

Moreover, words can also be connected to other words through lexical relations, including *antonymy* and relations of *derivation.*

WordNet also provides the polysemy count of a word, that is, the number of synsets that contain the word.

The Princeton WordNet is linked through the ILI (Interlingual Index) to the lexical/semantic networks developed, for European languages, within the EU's EuroWordNet[14] project. The EuroWordNet multilingual lexical database consists of wordnets for eight European languages, which are structured along the same lines as the Princeton WordNet. Currently, more than twenty languages share the same methodology and development structure and are linked to each other through the English language.

WordNet which is maintained by the Cognitive Science Laboratory of Princeton University under the direction of professor G. A. Miller and Pr. C. Fellbaumis is freely downloadable. The database contains about 150,000 words organized in over 115,000 synsets for a total of 207,000 word-sense pairs.

---

[12] www.wordnet.princeton.edu/

[13] Fellbaum, C. ed. 1998. *WordNet: An electronic lexical database*. London, England: The MIT Press, Cambridge.

[14] Ide, N., D. Greenstein, and P. Vossen. eds. 1998. Special Issue on EuroWordNe. *Computers and the Humanities*, 32(2–3):XXXII.

9.2.1.2 FrameNet

The Berkeley FrameNet Project[15] aims at building an online lexical resource for English, based on the principles of Frame Semantics [23] and on the notion of thematic role, supported by the corpus evidence. A semantic frame is a script-like structure of inferences, which are linked to the meanings of linguistic units (lexical items). Each frame identifies a set of frame elements (FE), which are frame-specific semantic roles. The description of each lexical item identifies the frames which underline a given meaning and the ways in which the frame elements are realized in structures headed by the word. FrameNet includes a rich network of relations between frames, such as the Inheritance (IS-A relation): the child frame is a subtype or the parent frame, and each FE in the parent is bound to a corresponding FE in the child; the Using: the child frame presupposes the parent frame as background; the Subframe: the child frame is a sub-event of a complex event represented by the parent and finally the Perspective on: the child frame provides a particular perspective on an un-perspectivized parent frame [2, 23].

The FrameNet database documents the range of semantic and syntactic combinatory possibilities of each word in each of its senses, through manual annotation of example sentences and automatic summarization of the resulting annotations. The FrameNet database is available in XML, and can be displayed and searched via the web and other interfaces. The FrameNet I data has also been translated into the DAML+OIL extension to XML and the Resource Description Framework (RDF), which makes FrameNet information machine readable and understandable [22]. Hundreds of researchers, teachers, and students around the world now use the database.

9.2.1.3 CYC

Cyc[16] is an artificial intelligence project that attempts to assemble a comprehensive ontology and database of everyday common sense knowledge, with the goal of enabling AI applications to perform human-like reasoning.

The Cyc project, started in 1984, is based on the idea that effective machine learning depends on having a core of knowledge that provides a context for information.[17]

More specifically, the purpose of the Cyc project is to provide computers with a store of formally represented "common sense": real world knowledge that can provide a basis for additional knowledge to be gathered and interpreted automatically.

---

[15] `http://framenet.icsi.berkeley.edu/~framenet`

[16] See the Cyc's web site: `http://www.cyc.com`

[17] Matuszek C., J. Cabral, M. Witbrock, and J. DeOliveira. March 2006. An introduction to the syntax and content of Cyc. In *Proceedings of the 2006 AAAI Spring Symposium on Formalizing and Compiling Background Knowledge and Its Applications to Knowledge Representation and Question Answering*, Stanford, CA.

Over three million facts and rules have been formally represented in the Cyc knowledge base by ontologists skilled in CycL, Cyc's formal representation language. In addition, natural language generation and parsing capabilities have been developed to provide support for learning from English corpora. As a result, the Cyc knowledge base now contains enough knowledge to support experimentation with the acquisition of additional knowledge via machine learning.

The Cyc system is made up of three distinct components: the knowledge base (KB), the inference engine, and the natural language system. The Cyc KB contains more assertions (facts and rules) describing concepts, structured into a hierarchical graph of microtheories, or reasoning contexts.

The natural language component of the system consists of a lexicon, and parsing and generation subsystems. The lexicon is a component of the knowledge base that maps words and phrases to Cyc concepts, whereas various parsers provide methods for translating English text into CycL, a declarative language used in the project.

The original knowledge base is proprietary, but a smaller version of the knowledge base, intended to establish a common vocabulary for automatic reasoning, was released as OpenCyc under an open source license. OpenCyc is the open source version of Cyc technology.[18]

9.2.2 Lexical Resources for the Legal Domain

Semantically enriched vocabularies are valuable in aiding part-of-speech tagging, thus helping automatic semantic and syntactic analysis of texts, supporting conceptual and cross-lingual I.R., ensuring consistency in legislative drafting.

When building a legal vocabulary, we have to consider that two different types of semantic information are associated with elements from legal texts. On the one hand, there is ontological structuring in the form of a conceptual model of the legal domain. A legal "language", consisting of a complex structure of concepts, forms an abstraction from legal textual material. On the other hand, there is a vocabulary of lexical items that lexicalise concepts (a lexicon), which are not necessarily restricted to the legal domain, and are associated with specific linguistic information (e.g., nouns versus verbs and syntactic preference). Variable dependency of ontological structure on language constraints indicates a continuum between formal structure and linguistic description. The formal resources are language independent ontologies reflecting the structure of the interested domain. On the contrary, the linguistic resources have a relevant ontological dependency on domain-specific lexicons and grammars. This means that, in the latter case, the structure of the ontology is fully determined by the structure of the language. A knowledge base that models legal knowledge needs to take both types of information into account, and to establish a modularly organized integration of the two.

[18] `http://www.cyc.com/cyc/technology/whatiscyc`.

In the following paragraphs, terminological resources created by the EU Institutions to support the multilinguality issues, and projects developing semantic resources for legal domains are described.

9.2.2.1 European Institutional Terminological Repositories: Eurovoc and Iate

The most prominent thesaurus is *Eurovoc*.[19]

EuroVoc is a multilingual thesaurus originally built specifically for processing the documentary information of the EU institutions. It is a multi-disciplinary and multilingual thesaurus, covering sufficiently wide-ranging fields to encompass both Community and national points of view, with a certain emphasis on parliamentary activities.

Recently, Eurovoc has moved to the semantic web approach adopting ontology-based thesaurus management. More specifically, EuroVoc currently uses semantic web technologies reflecting W3C recommendations and the latest trends in thesaurus standards. An ontological approach has been adopted and, in practice, the EuroVoc ontology is an extension of the SKOS Model (Simple Knowledge Organization System).

Currently, EuroVoc is split into 21 domains and 127 microthesauri. Each domain is divided into a number of microthesauri. A microthesaurus is considered to be a concept scheme with a subset of other concepts that are part of the complete EuroVoc thesaurus. Since the role of the thesaurus is to remove ambiguities, ensuring that each concept is contextualised in such a way that its meaning is univocal, each concept is limited to one meaning in the field and is connected to the microthesaurus to which it belongs through its semantic relationships, by additional information (scope notes, definition notes or history notes), as well as by its equivalents in the other languages covered in EuroVoc.

EuroVoc terms provide the lexical representation of the term in a given language and can be:

- Preferred terms (descriptors), used for indexing and denoting in an unambiguous way the name of the concepts;
- Non preferred terms (non descriptors), used as access points in the thesaurus, which guide users to the appropriate preferred term, with an instruction (USE, UF). They were never intended to be indexing terms.

If the meaning is not clear enough, a note can accompany a concept to clarify its meaning or use in a specified language, by:

- A scope note, describing the intended use of term within the thesaurus; introduced by the symbol "SN";
- A definition note, clarifying the meaning of the concept; introduced by the symbol "DEF".

[19] eurovoc.europa.eu/.

This new model follows a concept-based approach where concepts are language-independent of terms which represent them.

The "eu:ThesaurusConcept" represents the class of all EuroVoc concepts and is defined as a subclass of skos:Concept. Two classes have been settled on to point out the difference between the equivalence (USE/UF) and compound equivalence (USE+/UF+) relationships. Specific associations have been modelled to represent the relationships between a term (full name) and its acronym or short name. The latest version of Eurovoc 4.3.- has been published and made available over the Internet in 22 official EU languages (Bulgarian, Czech, Danish, Dutch, English, Estonian, Finnish, French, German, Greek, Hungarian, Italian, Latvian, Lithuanian, Maltese, Polish, Portuguese, Romanian, Slovak, Slovenian, Spanish and Swedish), as well as in one candidate country language (Croatian) and in another language (Serbian). All language versions have the same status: each preferred term (descriptor) in one language necessarily matches a preferred term in each of the other languages. A thesaurus concept includes by default all the language equivalents of the preferred term. However, equivalence between the non preferred terms (non descriptors) in the different languages does not necessarily exist. Each language is characterized by its wealth and its semantic and cultural differences, and a concept in one language is not always represented in another language.

Using the thesaurus has the following advantages:

- terminological standardization of indexing vocabularies, allowing more accurate documentary searches;
- multilingualism: establishing language equivalences between identical concepts expressed in different languages allows documents to be indexed in the language of the documentalist and searches to be made in the user's language.

However, EuroVoc has limitations. EuroVoc has been designed to meet the needs of general documentation systems on the activities of the European Union; it is not suitable for indexing or searching for specialised documents like legal documents. EuroVoc cannot claim to cover the various national situations at a sufficiently detailed level; however, efforts are being made to take into account the needs of users outside the EU institutions. Nevertheless, being the only available standardized semantic resource, Eurovoc is currently widely utilized for indexing national legislation (Italy, Croatia and others) by the Parliaments of EU Member States.

A second EU terminological resource is IATE (Inter-Active Terminology for Europe), the EU inter-institutional terminology database recently opened up for public use.[20] It originates from the integration of the Eurodicautom database, TIS, Euroterms and all the terminology produced created by the institutional agencies and translation centers of the EU Institutions (Commission, Parliament, European Court of Justice, European Court of Auditors). The aim is to support European translators in keeping track of the translations of words and phrases in different

[20] `http://iate.europa.eu/`.

languages, and to establish potential candidates for the translations of certain terms. The innovative aspect is the web-based infrastructure enhancing the availability and standardisation of the information and the dynamic evolution of the database, which now contains more than 1 million multilingual entries.

9.2.2.2 The TESEO—The Thesaurus of the Italian Parliament

TESEO is the semantic tool used by the Italian Parliament to classify documents of databases storing legislation and other relevant contents related to the legislative drafting.[21] It is a general thesaurus able to describe social, legal and scientific phenomena. It is divided into 33 thematic areas covering almost all issues of legislative activity and is made up of 3661 descriptors organized according to hierarchical, equivalence and associative relationships. Citizens can access the Parliament databases by navigating the theasurus and choosing the most appropriate descriptor to be used in their search. TESEO has also been adopted at regional level by some local public authorities.

9.3 Projects

9.3.1 The LOIS Project

LOIS is a concluded Demonstration Project co-financed by the European Commission under the e-Content Program. The main objective of LOIS is the localization of WordNets describing the legal domain in six different European languages, namely Italian, English, German, Czech, Portuguese and Dutch. As its methodological starting point, LOIS adopts the structure of WordNet and EuroWordNet (EWN).[22] Like these, in LOIS, a *synset* is a set of one or more uninflected word forms (lemmas) with the same part-of-speech that can be interchanged in a certain context. A synset is often further described by a gloss. The synsets (or concepts) of national legal WordNets are linked across them, in order to guarantee cross lingual access to European legislation and other legal documents (such as court cases).

The LOIS database is compatible with the *EuroWordNet* architecture,[23] and forms an extension of the EWN semantic coverage into the legal domain. Therefore, LOIS consists of a number of modules that directly or indirectly link into EWN modules through each individual language component. Within this framework, LOIS contributes to the creation of a European Legal WordNet, where

---

[21] `http://www.senato.it/guida/29346/30502/30503/genpaginamenu.htm`.

[22] See paragraph 9.3.1.

[23] Within the LOIS database, synsets are related to each other by means of semantic relations, the most important of which are hypernymy/hyponymy (between specific and more general concepts), meronymy (between parts and wholes), and antonymy (between semantically opposite concepts); even if less used, LOIS also includes all EWN relations

lexical items may be mapped from language to language according to their semantic meaning, at least as far as the structure of WordNet can be considered as semantically oriented. The goal of LOIS, however, is not only to localize resources for the exploitation of third parties. LOIS also aims at creating a paradigm for accessing legal resources both from a monolingual and cross lingual point of view.[24]

The information retrieval engine which is at the base of LOIS, is able to exploit such links, in a way that the query of a user who is unable to use technical terms, also retrieves documents which contain technical terminology. Therefore, citizens and/or professional users are able to enter queries in legal documentation database collections in their native language and also to retrieve documents written in different languages. Localization has been carried out in such a way that cross-lingual relationships between different synsets are maintained.[25]

Currently, the LOIS database covers six legislative systems coinciding with six languages. In line with the discussion on legal language above, each LOIS national legal wordnet is composed of two types of database modules:

- a *lexical database*, which conceptualises general language entities pertaining to legal theory and legal dogmatics, a set of patterns (models) in line with which law is drafted and operates, structured according to the EWN methodology;
- a *legislative database*, populated by legal concepts defined in European and national legislation and structured according to legal (supra)national models.[26]

In order to connect the linguistic expressions of concepts to the underlying conceptual domain entities, an intermediate structure or a *core ontology* has been adopted to distinguish language-independent concepts and relations from concepts and relations which are not. This methodology allows users to distinguish language-independent and language-dependent concepts and relations.

9.3.2 The Syllabus Project

The Legal Taxonomy Syllabus Project realized under the umbrella of EC funding is a tool aimed at helping to increase European terminological consistency by taking into account the problem of knowledge representation in the legal domain conceived as law governing actions in the Eu Member States as well as in the EU context.

---

[24] Sagri, M.T., and D. Tiscornia. 2003. In Semantic tools for accessing legal information. Atti del Convegno IADIS: E-Society 2003 (Lisbona, 3-6 Giugno 2003), eds. A. Palma dos Reis and P. Isaías (a cura di), IADIS Press.

[25] Curtoni, P., V. Di Tomaso, L. Dini, L. Mommers, W. Peters, P. Quaresma, E. Schweighofer, and D. Tiscornia. 2005. Semantic access to multilingual legal information. In *Workshop on "Free EU Information on the Web: The Future beyond the new EUR-Lex"*, Brussels.

[26] Peters, W., M.T. Sagri, D. Tiscornia, and S. Castagnoli. 2006. The LOIS Project. *The Fifth International Conference on Language Resources and Evaluation, LREC*, Genova.

This tool was developed to support the Uniform Terminology project[27] with the collaboration of the entire Law Department of Turin University.[28]

Syllabus is an open-access database linking European terms with national transposition law and also linking terms horizontally (i.e., between national legal orders). It provides full text reference to relevant EU legislation and to that of the Member States.

Documents are stored in a database including case law linked to the relevant legislation and to short commentary notes necessary to describe differing legal doctrine. As a starting point, the Legal Taxonomy Syllabus covers consumer law with national law references limited to France, Germany, Italy, Spain and the UK.

Syllabus aims at offering lawyers, translators, legislators and scholars a useful tool for enhancing terminological coherency in different stages of the law cycle (from drafting to the application of the law).

Specific functions enable lawyers to search for relevant case law in other Member States through a single click. Syllabus does not only provide translators with an actual translation but provides the respective legislative context of each term. Furthermore, the system allows the user to perform cross-sector analyses on the use of legal terms and concepts, integrating the classification systems employed by existing databases with the ontologies, which are oriented towards the multilingual terminology but only in one dimension, that of the European Union or which are structured on the subdivisions and sections of the European Treaty that have no relevant connection with the classifications implied in the legal discourse within the Member States.

9.3.3 The DALOS Project

The DALOS project, financed under the e-Participation program, aims at providing legal drafters and decision-makers with linguistic and knowledge management tools to be used in legislative processes, in particular within the phase of legislative drafting. This will contribute to the harmonisation and consistency of legislative texts by providing drafters with easy access to pertinent ontological resources so they can obtain immediate clarifications on the legal terms used, navigate through the network of legal terms, consider ways in which the same concept is expressed in different languages. This enriches the linguistic-ontological resources both via interaction with the legal experts who are directly involved and via the integration of ontology learning tools, able to cluster relevant terms from legislative texts and to organize them in taxonomical chains integrating ontological tools within the legislative process. It also facilitates accessibility to legislative texts by European citizens, thus promoting their participation in the legislative process and their involvement in

[27] Rossi, P., and C. Vogel. 2004. Terms and concepts; towards a syllabus for European private law. *European Review of Private Law (ERPL)*, 12(2):293–300.

[28] `http://www.copecl.org`

the process of comprehending the law, improving the quality and the readability of legislative texts, thus contributing also to the "certainty of the law of law".

Moreover, once the text is delivered, ontological knowledge will facilitate retrieval by European citizens and also the interpretation and implementation of legal documents. These results, besides a well structured multilingual domain-specific ontology, require a set of computer tools, clustered around such an ontology. These tools allow law makers to monitor the connection between the language and terminology used in the text and the harmonised concept repository, thus allowing them to get immediate feedback on the quality and accessibility of the language used. On the other hand, tools for terminology extraction and ontology learning can also help to expand existing ontologies and terminological repositories in a controlled and harmonized way. In DALOS, these tools manage multilingual issues: they are addressed towards the harmonization of legal concepts and related terminologies used in European legislation as well as in the legislation of different European countries. To obtain this result the project exploited linguistic ontological resources developed within previous European projects. In particular, there is a link to the LOIS project (EDC 22161- see `http://www.loisproject.org`). Using these resources legislative drafters will be able to query linguistic and ontological resources, searching for appropriate and standardized terms or locutions, corresponding to specific legal concepts. The DALOS prototype is focused on the specific area of protection of consumers' economic and legal interests.

The final outcome of the DALOS project is a linguistic tool assisting the process of drafting legislation by providing ontology-based and statistically selected suggestions for terminological re-use and knowledge management.

9.3.4 The Euroterm Project (EDC-2214)

Due to the difficulties multi-languages poses for the EU Institutions and Member States in all sectors of Public Sector Information, EuroTerm[29] ("Extending the EuroWordNet with Public Sector Terminology"[30]) is essentially dedicated to extending EuroWordNet with environmental terminology for the following languages: Greek, Dutch and Spanish, by adding specific public sector terms. Therefore, this project allows for the creation of a multi-language lexicon database to aid access to information and to contribute to the use and development of European digital contents. The domain-specific WordNets are stored in a common lexical database and linked to the central EWN database. There are some deviations from the EWN model due to the different structure of the lexical resources and the quality of the tools used for terminology acquisition. For the development of EuroTerm, a combination of the merge and expand model have been implemented. The merge model

[29] Christodoulakis, D. et al. 2002. Expanding EuroWordNet with domain-specific terminology using common lexical resources: Vocabulary completeness and coverage issues. In *Proceedings of the 1st Global Wordnet Conference (GWC), January 21–25*. Mysore: India.

[30] `http://www.ceid.upatras.gr/Euroterm/`

implies the independent development of each monolingual WordNet and then their linking to the most equivalent synset in the ILI, whereas the expand model implies the translation of English concepts into other languages. Both models have been followed in order to assure compatibility and maximize control over the data across the individual WordNets while maintaining language-dependent differences [52].

Each of the monolingual WordNets comprises $\sim 1,000$ synsets, stored in a common database, which are linked to the central EWN database under the domain label "Environment".

9.4 Legal Ontologies

According to Breuker and al., ontologies in the legal field keep on growing [14] and this is mainly due to the fact that the law itself does not appear to be ontologically founded, and therefore, calls for action and knowledge representation in order to be processed with ICTs. There are a number of legal ontologies available that approach formal modelling from different perspectives, such as the Functional Ontology and the Frame Based Ontology. Furthermore, there is also CLO (Core Legal Ontology) and many others. There are, in fact, many ways to formalize ontologies and the results to be achieved are strictly linked to the aims and purposes that the ontologies are going to reach [47]. A brief overview of some of the ontologies that have already been realised in the legal domain is offered in chronological order starting from the knowledge representation models developed during 1990s.

The oldest ontologies in the legal field is the *Stamper's Norma Formalism* based on the identification of some relevant concepts. The first concept is the "agent" which is an organism standing at the centre of reality. It gains knowledge, regulates, and modifies the world by means of actions. The second is the "behavioural invariant" which is a description of a "situation" whose features remain invariant. Finally, there are the "realisations" of a situation, specified as the combination of an agent and a behavioural invariant relized by an agent.

Another ontology is the *Language for Legal Discourse* (LLD) proposed by McCarty. The basic components of LLD are atomic formulae and rules. Together they allow for the creation of first-order expressions. Modalities, such as time and permissions, are stated as second-order expressions. A relevant distinction is the one made between count terms (to express tangible objects, such as houses, and persons) and mass terms (to express intangible objects, such as cash and stock). Rules are formed by connecting atomic formulae with logical connectives. Currently, the following modalities are supported: time, events and actions, and deontic expressions. To express temporal statements, LLD recognises states. The legal core epistemology is the ontology developed by van Kralingen and Visser. This *frame-based ontology of law* (FBO) is decomposed into the generic legal ontology (norms, acts, concept descriptions) and the statute-specific ontology. The distinction is based on the observation that some parts of an ontology are reusable across different legal subdomains. The legal ontology divides legal knowledge into three distinct entities: norms, acts and concept descriptions. For each of these entities the ontology defines a frame structure that lists all attributes relevant for the entity. Events and processes are present, where events represent an instantaneous change between two states, while processes have duration. Another relevant distinction is the one between institutional acts and physical acts. It should be stressed that concept descriptions deal with the meanings of the concepts found in the domain. The vocabulary with which the knowledge base is constructed is also defined.

FOLaw is a "functional" core ontology for law, supporting the building of legal knowledge systems, due to the fact that it reflects an understanding of types of knowledge and dependencies existing in legal reasoning described by Valente. This core-ontology, served a number of purposes. The first was to distinguish the various types of knowledge in legal reasoning, and, in particular, those types that are typical for that kind of reasoning. Related to this role the dependencies between these types of knowledge in legal reasoning are clarified.

The major types of knowledge identified are normative knowledge, world knowledge, responsibility knowledge, reactive knowledge, creative knowledge and meta-legal knowledge.

Valente's functional ontology of law obviously adopts a functional perspective of law (FOLaw). The main function of a legal system is to regulate social behaviour (law as a social control system). By using this functional view of the law, categories of legal knowledge are distinguished and are represented in the ontology.

The *LRI core ontology* has been developed in the context of the E-court and E-power projects with the aims of constituting a clear core ontology for legal domains. It is based on the intuition that, typical legal terms have still a strong common sense flavour, and there is still a type of knowledge, pivotal for law, that may contain the same concepts that are typical but may not be exclusive to the legal domain. It includes Valente's FOLaw functional ontology, but differs from it by being a more generic ontology with reference to legal roles, procedures, documentation, communication and legal sources. In doing so, it deals with substantive law (as FOLaw already did) as well as with procedural law. Major categories covered are: roles, physical-concept, mental-concept, occurrence, abstract-concept.

Key distinctions made by LRI-Core include the distinction between events and processes: events are explained by processes; definition of the role of force or energy in processes, as opposed to distinguishing objects as endurants or perdurants (i.e., whether objects can lose their identity over time). The emphasis is on representing agents and the communications between them. There is an important difference between the mental world and the physical one. Physical processes occur causally, but mental processes are controlled by an intentional stance. The outcome of mental processes can be the intention to act.

The *LKIF* is a Legal Knowledge interchange Format developed within the Estrella Project[31] in order to *enable the translation between legal knowledge bases*

[31] Estrella project (IST-2004-027665), `http://www.estrellaproject.org`. See (Boer, A., R. Winkels, and F. Vitali. 2007. XML Standards for Law: MetaLex and LKIF. In *Proceedings of JURIX 2007*. Amsterdam: IOS Press.) for a specification of the Legal Knowledge Interchange Format.

written in different representation formats and formalisms and to act as a knowledge representation formalism that is part of a larger architecture for developing legal knowledge systems. Within the LKIF, an ontology of basic legal concepts, known as the LKIF-core, has been implemented enabling the interchange of knowledge (LKBS) by supporting legal inference, knowledge acquistion and knowledge exchange. Three layers can be distinguished in the ontology: Top Level (that borrows most classes from the LRI-Core), Intentional Level (that includes concepts and relations which describe behaviour *of rational agents that can be effectively influenced by the law* [31] and Legal Level (legal agents, actions rights and powers—modified by Rubino et al. [45], also described in the list of ontologies below—and legal roles and concept definitions).

The development of the CLO core ontology takes into account methodologies belonging to upper level ontologies, and proposals in the field of legal ontologies. The Core Ontology organises the legal concepts in classes on the basis of formal (meta) properties defined in the foundational ontologies. The basic entities that populate the domain of law can be considered universal and clearly identifiable, and, as such, they are pointed out through a minimal generalised series of properties and relations (intentional meaning). The CLO organises legal concepts and relations based on the formal properties defined in DOLCE+. The legal world is conceived of as a representation, or a description of reality, an ideal view of the behaviour of a social group, according to a system of rules that are commonly accepted and acknowledged.

Finally, the *JurWordNet* will be analysed. This initiative is the result of a joint work between ITTIG-CNR, and the Laboratory for Applied Ontology (LOA) at ISTC-CNR, and its objective is to realise the extension to the legal domain of the Italian ItalWordNet (IWN) database, providing a knowledge base for the multilingual access to sources of legal information. In JurWordnet entries are linked by lexical relations to other concepts and, by "hypo-plugs" links, to ItalWordnet, to maintain conventional legal language.

Legal concepts are organised by the Legal Core Ontology in classes based on formal (meta) properties defined in DOLCE+.

As in the original WordNet, meanings in JurWordNet are represented by synsets. A synset is a set of terms (house, home, dwelling domicile), linked by a relation of meaning equivalence (expressing approximately the same conceptualization). Proper synsets in the legal lexicon are rare so it was crucial to create mapping relations to common language, in order to also allow searches to be made by non-experts using terms from common language instead of legal terminology. Besides taxonomic (hyponymy) relations, the synsets of the legal lexicon also have associative horizontal relations such as the meronymy and the role.

Consistently with WordNet projects,the developing methodology favours the use and harmonization of already existing lexical resources. Relevant concepts have been extracted in a bottom-up way, from a corpus of legal documentation.

The categories that bring together the top level of JurWordNet's taxonomical trees are the basic legal entities which are held to be common to all the legal systems. Having a nucleus of shared legal knowledge allows for the matching, integration, and comprehension of legal concepts created by particular legal systems, and takes for granted that the criteria used to organize the concept into classes are mainly based on the law.

9.5 Semantic Mark-Up Trends

The legal domain has very specific features to be considered when structuring knowledge and information relevant to the field. This is mainly due to the fact that the law talks about its contents in a technical way using specific language and jargon. Nevertheless, as regulations do impact on the common sense scenario affecting the human behaviour, "words" expressing rules do need to be unambiguous and clear in order to be perceived in all their complexity.

Semantic mark-up allows users to identify those terms and concepts playing a fundamental role within the provisions and to link them to some other information (semantic resources) with the aim of clarifying the meaning and the context in which the law impacts by changing the scenario. Marking-up legislative texts embedding into them (to the entire document or to a selected part of it) semantics for providing additional information (metadata) complies with the existing semantic gap.

The complexity of this scenario affects the methodology for approaching a possible representation of legal knowledge and the implementation of semantic resources able to foster the management from a conceptual point of view. The great opportunity offered by XML to include directly relevant information by legislators ex ante or ex post in the document enhances the coherent up-keeping of legal orders with respect to specific domains, the interoperability among applications, the realization of self-explaining texts and the possibility to have tools retrieving provisions and not only legislative text as a whole from the conceptual point of view and finally the automatic consolidation of texts. Moreover, the possibility of accessing and retrieving provisions or arguments directly increases the certainty of the law of the law and the uniform drafting and application of it. Of course, the best solution is to have the ex ante mark-up of the information by legislators as this provides an authentic interpretation and explanation of rules contained in a text. Currently, when considering semantic resources for marking up legislative texts, specific attention should be devoted to the fact that the frontier of the separate use of the different available semantic resources is tailing off more and more, leaving the floor to a combined use of them. It is possible that a lexicon (considered as a lightweight ontology) with a semantic hierarchy might serve as the basis for a useful ontology, and that an ontology may serve as grounding for a lexicon. This is particularly the case in technical domains, in which vocabulary and ontology are more closely tied than in more general domains [30]. In terminological lexicons, terms and concepts usually coincide, creating an intersection between the linguistic meaning and the formal ontological conceptual structure. The importance of incorporating linguistic resources in ontology engineering has been stressed by [32]: *Linguistic resources (such as lexicons, dictionaries and glossaries) can be used as consensus references to root ontology concepts. The importance of using linguistic resources in this way lies in the fact that a linguistic resources renders the intended meaning of a linguistic term as it is commonly agreed among the community of its language.* Therefore, on the one hand, linguistic resources (such as lexicons, dictionaries, and thesauri) are indeed important resources for identifying concepts and can be used as consensus references to root an ontology. On the other hand, it can be affirmed that lexical resources and semantic resources such as ontologies need each other and are complementary to each other as ontologies allow us to represent the complex relationship between the lexical and the semantic meaning of a term. More specifically, first and foremost, the representation made by ontologies enables us to migrate from the term to the concept, which is something more consistent from the semantic point of view and, secondly, they enable the disambiguation of the meaning of the concept by setting it in a specific domain. This procedure seems to be very useful in the legal domain where the lexical meaning of a term hardly ever corresponds to the semantic one. Therefore, the need to narrow or to extend the lexical meaning can also be realized from the formal point of view by representing the domain by using ontologies.

Nevertheless, ontologies alone seem to be unfit for the management of electronic data and sources. The ontological approach is, however, helpful as a starting point for enhancing existing tools. Recent trends in the information technology domain demonstrate that these new tools might work better if combined with other techniques that are somehow also linked to previously constructed tools. In this direction, good results have been achieved in the Eurovoc re-engineering process using the ontological approach: the thesaurus has been revised implementing SKOS (Simple Knowledge Organization System) model. Finally, the systematic semantic mark-up of legislation permits the coupling of traditional searches for legal texts with the conceptual search by normative provisions and their contents.

References

1. Agnoloni, T., L. Bacci, E. Francesconi, G. Giardiello, P. Spinosa, and F. Uccheddu. 2006. XmLegesEditor v.2.0 rc5. Editore per la redazione di testi normativi, Ittig-Cnr, Firenze.
2. Baker, Collin F., Charles J. Fillmore, and John B. Lowe. 1998. The Berkeley framenet project. In *COLING-ACL'98: Proceedings of the Conference*, 86–90, Montrìal. Association for Computational Linguistics.
3. Bartalesi, et al. 2008. The LME project: legislative metadata based on semantic formal models, in Journal International Journal of Metadata, Semantics and Ontologies, Volume 4 Issue 3, August 2009. In *Proceedings of LEGONT'97*, Melbourne, Australia.
4. Bartolini, R., A. Lenci, S. Montemagni, V. Pirrelli, and C. Soria. 2004. Semantic Mark-up of Italian legal texts through NLP-based technique. In *Proceedings of LREC 2004*, Lisbon, Portugal.
5. Bench-Capon, T.J.M., and P.R.S. Visser. 1997. Ontologies in legal information systems; the need for explicit specifications of domain conceptualisations. In *Proceedings of the 6th International Conference on Artificial Intelligence and Law (ICAIL'97)*, 132–141. ACM, New York, NY.
6. Berrueta, D., J.E. Labra, and L. Polo. 2006. Searching over public administration legal documents using ontologies, Frontiers in artificial intelligence and applications, Vol. 140, 167–175.

7. Biagioli, C. 1997. Towards a legal rules functional micro-ontology. In *Proceedings of LEGONT'97*, Melbourne, Australia.
8. Biagioli, C., and D. Grossi. 2008. Formal aspects of legislative meta-drafting. In *Proceedings of Jurix08*, Florence, Italy.
9. Biasiotti, M.A., and M. Fernandez Barrera. 2009. Enriching Thesauri with Ontological Information: Eurovoc Thesaurus and DALOS domain Ontology of consumer law. In *Proceedings of the Third Workshop on Legal Ontologies and Artificial Intelligence Techniques (LOAIT 2009)*, Barcelona, Spain, June 8, 2009.
10. Boer, A., R. Winkels, and R. Hoekstra. 2001. The clime ontology. In Winkels, R., editor. In *Proceedings of the Second International Workshop on Legal Ontologies (LEGONT) in JURIX 2001, Amsterdam (Netherlands)*, 37–47, Amsterdam, Netherlands.
11. Breuker, J., and R. Hoekstra. 2004. Core concepts of law: Taking commonsense seriously. In *Proceedings of Formal Ontologies in Information Systems FOIS-2004*, 210–221. IOS-Press.
12. Breuker, J., and R. Hoekstra. 2004. Epistemology and ontology in core ontologies: FOLaw and LRI-Core, two core ontologies for law. In *Proceedings of EKAW Workshop on Core ontologies*, Northamptonshire, UK.
13. Breuker, J., A. Valente, and R. Winkels. 2005. Use and reuse of legal ontologies in knowledge engineering and information management. In *Law and the semantic web. Legal ontologies, methodologies, legal information retrieval, and applications*, eds. V. Benjamins, P. Casanovas, J. Breuker, and A. Gangemi, 35–64. Springer.
14. Breuker, J. et al. 2008. The flood, the channels and the Dykes. In *Law, ontologies and the semantic web*, eds. J. Breuker et al. The Netherlands. Springer, IOS Press.
15. Buitelaar, P., P. Cimiano, and B. Magnini. 2005. Ontology learning from text: An overview. In *Ontology learning from text: Methods, evaluation and applications*, eds. P. Buitelaar, P. Cimiano, and B. Magnini, volume 123 of Frontiers in Artificial Intelligence and Applications Series. IOS Press.
16. Cimiano, P., and J. Voeìlker. 2005. Text2onto - a framework for ontology learning and data-driven change discovery. In *Proceedings of the 10th international conference on applications of natural language to information systems (NLDB)*, eds. A. Montoyo, R. Munoz, and E. Metais, volume 3513 of Lecture Notes in Computer Science, 227–238. Alicante, Spain: Springer.
17. Corcho, O., M. Fernandez, and A. Gomez-Perez. 2003. Methodologies, tools and languages for building ontologies: Where is the meeting point? In *Data & knowledge engineering* 46.
18. Cunningham, H., D. Maynard, K. Bontcheva, and V. Tablan. 2002. GATE: A framework and graphical development environment for robust NLP tools and applications. In *Proceedings of the 40th Anniversary Meeting of the Association for Computational Linguistics (ACL'02)*, 168–175, USA: Philadelphia.
19. Delgado, Jaime et al. In IPROnto: An ontology for digital rights management. In *Proceedings of Jurix 2003: The Sixteenth Annual Conference on Legal Knowledge and Information Systems.*
20. Després, S., and S. Szulman. 2006. Terminae method and integration process for legal ontology building. In IEA/AIE, eds. M. Ali, and R. Dapoigny, volume 4031 of Lecture Notes in Computer Science, 1014–1023. Springer.
21. Dick, J.P. 1991. Representation of legal text for conceptual retrieval. In *Proceedings of the 3rd International Conference on Artificial Intelligence and Law, Oxford, England*, 106–115. New York: ACM Press.
22. Farquhar, A., R. Fikes, and J. Rice. 1997. Tools for assembling modular ontologies in ontolingua. In AAAI - National Conference on Artificial Intelligence, vol. 14, 436–441. Wiley.
23. Fillmore, C.J., and Collin F. Baker. June 2001. Frame se- mantics for text understanding. In *Proceedings of Word- Net and Other Lexical Resources Workshop*, 59–64, NAACL, Pittsburgh.
24. Fortuna, B., M. Grobelnik, and D. Mladenic. 2007. Ontogen: Semi-automatic ontology editor. In *Proceedings of human interface and the management of information. Interacting in information environments, symposium on human interface 2007, held as part of HCI international*

2007, Beijing, China, July 22–27, eds. M. J. Smith, and G. Salvendy, volume 4558 of Lecture Notes in Computer Science, 309–318. Springer.

25. Gangemi, A., N. Guarino, C. Masolo, and A. Oltramari. 2002. Luc Schneider: Sweetening ontologies with DOLCE. *EKAW* 166–181.
26. Gangemi, A., M.-T. Sagri, and D. Tiscornia. 2003. Metadata for content description in legal information. In *14th International Workshop on Database and Expert Systems Applicat-Springer, IOS Press, 2008, The Netherlandsions (DEXA'03), September 1–5*, Prague, Czech Republic, 745, IEEE Computer Society, Washington, DC.
27. Gruber, T.R. 1993. Toward principles for the design of ontologies used for knowledge sharing. Technical Report KSL 93-04, Knowledge Systems Laboratory, Stanford University.
28. Gruber, T.R. 1991. The role of common ontology in achieving sharable, reusable knowledge bases. In *Principles of knowledge representation and reasoning: Proceedings of the second international conference*, eds. J.A. Allen, R. Fikes, and E. Sandewall, 601–602. Cambridge, MA: Morgan Kaufmann.
29. Guarino, N. 1998a. Formal ontology in information systems. In *Proceedings of the First Conference (FOIS'98)*, IOS Press Trento, Italy, 6–8 June 1998. Guarino, N. 1998b. Formal ontology in information systems. In *Formal ontology in information systems. Proceedings of FOIS'98, Trento, Italy, 6–8 June 1998*, ed. N. Guarino, 3–15. Amsterdam: IOS Press.
30. Hirst, G. 2004. Ontology and the lexicon. In *Handbook on Ontologies*. S. Staab and R. Studer eds., 209–229. Heidelberg: Springer.
31. Hoekstra, R., J. Breuker, M. Di Bello, and A. Boer. 2007. The LKIF Core ontology of basic legal concepts. In *Proceedings of the workshop on legal ontologies and artificial intelligence techniques* (LOAIT 2007), eds. P. Casanovas, M.A. Biasiotti, E. Francesconi, and M. Teresa Sagri, June 2007.
32. Jarrar, M. 2006. Towards the Notion of Gloss, and the Adoption of Linguistic Resources in Formal Ontology Engineering. In *Proceedings of the 15th International World Wide Web Conference*. WWW2006, ACM Press, Barcelona.
33. Jarrar, M.K., and P. Dongilli. 2006. Multilingual verbalization of norm conceptual models and axiomatized ontologies. Starlab technical report, STARLab, Vrije Universiteit Brussel.
34. Lame, G. 2001. Constructing an IR-oriented legal ontology. In *Second International Workshop on Legal Ontologies, JURIX 2001*, Amsterdam, Neederlands, December 2001.
35. Li, Y., K. Bontcheva, and H. Cunningham. 2005. SVM Based Learning System For Information Extraction. In *Deterministic and statistical methods in machine learning*, eds. J. Winkler, M.N. and N. Lawerence, LNAI 3635, 319–339. Berlin: Springer.
36. Masolo, C., S. Borgo, A. Gangemi, N. Guarino, A. Oltramari, and L. Schneider. 2002. Preliminary report wonderweb deliverable D17. The WonderWeb Library of Foundational Ontologies and the DOLCE ontology. (ver. 2.0, 15-08-2002).
37. Masolo, C., A. Oltramari, A. Gangemi, N. Guarino, and L. Vieu. 2003. La prospettiva dell'ontologia applicata. *Rivista di estetica*, 22(1/2003), XLIII:170–183.
38. McGuinness, D.L., and J.R. Wright. 1998. Conceptual modelling for configuration: A description logic-based approach. *Artificial Intelligence for Engineering Design, Analysis, and Manufacturing*, 12:333–344.
39. McGuinness, D.L., R. Fikes, J. Rice, and S. Wilder. 2000. The chimaera ontology environment. In *Proceedings of the Seventeenth National Conference on Artificial Intelligence (AAAI 2000)*, Austin, TX, July 30–August 3.
40. Missikof, M., R. Navigli, and P. Velardi. 2002. Integrated approach to web ontology learning and engineering. *Computer*, 35(11):54–57.
41. Musen, M.A. 1992. Dimensions of knowledge sharing and reuse. *Computers and Biomedical Research*, 25:435–467.
42. Navigli, R., and P. Velardi. 2004. Learning domain ontologies from document warehouses and dedicated web sites. *Computational Linguistics* 30(2):151–179.
43. Peters, W., M.T. Sagri, D. Tiscornia, and S. Castagnoli. 2006. The LOIS project. In *The Fifth International Conference on Language Resources and Evaluation*, LREC, Genova.

44. Rosch, E.H. 1978. Principles of categorization. In *Cognition and categorization*, eds. E. Rosch and B. Lloyd, 27–48. Hillsdale, NJ: Erlbaum Associates.
45. Rubino, R., A. Rotolo, and G. Sartor. 2006. An OWL Ontology of Fundamental Legal Concepts. In *Proceeding of the 2006 conference on Legal Knowledge and Information Systems: JURIX 2006: The Nineteenth Annual Conference*. T. M. van Engers ed., 101–110., The Netherlands: IOS Press, Amsterdam.
46. Sartor, G. 2006. Fundamental legal concepts: A formal and teleological characterisation, artificial intelligence and law. Technical report. European University Institute, Florence/Cirsfid, University of Bologna.
47. Sartor, G., P. Casanovas, M.A. Biasiotti, and M. Fernández-Barrera. eds. 2011. *Approaches to legal ontologies. Theories, domains, methodologies, Series: Law, governance and technology series*, Vol. 1. The Netherlands: Springer, IOS Press.
48. Saskia van de Ven, Rinke Hoekstra, and Radboud Winkels. June 2007. MetaVex: Regulation drafting meets the semantic web. In Proceedings of the workshop on semantic web technology for law (SW4Law 2007), eds. M. Klein, P. Quaresma, and N. Casellas, 42–55. Berlin: Springer.
49. Sclano, F., and P. Velardi. 2007. Termextractor: a web application to learn the common terminology of interest groups and research communities. In *Proceedings of the 9th Conference on Terminology and Artificial Intelligence (TIA'07)*, Sophia Antinopolis, October.
50. Smith, B. 2003. The cambridge companion to searle. Cambridge: Cambridge University Press.
51. Spyns, P., and A. Lisovoy. 2003. The dogma modeller manual. EuroLan 2003 tutorial material STAR-2003-11, STAR Lab, Vrije Universiteit Brussel.
52. Stamou, S., A. Ntoulas, J. Hoppenbrouwers, M. Saiz-Noeda, and D. Christodoulakis. 2002. EUROTERM: Extending the EuroWordNet with Domain-Specific Terminology Using an Expand Model Approach. In *Proceedings of the 1st Global Wordnet Conference (GWC)*, January 21–25, Mysore, India.
53. Valente, A., and J. Breuker. 1995. ON-LINE: An architecture for modelling legal information. In *Proceedings of the fifth international conference on artificial intelligence and law*, eds. T. Bench-Capon, 1079–1125. New York: ACM Press.
54. Velardi, P., R. Navigli, A. Cucchiarelli, and F. Neri. 2005. Evaluation of OntoLearn, a methodology for automatic population of domain ontologies. In *Ontology learning from text: Methods, evaluation and applications*, eds. P. Buitelaar, P. Cimiano, and B. Magnini, volume 123 of Frontiers in Artificial Intelligence and Applications Series, 92–106. The Netherlands: IOS Press.
55. Wyner, A. June 2009. Lagal Ontologies Spin up a Semanti Web, June 08, 2009. `http://www.law.com/jsp/lawtechnologynews/PubArticleLTN.jsp?id=1202431256007`.
56. Yehia-Dahab, M., H.A. Hasan, and A. Rafea. 2008. Textontoex: Automatic ontology construction from natural english text. *Expert Systems with Applications*, 34:1474–1480.

Chapter 10
A Review of Systems and Projects: Management of Legislative Resources

Enrico Francesconi

10.1 European Initiatives

In the last few years a number of important initiatives in the field of legislative document management have been developed. Different national initiatives have introduced standards for legal source description as "MetaLex" (Section 10.1.1) and SDU BWB (Section 10.1.2) in the Netherlands, "LexDania" in Denmark (Section 10.1.3), the "NormeInRete" and "Normattiva" projects in Italy (Sections 10.1.4 and 10.1.5), "CHLexML" in Switzerland (Section 10.1.6), "eLaw" project in Austria (Section 10.1.7), until the open government UK initiative that gave rise to legislation.gov.uk Web publishing service of original (as enacted) and revised versions of legislation (Section 10.1.9).

Such initiatives, mainly promoted by national institutions including also research institutes and universities, have promoted XML standards as well as schemes for legal document identification in order to manage and publish legislation.

Finally the CEN MetaLex initiative aiming to define a European standard for legislation is presented in Section 10.1.10.

10.1.1 MetaLex

MetaLex was developed as part of the E-POWER project. This project was aimed at using ICT to support citizens and governments in dealing with an increasing number of regulations. European citizens and enterprises are more and more facing rules and regulations, affecting various aspects of their daily life and business. Regulations coming from international, European, national and local authorities is continuously increasing, despite the attempts to harmonize and deregulate particular domains, representing a problem also for public administrations. Hence the need to develop consistent and coherent legislative workflow systems aimed to

E. Francesconi (✉)
ITTIG-CNR, Institute for Legal Information Theory and Techniques, National Research Council of Italy, 50127 Florence, Italy
e-mail: francesconi@ittig.cnr.it

G. Sartor et al. (eds.), *Legislative XML for the Semantic Web*, Law, Governance and Technology Series 4, DOI 10.1007/978-94-007-1887-6_10,

© Springer Science+Business Media B.V. 2011

upholding and applying valid laws. ICT support in the legislative workflow domain can help both the government and citizens in dealing with this increasing body of law.

A precondition for relying on ICT solution in the legislative domain is the availability of legal sources in a structured and standard format. MetaLex was developed to fit this need [6, 7], providing a generic and extensible framework for the XML encoding of the structure and contents of written public decisions and public legal documents of a general and regulatory nature.

Currently, MetaLex is used by the Dutch Tax and Customs Administration, Be Value, the Belgian Public Centers for Welfare and others.

10.1.2 SDU BWB

Another institutional initiative in The Netherlands is represented by the Dutch SDU BWB standard: it is an XML format currently used for encoding the laws in the Dutch Basiswettenbestand (BWB) database, that is a large database containing almost all Dutch laws and decisions. The standard is based on a DTD originally developed by SDU publishers, and now maintained by the Dutch government.

10.1.3 LexDania

The LexDania project defined a national Danish system for the creation and interchange of legislative documentation. LexDania was initiated by the Danish Ministry of Science, Technology and Innovation then continued by the Retsinformation (Ministry of Justice) and the Folketinget (Danish Parliament). The work was conducted in two phases. In a first phase, a research on international activities and an investigation in other national standards and projects was done. In a second phase, the development of an XML standard followed: it is based on a the data model/methodology of the General Danish Public Information Online (OIO) XML strategy. This strategy consists in choosing a set of central types and elements, creating sets of "building blocks" for national use, (re-)using building blocks to create specific legislative schemas [18–23].

The project has been focused on developing a system of schemas for the systematic creation and maintenance of document type and application schemas. The system has an unique approach to building schemas. A structure of stratified layers is used to incrementally construct the schemas from functional features—rather than document characteristics. The structure is accompanied by a methodology explaining ways of constructing consistent and compliant schemas for specific purposes.

10.1.4 NormeInRete

The project NormeInRete [11] (translation: Legislation on the Net), or NIR, started in 1999 with the leadership of CNIPA[1] together with the Italian Ministry of Justice. It gathered several Italian public institutions and research organizations.

NormeInRete reached the following results:

- a Web portal (`www.normeinrete.it`) providing a unique access point for searching the Italian legislative corpus. It offered search and retrieval services operating on Italian laws since 1904, and utilities for automatic hyperlinking. The portal included e-learning facilities, a software download section to deliver open source utilities developed by the project team, and a best-practices section to encourage re-use experiences, in order to create a virtual space for knowledge sharing within the Public administrations community;
- a standard for persistent identification of legal documents, compliant with the IETF Uniform Resource Name [15], and an infrastructure for identifiers resolution and management [17].
- a standard for XML representation of legal documents [14]. DTDs and XML schemas for Italian legislation were defined; these schemas include structural information as well as administrative and semantic metadata [5] providing meaningful information for advanced retrieval and to automate legislative documents life-cycle management;
  The availability of XML documents marked-up according to shared formats allows to provide advanced search and retrieval functions operating effectively on heterogeneous databases in a distributed environment.

The NormeInRete standards have been issued as technical norm by the Italian Authority for information technology in Public Administration (AIPA, later CNIPA and DigitPA), and published on the Italian Official Journal [1, 2].

Nowadays, both standards have been adopted by several Italian public administrations, and by a growing number of private operators.

NormeInRete was the result of several years of collaboration between law scholars, software developers and public administrators both at the national and regional levels. An open forum for discussion was available to collect requirements and suggestions on the existing schemas.

10.1.5 Normattiva

As an evolution of the NormeInRete project, in 2010 the Normattiva[2] portal has been launched, with the aim to provide citizens with a complete and free-of-charge

---

[1] Centre for Information Technology in Public Administration

[2] `http://www.normattiva.it`

access service to the in-force legislation. In particular the Normattiva service can be accessed to search for legislative documents:

- in their original version, as published in the Official Journal;
- in-force, therefore applicable, on the query date;
- in-force on a certain date chosen by the user.

The service, in its final version, will give access to the whole Italian normative corpus (laws, decree, legislative decree, other numbered acts), up to 75.000 acts. Publishing readiness and accessibility services to legal documents and single provisions based on concepts and subject matters will be specific characteristics of the service. In particular this kind of conceptual document retrieval will be made available through a semantic indexing service based on Eurovoc.

Normattiva has already inherited the identification method developed within the NormeInRete project, based on the URN standard. Similarly, in the near future, the Normattiva archive is expected to adopt the XML standards developed by NormeInRete as well.

10.1.6 CHLexML

The first phase of the activities about legal standards, with particular attention to multilingual issues in the Swiss Confederation, were coordinated by COPIUR "Coordination Office for the Electronic Publication of Legal Data Federal Office of Justice" in Bern, Switzerland.

COPIUR started its work in October 1998. Initially attached to the Federal Chancellery, it later joined the Service of "Legal Data Processing and Computer Law" (Rechtsinformatik und Informatikrecht/ Informatique juridique, droit et informatique/ Informatica giuridica, diritto dell'informatica) at the Federal Office of Justice. The Service initiated and led informatics and organizational projects of national importance in areas like registers, electronic exchange of legal documents and electronic publication of legislative data. COPIUR evaluated and promoted new information technologies in the legislative field, dealing mainly with the elaboration of uniform norms, standards [10], and information structures. The aim was to harmonize federal, cantonal as well as private sector publications, in order to give the public a rich, uniformly presented and simply accessible online-offer of legislative data. COPIUR also aimed to represent the federal administration at the appropriate national and international coordination bodies. In 2002 COPIUR was integrated within the legal informatics federal service. At the end of 2006 it was closed as independent administrative unit.

COPIUR managed two relevant projects.

The first one was CHLexML (`www.chlexml.ch`), or the establishment of a comprehensive XML schema to be used for the publication of all (federal, cantonal and even communal) legislative acts. The schema was finalised by a working group of the Swiss association for juridical informatics led by COPIUR and the Federal Chancellery.

The second project, LexGo (`www.lexgo.ch`), aimed to align the 27 classification systems (all different) used by the 27 (federal and cantonal) systematic collections of law in order to simplify and improve search results. Based on the common systematic for the classification of legal acts elaborated by the Institute of Federalism of Fribourg, LexGo has created 27 matrix tables (Konkordanztabellen, tableaux de concordance) aligning all cantonal and federal legislative acts to the common systematic. LexGo allows users to find, for example, all federal and cantonal norms related to a given subject.

In 2006 the Federal Chancellery, within the initiatives aimed to modernize the publication of legislative documents, launched a project to change the Centre for Official Publication platform on a new technical one. This initiative has been recently (2010) relaunched in order to provide a system capable of fulfilling the requirements for a modern editing and publishing system.

This new project has defined a strategy aimed to obtain by 2015 that the electronic version of the official publications of the Federal Chancellery is the legally authoritative version and takes precedence over the printed version of the given publication.

10.1.7 eLaw

In the domain of legislative standards the Austrian institutional initiative is the eLaw Project. It aims at a reform of legal text production, creating one continuous electronic production channel with a uniform layout prepared on the same electronic text basis from draft to publication (promulgation) on the Internet. The workflow system includes government bills, committee reports, legal enactments of the Nationalrat and decisions of the Bundesrat. Parliament returns consolidated electronic texts of legal enactments to the Federal Chancellery, ready for publication. The authentic electronic publication on the Internet (since 2004) is available for everybody free of charge.

The eLaw (e-Recht “Electronic Law”) project aims at creating one continuous electronic production channel from the invitation to comment on draft legislation to promulgation (on the Internet). As a result, it is only required to enter amendments to the text during the legislative stages (for example by a committee, or in the plenary of the Nationalrat). As the first result of the project, texts of laws on paper are to be replaced by electronic texts, that is to say, printed government bills, committee reports and other parliamentary printed matter will cease to exist.

Electronic document workflow management allows to query documents at all the legislative stages and to track them in a fully transparent process. Primarily for the purpose of cost-cutting, the texts of legislation has to be given a uniform layout and has to be prepared on the same electronic text basis from draft to publication in the Federal Law Gazette on the Internet. As a result, the Federal Chancellery sends government bills to Parliament, Parliament returns the consolidated electronic version of the legal enactment adopted by the Nationalrat once parliamentary procedures have been completed. The State Printing Office (Wiener Zeitung) is therefore no longer necessary.

To translate eLaw into reality, two projects were launched by the Administration of Parliament in view of the complex task on hand and the brief period available by decision of the federal government:

- the "Implementing E-Law" project (in April 2001) to ensure one continuous electronic channel for the legislative procedure in the Nationalrat and the Bundesrat, as well as
- the "Roll-out Plan for laptops" to be used by Members of Parliament (in December 2002).

The basic ideas of the eLaw project have been:

- To provide an electronic workflow for producing legal texts beginning with the draft bill and ending with the ePublication of the Federal Law Gazette (e.g. law, regulation, announcement, treaty)
- To replace printed legal texts by digitally signed electronic documents
- Official publication of the Austrian Federal Law Gazette in the Internet

The exchange of documents with the federal administration, where a separate workflow is in place, it is based on compatible formats and an independent interface, and detailed procedures have been developed for the exchange of data between parliament and government.

The system offers the people involved in the legislative process not only electronic information but also participation opportunities; in this context, a special upload mask was created for Members of Parliament and their assistants to enter the electronic versions of motions into the system. In a competence center established in Parliament, a specific staff supports the rapporteurs of the committees and the committee secretaries of the Parliamentary Administration in preparing the committee reports.

10.1.8 LAMS and UKMF

In the early 2000 two main institutional initiatives were launched by UK institutions.

The "Legal and Advice Sectors Metadata Scheme" (LAMS[3]) initiative, developed by the Lord Chancellor's Department in UK as part of the Community Legal Service (CLS) launched in April 2000, aimed at promoting common standards across Internet sites developed by organisations in the Legal and Advice Sectors.

It was specifically concerned with the standardisation of websites holding information on legal matters to the extent that they should classify information according

---

[3] `www.lcd.gov.uk/consult/meta/metafr.htm`

to a common framework. The proposals were intended to deliver benefits to both providers and users of these websites.

LAMS was conform closely to the standard metadata element set of "Simple" Dublin Core. This gives the greatest possibility of gaining the advantages offered by the adoption of an existing metadata scheme.

Similarly UK Metadata Framework (UKMF) aimed at describing all resources within the government sector to provide policy-makers with effective accessibility to the resources on a particular policy issue, regardless of the department to which those resources belong.

10.1.9 UK "Open Data" Initiative

UK Government has recently launched its "open data" initiative which aims at publishing governmental public sector information as linked data, basically data in which real-world things are given addresses on the web (URIs), and are published in machine-readable formats (based on RDF) at those locations. The linked data approach allows other datasets to point to those resources using their URIs and find out more about them without that information being copied into the original dataset.

The main types of information already published by UK Government as linked data are related to:

- Reference data, covering the central working of government, including organisational structures where these have been made available as RDF;
- Ordnance Survey, including postcode units and administrative areas;
- Transport data, including the transport infrastructure and data about traffic flow;
- Education data, covering all schools and nurseries;
- Combined Online Information System (COINS), database of UK Government expenditure provided by government departments;
- Legislation.

In particular legislation is published under `www.legislation.gov.uk`, managed by The National Archives on behalf of HM Government, containing revised enacted UK legislation from 1267, as well as its changes over time.

Legislation.gov.uk publishes most types of UK legislation: from public general and local UK acts, till those of the UK national assemblies. The revised versions of legislation are maintained by the Statutory Publications Office – part of the Office of the Legislative Counsel in Northern Ireland within the Office of the First Minister and Deputy First Minister.

Legislation.gov.uk Web site allows user to select any legislation type and browsing or select, over the UK map, a geographical area to see which legislation types are applicable. Moreover a timeline of changes reporting the different points in time where a change occurred can be shown: the dates will coincide with the earliest date on which the change (e.g. an insertion, a repeal or a substitution) that was applied came into force. The first date in the timeline is usually the earliest date when a provision came into force.

Legislation is available in different versions:

- Latest Available (revised): The latest available updated version of the legislation incorporating changes made by subsequent legislation;
- Original (As Enacted or Made): The original version of the legislation.

Legislation item can be shown in different formats:

- the original print PDF of the "as enacted" version that was used for the print copy
- lists of changes made by and/or affecting this legislation item
- all formats of all associated documents
- correction slips
- links to related legislation and further information resources

From a technical point of view, www.legislation.gov.uk provides an API to give developers full and open access to the underlying data, free for re-use under data.gov.uk licence terms. Such data are managed through a native XML database and resources are identified by three types of URI: identifier URIs, document URIs and representation URIs.

Identifier URIs are of the form `http://www.legislation.gov.uk/id/type/year/number` and are used to denote the abstract concept of a piece of legislation – the notion of how it was, how it is and how it will be. These identifier URIs are designed to support the use of legislation as part of the Web of Linked Data.

Document URIs are used to refer to particular documents on the web: versions of the legislation. Document URIs follow the template:
`http://www.legislation.gov.uk/type/year/number`
`[/section][/authority][/extent][/version]`

Representation URIs are for the different types of possible rendition of the document (html, pdf or xml) and its a particular format follows the template:
`http://www.legislation.gov.uk/type/year/number`
`[/section][/authority][/extent][/version]/data.ext`

Finally RDF is used to describe semantics while the Dublin Core model and terms is used for metadata.

10.1.10 The Metalex/CEN Initiative

On the basis of such experiences, in 2006 an initiative was launched at CEN (European Committee for Standardization) for a Workshop on Open XML interchange format for legal and legislative resources. This initiative discussed also the definition of a unique identifier for legal measures.

A CEN Workshop Agreement (CWA) on an Open XML interchange format for legal and legislative resources has been accepted by the CEN [8] and associated standard organisations as a publicly available specification.

The CEN MetaLex standard is considered as an interchange format between other, more jurisdiction-specific XML standards. As such it is very abstract, therefore it is considered a basis to develop the new standards. It is based on best practices from amongst others the previous versions of the MetaLex schema, the Akoma-Ntoso schema, and the NormeInRete schema. Other relevant parties are LexDania, CHLexML, FORMEX, etc.

10.1.11 FORMEX

FORMEX[4] is the format used since 1985 by the Publication Office of the European Union to exchange data with its contractors. It defines the logic markup for documents which are published in the different series of the Official Journal of the European Union.

The first three FORMEX versions were based on SGML (Standard Generalized Markup Language – ISO 8876-1986); the last SGML version (version 3) entered into force on April 1999.

However SGML had not the success that was expected, because of the complexity of its grammar and the difficulties of developing tools supporting users. Therefore user organizations were involved to discuss the state and the future of FORMEX: these meetings made the proposal to migrate to XML and to replace DTD with XML schema. This lead to a redefinition of FORMEX and the new (version 4) entered into force on May 2004.
One of the FORMEX new features is represented by renouncing to ISO 2022 character set definition and in the adoption of Unicode (UTF-8). This has reduced problems with encoding of special characters and symbols of the different EU languages.

The adoption of XML also gave the opportunity of reviewing the existing specifications: the 1200 tags contained in FORMEX version 3, have been replaced with around 260 tags in FORMEX version 4.

The specifications consist of two parts:

1. physical specifications containing information data exchange, filenames construction and, in particular, on character set;
2. XMLSchema FORMEX grammar for document markup.

10.2 African Initiatives: The Akoma-Ntoso project

In the last few years the UNITED NATIONS Department for Economic and Social Affairs (UN/DESA) project "Strengthening Parliaments' Information Systems in

[4] Formalized Exchange of Electronic Publications

Africa" launched an initiative addressed to empower legislatures with ICTs solutions to better fulfil their democratic functions, to increase the quality of parliamentary services, as well as to facilitate parliamentarians work and the civil society to access parliamentary processes. In the first stage, the project has been actively supported by the NormeInRete community, and has been influenced by NormeInRete project results.

A key role has been played by the AKOMA NTOSO[5] (Architecture for Knowledge-Oriented Management of African Normative Texts using Open Standards and Ontologies) project, which has provided a set of guidelines for e-Parliament services in a Pan-African context.

The project aimed to promote interoperability between Parliament information systems across Africa by defining technical recommendations and document standards. In particular, Akoma-Ntoso proposes an XML document schema for several Parliamentary document types (including bills, acts and parliamentary records, etc.), for fostering interoperability across African Parliaments, open access to Parliamentary information, transparency and accountability of Parliaments by open source multi-platform applications based on open standards

The Akoma-Ntoso Framework is able to support individual country Parliaments to use the defined guidelines and tools to supplement national e-Government initiatives in a Pan-African dimension, thus promoting interoperability of Parliaments.

As regards document standards, the Akoma-Ntoso Framework reached three main objectives [24]:

- to define a common standard for data interchange between parliaments;
- to define the specifications for a base document model on which parliamentary systems can be built;
- to define an easy mechanism for citation and cross referencing of data between parliaments.

Such framework is able to provide two basic types of interoperability:

- *semantic interoperability*, guaranteeing that the meaning of exchanged information is understandable by both humans and applications receiving the data;
- *technical interoperability*, guaranteeing that all Akoma-Ntoso-related applications and interfaces are based on a shared core of technologies, languages and technical specifications.

10.3 Asian Initiatives

Asian context is characterized by studies carried on mainly by university departments to define XML standards for legal acts.

---

[5] The "Akoma-Ntoso" ("linked hearts" in English) symbol is used by the Akan people of West Africa to represent understanding and agreement

For example, recently, the Graduate School of Information Science of Nagoya University in Japan has carried out a study on legislative consolidation on a statute database [16].

In Japan some electronic databases of statutes (e.g., [9]) have been established; however, they include only the current versions at the time when retrieved, when the database was established, or when the statutes were enforced.

To store every version of statutes, a large number of documents has to be restored in a digitalized form.

Document digitalization is an essential pre-condition to implement effective accessibility to a large and increasing amount of statutes Among the acts enacted by the Diet, about 1800 are currently accessible, more than 12,000 acts have been enacted during the last 120 years, and about 200 new acts including about 150 amendment acts are enacted every year. In addition, about 5500 orders and regulations enacted by the cabinet and ministries are currently in effect.

Another problem is represented by statute amending, which is performed by enacting an amendment statute, where the details of the amendment are described in terms of amending sentences, which can be used to generate a new consolidated version of the act, by recursively apply amendments.

In Japan, consolidation has so far been achieved manually by experts on legislation as paper-based work, and the knowledge of how to carry out this task is acquired from technical guidebooks on legislation (e.g., [12]) or from other experts.

Automatic consolidation system for statutes is therefore desirable: in this context the Nagoya University has proposed an automatic consolidation system for Japanese statutes based on the formalization of amendment clauses, which are parts of amendment sentences, formalized according to sixteen kinds of regular expressions.

The whole system utilizes XML techniques, exploiting the native structure of a Japanese statute including title, contents, the main provision, supplementary provisions, etc. Such elements, as the main provision, can have a further hierarchical structure containing parts, chapters, sections, sub-sections, and divisions. In addition, the elements below chapters are also hierarchical, whose substructure includes articles, paragraphs, items, sub-items, etc.

A DTD has been therefore designed to for Japanese statutes: it is also able to describe amending contents, thus allowing to implement amending actions as operation to strings in the texts or to the document structure.

Amending actions are classified into the following ten kinds:

1. Actions on strings in a statute text: (a) Replacement, (b) Addition, and (c) Deletion
2. Actions on structure elements of a statute such as sections, articles, items, etc.: (a) Replacement, (b) Addition, and (c) Deletion
3. Actions on numbers of structure elements: (a) Renumber, (b) Attachment, and (c) Shift
4. Simultaneous execution of several actions in the above, especially replacement of title strings and renumbering structure elements.

By using a regular expression formalism, the previous actions can be managed and the automatic consolidation system is able to produce the consolidated acts. Experiments have been executed on statutes, consisting of the first versions of seventeen acts enacted since 1947, proving the validity of the approach [9].

10.4 US Initiatives

US is characterized by both institutional and non-institutional initiatives aiming at promoting legal standards, in particular some important private initiatives are currently acting to promote standards for semantic web in legal communities.

10.4.1 An Institutional Case: XML at the US House of Representatives

An important experience of legal documents standardization has been carried out in the legislative drafting service (HOLC) of the US House of Representatives, provided by the Office of the Legislative Counsel. The Office provides drafting and related assistance to the Members of the House, the House committees, and the conference committees between the House and the Senate. The signed paper version submitted to the Clerk of the House on the House Floor is the official document of record.

HOLC consists of approximately 35 attorneys and a support staff of about 15 individuals, and is headed by the Legislative Counsel of the House who is appointed by the Speaker of the House.

The drafters provide their clients with typeset drafts or PDF files that can be printed in the client's office, since the paper version is still the official document of record. Currently the paper version of legislation is created in one of the following two ways:

- using Xywrite, a DOS editor which enables the drafter to create a file, processable through a typesetting program developed by the Government Printing Office (GPO). The output of the typesetting program is an Adobe PostScript then transformed into a PDF file;
- using Corel's XMetaL application, which enables the drafter to create an XML file that is converted to the typesetting coded file and processed as in the previous way.

As reported at `http://xml.house.gov/drafting.htm` he transition to XML for the drafting of legislation has been both challenging and felt highly rewarding for the House, and nowadays the House has been using the XML authoring environment for House-only resolutions since January 2001 and began drafting bills in XML in September 2002. Public can access legislative documents through the Library of Congress' Thomas website (http://thomas.loc.gov/) and GPO's GPO Access website (http://www.access.gpo.gov/). DTDs, schemas, and examples of XML bills and resolutions are available at http://xml.house.gov/.

In particular DTD and XMLSchema versions of XML standards for bills, resolutions and amendments have been defined. In conjunction to the definition of such schema an XML authoring environment for drafting legislation has been developed based on the context provided by the underlying XML structure. The goal for the new environment has been to minimize drafters' attention to the typesetting product and to the legislative language itself, while providing "just-in-time" knowledge support during the drafting process, as well as a WYSIWYG (non-Tags-On) environment.

10.4.2 A Non-institutional Case: Legal-RDF

On of the most significant non-institutional initiatives in the field of legal standardization is "Legal-RDF"[6] [13].

Legal-RDF is "a non-profit organization, sponsored by legal firms, software companies, and other stakeholders interested in software tools that leverage the semantic web".

The strategy of the Legal-RDF community is to construct two databases – a comprehensive open-source ontology set as well as a statutory and administrative codes described according to such ontology. In this perspective Legal-RDF created a semantic model based on seven ontologies organized into components that, once taken together, allow the description of legal contents. These databases are then accessed by reasoning software to support orderly industry growth.

10.5 Australian Initiatives

10.5.1 EnAct

Australia has introduced ICT for legislative processes since the second part of the 1990s with the EnAct project. It involves Tasmania, Canada, some federal state of US and New Zealand.

EnAct is a legislation drafting, management and delivery system enabling the Tasmanian Government to provide improved legislation information services to the community [4]. EnAct provides facilities for automating much of the legislative drafting and consolidation process, enabling cost effective public access to reliable, up-to-date, consolidated Tasmanian legislation. It is based on the "point-in-time"

[6] http://www.hypergrove.com/legalrdf.org

capability allowing users to search and browse consolidated legislation since 1 February 1997.

The EnAct repository uses SGML to store legislation fragments and associated metadata, including timestamp marking the time interval (start and end time) over which the related content is valid. The logical structure of the SGML fragments is exploited an by an SGML parser allowing repository indexing.

As regards consolidation, the drafters are given a working environment in which they can mark amendments directly on the act using strike-through and underline markings. These markings are captured in an internal representation of the changes represented in SGML and called Change Description Document (CDD). These changes are then used to generate amendment wordings [3, 4], thus keeping amending and amended documents together for a better consolidation process management.

Cross-references are described as hyperlinks including queries in the database, rather than using a specific document identifier. Similarly hyperlinks used to associate history notes, related to amending Acts, to the amended Acts themselves.

Moreover a table of contents summarizes conventional sections and headnotes of a text as well as a list of links to successive versions of the corresponding fragments, providing a quick and effective overview of the history of a provision. Finally, at the end of a document two tables show, respectively, the name and the time of commencement of all amending Acts applied to that Act, as well as the lists each provision that has been amended and how it was amended.

In addition to the public web site, the Printing Authority of Tasmania (PAT) also uses the same repository to generate "on-demand" authorized reprints. Such database is not the only repository in the EnAct system. A working database is also maintained in the Office of Parliamentary Counsel: it contains the content of the public repository, as well as the politically sensitive draft Bills in preparation. It is also able to provide workflow information about the status of Bills and other draft legislation.

10.5.2 JSMS

Justice Sector metadata Scheme (JSMS) is a development of the AGLS metadata scheme, which is a set of descriptive properties to improve visibility and availability of online resources. AGLS is published as Australian standard (AS 5044-2010).

JSMS is designed for the use of organisations in New South Wales, Australia, which are publishing legal materials on the Internet. JSMS makes some minor qualifications to the "Simple" Dublin Core metadata elements adopted by AGLS.

10.6 The Legal XML Consortium

Legal XML is a non-profit organization composed by volunteer members from private industry, non-profit organizations, government, and academia. The Legal XML mission is to "develop open, non proprietary standards for legal documents and associated applications". It is a collection of standards developed by different Technical Committees, covering a wide spectrum of legal materials. Formed in 1998, Legal XML is the result of the collaboration of attorneys, court administrators and IT staff, academics, and companies. Early Legal XML work focused on electronic filing of court documents. The group's first specifications, "*Court Filing 1.0 and 1.1*", "*Court Document 1.1*", and "*Query and Response 1.0*" addressed key areas of concern for attorneys and managers of court case records.

In 2002 Legal XML joined OASIS (the Organization for Advancement of Structured Information Systems), not-for-profit consortium for development, convergence and adoption of open standards for the global information society.

Much of the work done in Legal XML regards national organizations and associations outside OASIS. Such work is presented to those groups for considering their adoption as business and technical standards. Specifications from the Electronic Court Filing Technical Committee (ECFTC) were submitted for review and have been adopted by the Joint Technology Committee (JTC) of the Conference of State Court Administrators (COSCA) and National Association for Court Management (NACM).

References

1. AIPA. 2001, November. Definizione delle regole per l'assegnazione dei nomi uniformi ai documenti giuridici. Circolare n. AIPA/CR/35. In Italian.
2. AIPA. 2002, April. Formato per la Rappresentazione Elettronica dei Provvedimenti Normativi tramite il Linguaggio di Marcatura XML. Circolare n. AIPA/CR/40 (in Italian), `http://www.cnipa.gov.it/site/_contentfiles/00127500/127544_CR_40_2002.pdf`.
3. Arnold-Moore, T. 1997. Automatic generation of amendment legislation. In *Proceedings of the International Conference of Artificial Intelligence and Law*, pp. 56–62, Melbourne, Vicoria, Australia, ACM, 1997. ISBN 0-89791-924-6.
4. Arnold-Moore, T., J. Clemes, and M. Tadd. 2002. Connected to the law: Tasmanian legislation using enact. Technical report, TeraText.
5. Biagioli, C. 1997. Towards a legal rules functional micro-ontology. In *Proceedings of the First International Workshop on Legal Ontologies, LEGONT'97*. University of Melbourne, Law School, Melbourne, Victoria, Australia.
6. Boer, A., R. Hoekstra, and R. Winkels. 2002. Metalex: Legislation in xml. In *Proceedings of JURIX 2002: Legal Knowledge and Information System*, 1–10.
7. Boer, A., R. Winkels, R. Hoekstra, and T. van Engers. 2003. Knowledge management for legislative drafting in an international setting. In *Proceedings of JURIX 2003: Legal Knowledge and Information System, 91–100*, Faculty of Law & Institute of Information and Computing Sciences Utrecht University, The Netherlands.
8. Boer A., R. Hoekstra, E. de Maat, E. Hupkes, F. Vitali, M. Palmirani, and B. Rátai. 2009. CEN MetaLex Workshop Agreement.
9. Horei Data Teikyo System, Ministry of Internal Affairs and Communications, M. and C. H. D. T. System. http://law.e-gov.go.jp/cgi-bin/idxsearch.cgi.
10. Khaled, O.A., H. Chabbi, and M. Ramalho. 2004, July. *ÉTUDE URN*. University of Applied Sciences of Western Switzerland, EIA-FR.

11. Lupo, C., and C. Batini. 2003. A federative approach to laws access by citizens: The "NormeinRete" system. In *Proceedings of second international conference electronic government (EGOV)*, ed. R. Traunmuller, 413–416. Springer.
12. Maeda, M. 2003. *Workbook Hosei Shitsumu.* (revised ed.). Tokyo: Gyosei.
13. McClure, J. 2006. Legal-RDF vocabularies, requirements & design rationale. In *Proceedings of the V Legislative XML Workshop*, 149–159. European Press Academic Publishing, Florence.
14. Megale, F., and F. Vitali. 2001. I dtd dei documenti di norme in rete. *Informatica e Diritto* 1: 167–231.
15. Moats, R., and K.R. Sollins. 1997. URN syntax. Technical Report RFC 2141, Internet Engineering Task Force (IETF).
16. Ogawa, Y., S. Inagaki, and K. Toyama. 2007. Automatic consolidation of Japanese statutes based on formalization of amendment sentences. In *Proceedings of JSAI'07*, 363–376. Miyazaki, Japan
17. Spinosa, P. 2001. Identification of legal documents through urns (uniform resource names). In *Proceedings of the EuroWeb 2001, The Web in Public Administration.*
18. Tucker, H. 2004a, July. *Lex Dania - White Paper. A System of XML Schemas for Danish Legislative Documentation.*
19. Tucker, H. 2004b, July. *LexDania - Documentation. Guidelines for Writing Omni- and Doc-Type and Application Schemas.*
20. Tucker, H. 2004c, March. *LexDania - Documentation. Introduction to Concepts and Status of XML Linking.*
21. Tucker, H. 2004d, June. *LexDania - Documentation. Metadata.*
22. Tucker, H. 2004e, May. *LexDania - Documentation. XML and XSL Best Practices for Writing Schemas.*
23. Tucker, H. 2004f, April. *LexDania Documentation. Universal addresses.*
24. Vitali, F., and F. Zeni. 2007. Towards a country-independent data format: The Akoma-Ntoso experience. In *Proceedings of the V Legislative XML Workshop*, 67–86. European Press Academic Publishing, Florence.

Index

G. Sartor et al. (eds.), *Legislative XML for the Semantic Web*, Law, Governance and Technology Series 4, DOI 10.1007/978-94-007-1887-6,

© Springer Science+Business Media B.V. 2011

MIX
Papier aus verantwortungsvollen Quellen
Paper from responsible sources
FSC® C105338

If you have any concerns about our products,
you can contact us on
ProductSafety@springernature.com

In case Publisher is established outside the EU,
the EU authorized representative is:
Springer Nature Customer Service Center GmbH
Europaplatz 3, 69115 Heidelberg, Germany

Printed by Libri Plureos GmbH
in Hamburg, Germany